# TELFORD
## THROUGH TIME

## Allan Frost

Elder Hobbs,
    Thank you so much for visiting us. We have so enjoyed your company, your gospel messages and not forgetting your travelling 'experiences'. We hope that both you and your girlfriend will always keep in touch as you are a special person.
    Love Paul and Wendy Bonigal
        January 2012

AMBERLEY PUBLISHING

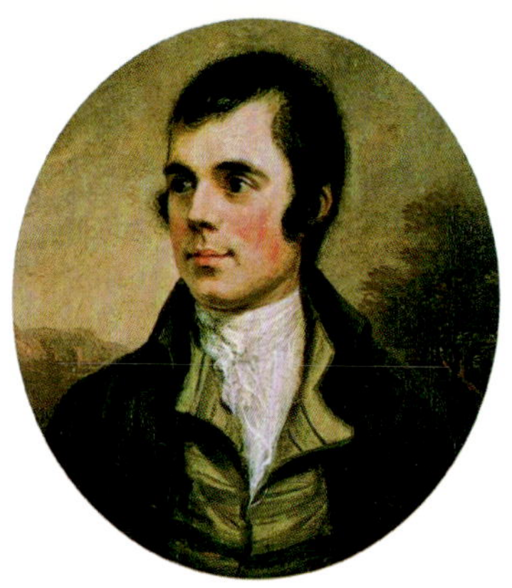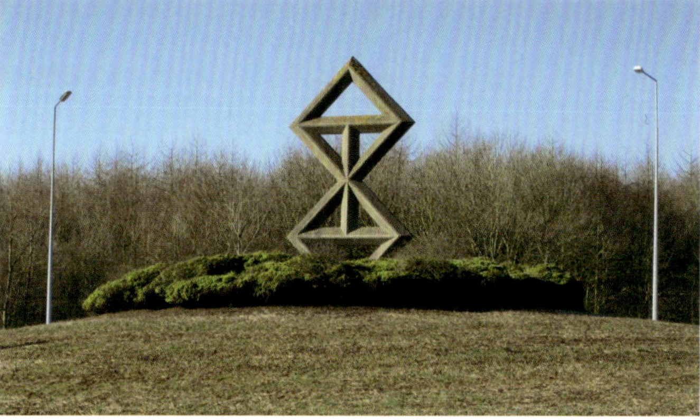

Thomas Telford (left) and a concrete representation of his stonemason's mark on a roundabout on the A5 near St. Georges. Telford (1757-1834) was born in the Scottish Borders and was apprenticed when aged fourteen to a stonemason. After working in Edinburgh, he moved to London and spent time at Portsmouth before becoming Surveyor of Public Works in Shropshire in 1787. He subsequently gained an unrivalled reputation throughout Britain and abroad as a civil engineer, particularly for his bridge, road and canal constructions. Evidence of his designs can be found locally at St. Michael's church, Madeley and St. Leonard's church, Malinslee, while Blist's Hill Museum in the Ironbridge Gorge boasts the reconstructed Shelton Toll House originally designed by Telford for use on the turnpiked stretch of the Holyhead Road just west of Shrewsbury.

*Dedicated to those who remember affectionately what east Shropshire was like before the Telford conurbation came into being.*

First published 2010

Amberley Publishing plc
Cirencester Road, Chalford,
Stroud, Gloucestershire, GL6 8PE

www.amberley-books.com

© Allan Frost, 2010

The right of Allan Frost to be identified as the Author of this work has been asserted in accordance with the Copyrights, Designs and Patents Act 1988.

ISBN 978 1 84868 577 2



British Library Cataloguing in Publication Data.
A catalogue record for this book is available from the British Library.

Typesetting and Origination by Amberley Publishing.
Printed in Great Britain.

# Introduction

Telford in Shropshire, England, is not a town, nor does it have a long, distinguished history. It is a conurbation devised by government planners in the 1960s to incorporate several ancient townships which do have a fascinating story to tell. Telford itself is named after renowned Scotsman Thomas Telford, whose reputation as a civil engineer, among other things, was unsurpassed during his lifetime.

In 1968, the then Labour Minister of Housing and Local Government, Anthony Greenwood, decreed that the so-called 'new town' be named Telford, despite considerable opposition from local residents who resented an outsider dictating the name without their consent.

Whereas Telford is, therefore, a little over forty years old, it has had a far-reaching impact on the area. Its history is characterised by a seemingly insatiable desire to build something – a housing estate, road, roundabout or factory – on every square metre of land. And to promote out-of-town shopping centres at the expense of investment in the traditional townships incorporated into the conurbation, even to the point of practically denying their existence.

Sadly, the successors to former local-community Urban and Rural District Councils (Telford Development Corporation, Wrekin District Council and now the Borough of Telford and Wrekin) seem to have neglected those townships (once arrogantly and unsympathetically described as 'district centres') over the last forty years; it is only in recent times that substantial regeneration projects have begun to make good at least some of the damage done to local economies. Contrary to an opinion often expressed, Telford does not simply comprise Ironbridge with its endlessly promoted museums, nor the ubiquitously named Telford Town Centre and Wonderland Park.

No. The most interesting parts of Telford are to be found in the towns which comprise the conurbation, and the land surrounding them. Whereas the original 'new town' was to be centred on Dawley, the 'designated area' was expanded in 1968 to encompass Madeley, Ironbridge, Hadley, Oakengates, Donnington... to name but a few.

Their status, like that of Wellington, which had been the dominant settlement in the area for several hundred years, was relegated to that of suburb. Even Newport and Lilleshall, situated several miles away, were eventually absorbed into the Borough. Furthermore, the sphere of influence over which the Borough has control now includes considerable tracts of east Shropshire farmland, and countless villages and hamlets north of the River Severn. Shropshire's internationally famous natural landmark, The Wrekin Hill, straddles the Telford administrative border to the west.

The modern conurbation has existed for very few years, but human occupation in the area extends as far back as the Stone Age. Since then, Man has sought refuge on its hills and cleared its woodland for employment, food and shelter. Many important events in British history have taken place here, including aspects of Roman and Norman Conquest, the English Civil War, and Agrarian and Industrial Revolutions.

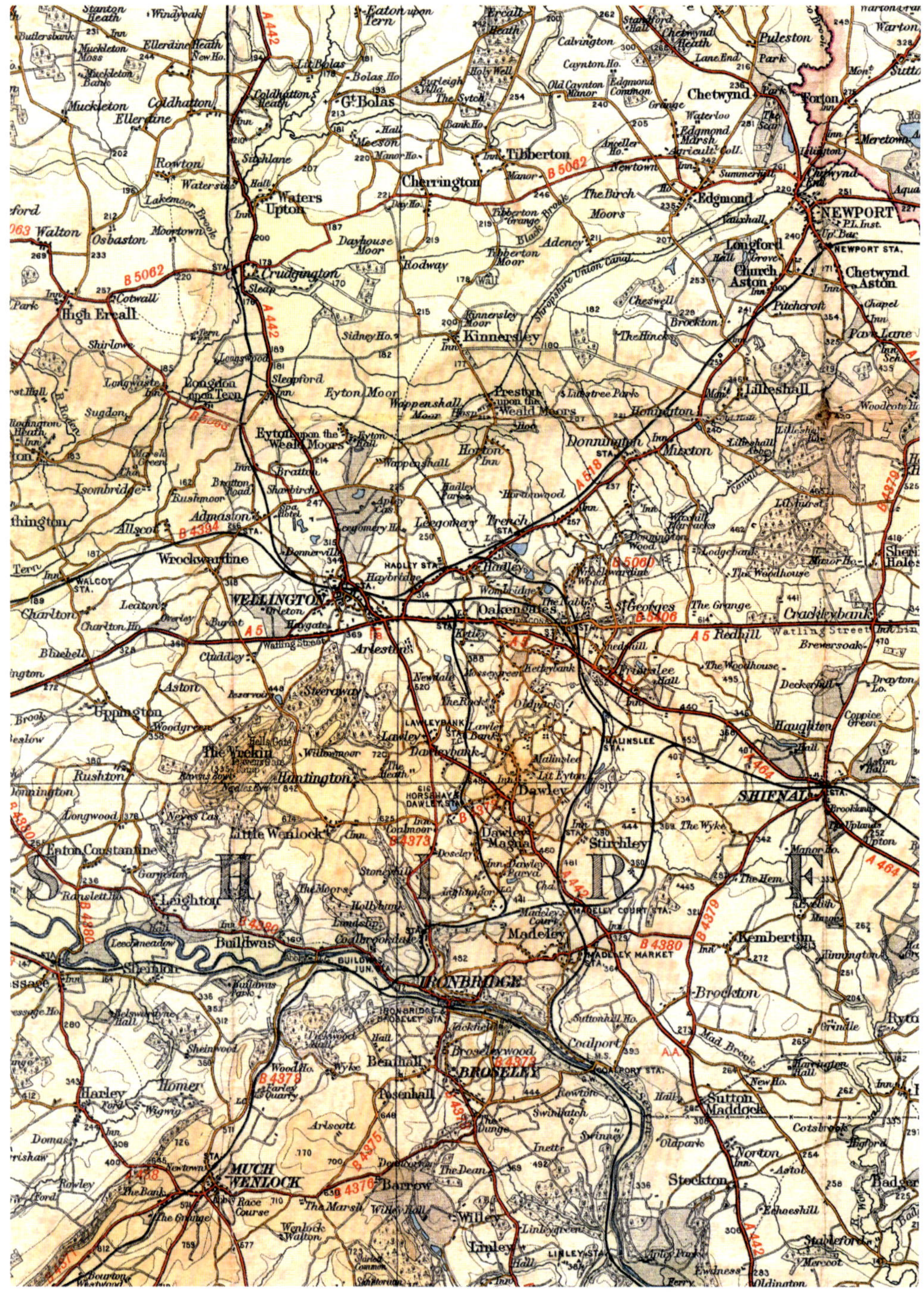

Extract from a 1940s Bartholemew's four miles to the inch map showing much of the present Telford area. Right: A 2007 map included in a *Transforming Telford* information pack. The white areas show the original Telford designated area and the later Newport addition; the yellow area signifies the extent of the present Telford & Wrekin Borough. Note that the M54 has replaced the A5 as the dominant east-west route through the district.

Some of its inhabitants have exerted important influence on industrial development, among them Abraham Darby and the family which eventually became Dukes of Sutherland; others have been heavily engaged in the unpredictable world of politics, like Richard Baxter from Rowton, the 'Protestant Divine' who served as chaplain to both King Charles I as well as Oliver Cromwell; a few have influenced social legislation (the Wellington-born authoress Hesba Stretton) and scientific achievement (William Withering, also from Wellington). These are merely a few of the many worth mentioning.

The Telford conurbation has had a major impact on the manner in which the district has developed. But whereas residents and newcomers may be forgiven for thinking Telford equals a shopping centre and museums in the Ironbridge Gorge, the number of local history groups which have sprung up over the last few years is in itself an indication that there is far more to Telford than meets the eye.

I hope this book will encourage readers to discover more.

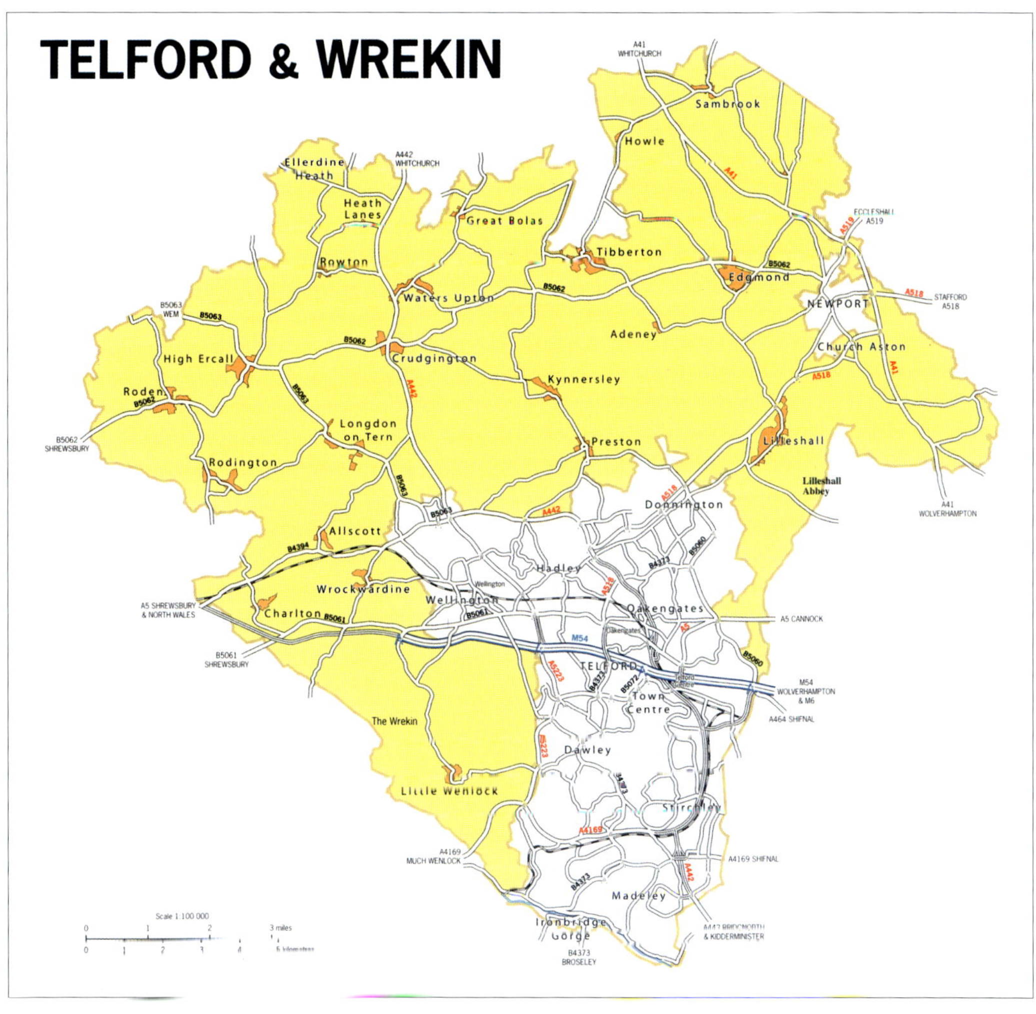

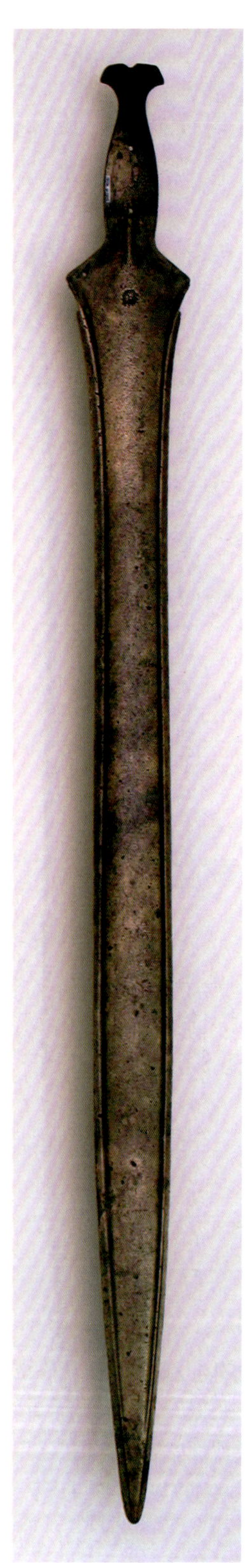

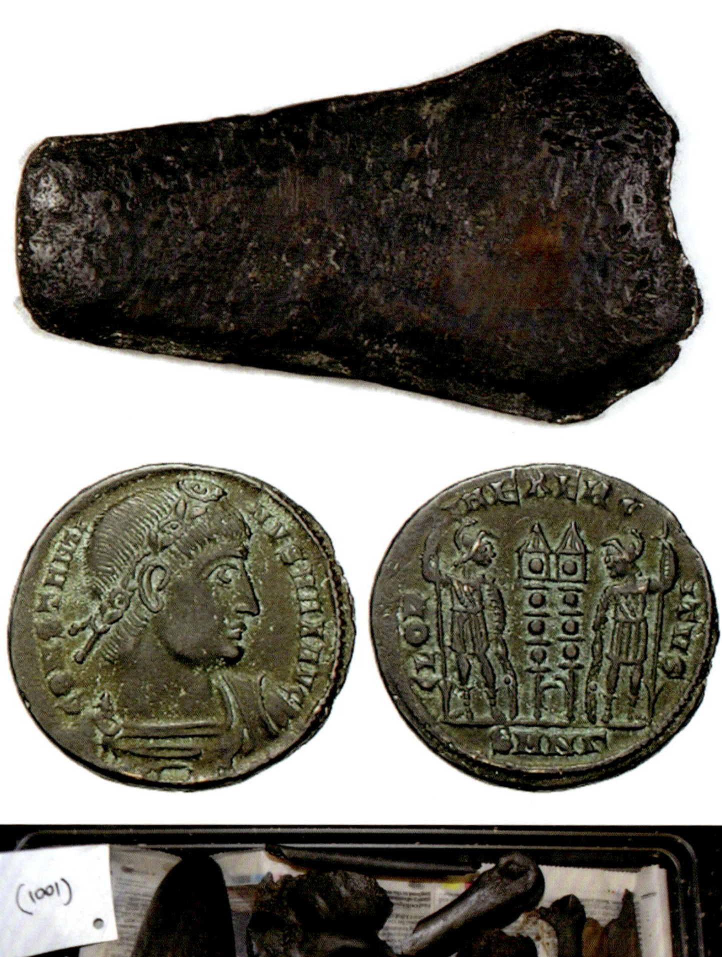

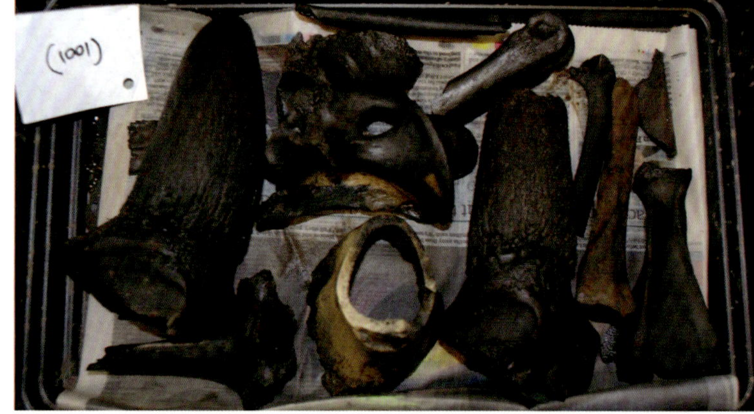

### Archaeological Discoveries

The Telford area has revealed items from Stone Age to Medieval times, proving a long period of human occupation. *Left*: An Iron Age bronze sword found in the River Severn at Jackfield in the 1970s. *Top*: A Bronze Age copper palstave discovered in a quarry on Ercall Hill in 1890. Centre: Roman coins of this type showing Emperor Constantinius the Great (AD307-337) were found near Kynnersley *c.* 1840. *Bottom*: Animal bones, evidence of Medieval tanning, found by SLR Consulting archaeologists at Edgbaston House, Wellington, in May 2010.

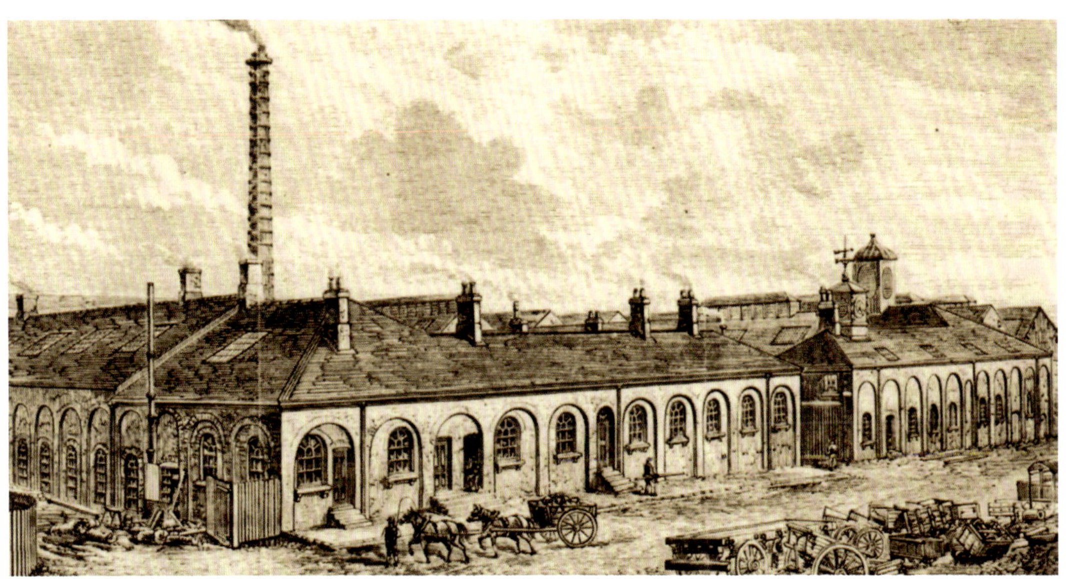

## Geology Rules!

The geology of The Wrekin area is regarded as the most complex in the world. Coal, iron and other minerals have been exploited for millennia, giving rise to a number of thriving businesses. Above: New Yard, built at St. Georges by the Lilleshall Company in the 1860s; the firm, which operated from 1802 to 1969, was globally famous for its extensive mining operations, engineering and other industries. Below: Ceramic tiles on the A442 near Oakengates represent severe faulting in nearby coal measures.

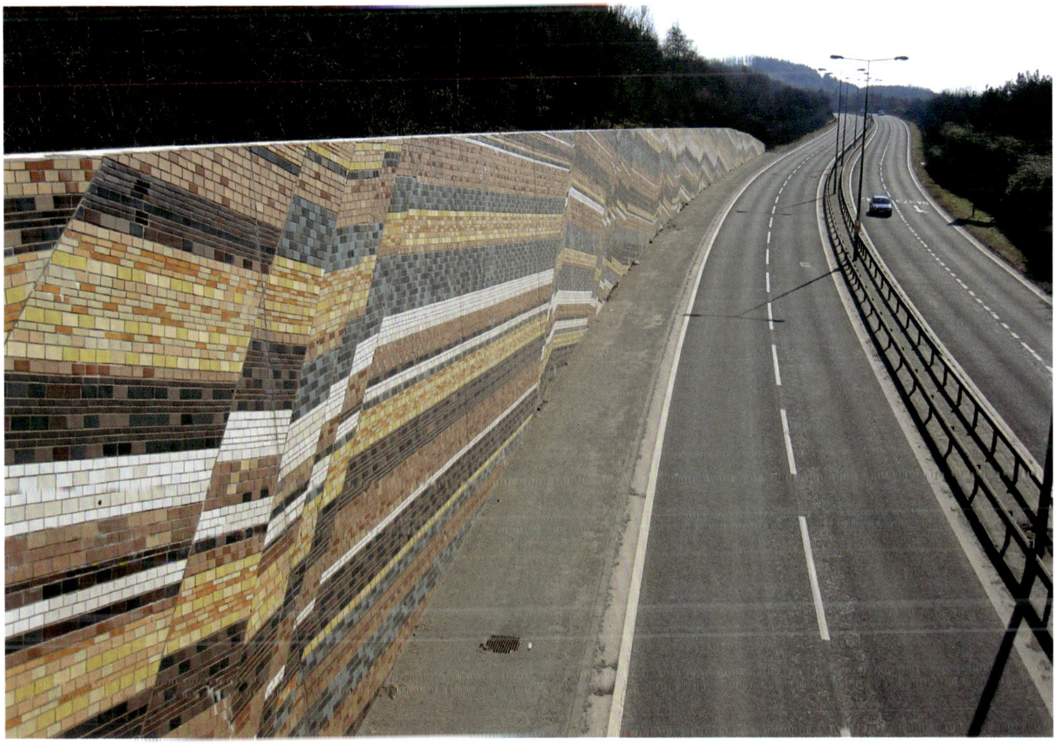

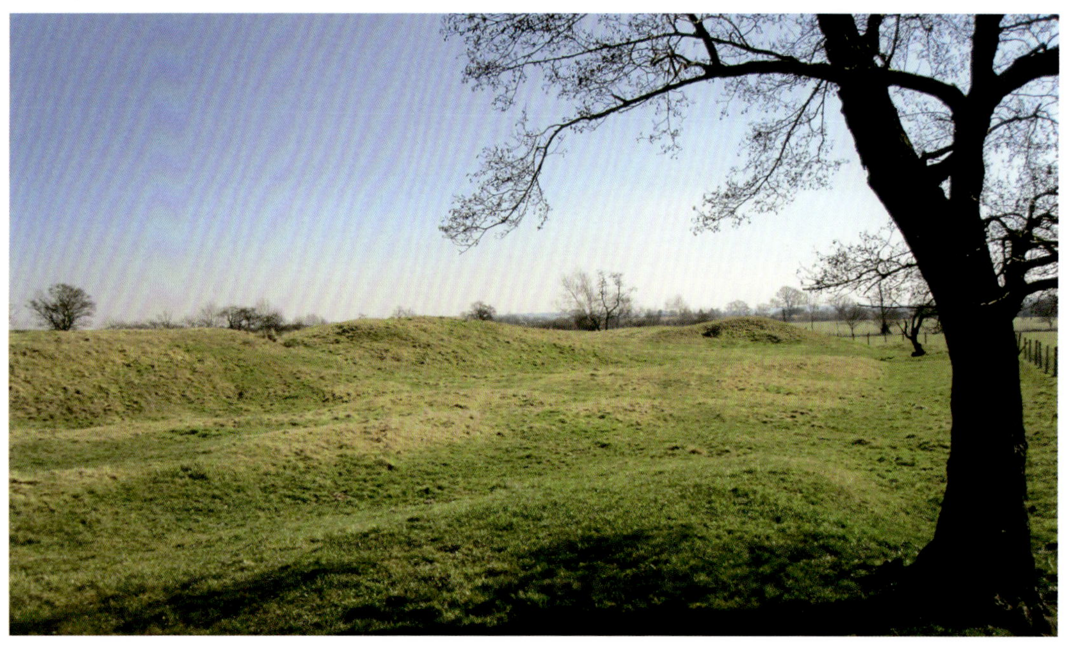

## Iron Age Hill Forts

*Above:* The fort at Wall, near Kynnersley, was built on a low mound surrounded by waterlogged peat bog. *Below:* A 1940s view of the impressive ramparts of The Wrekin Hill fort, capital of the Cornovii tribe.

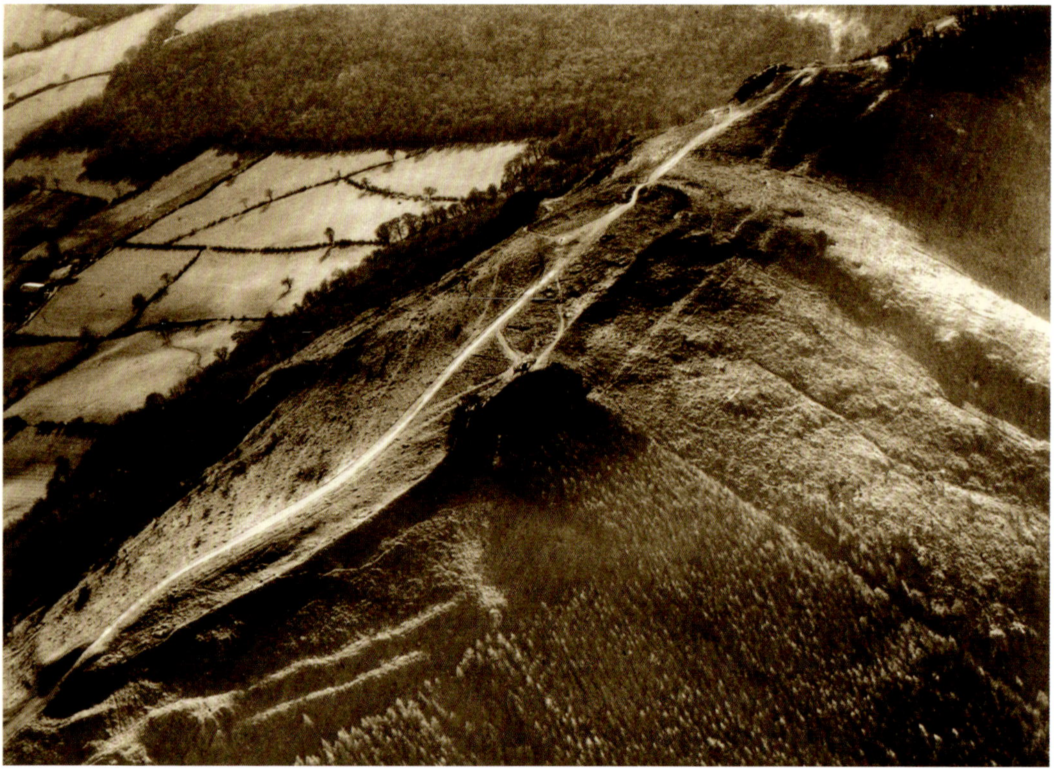

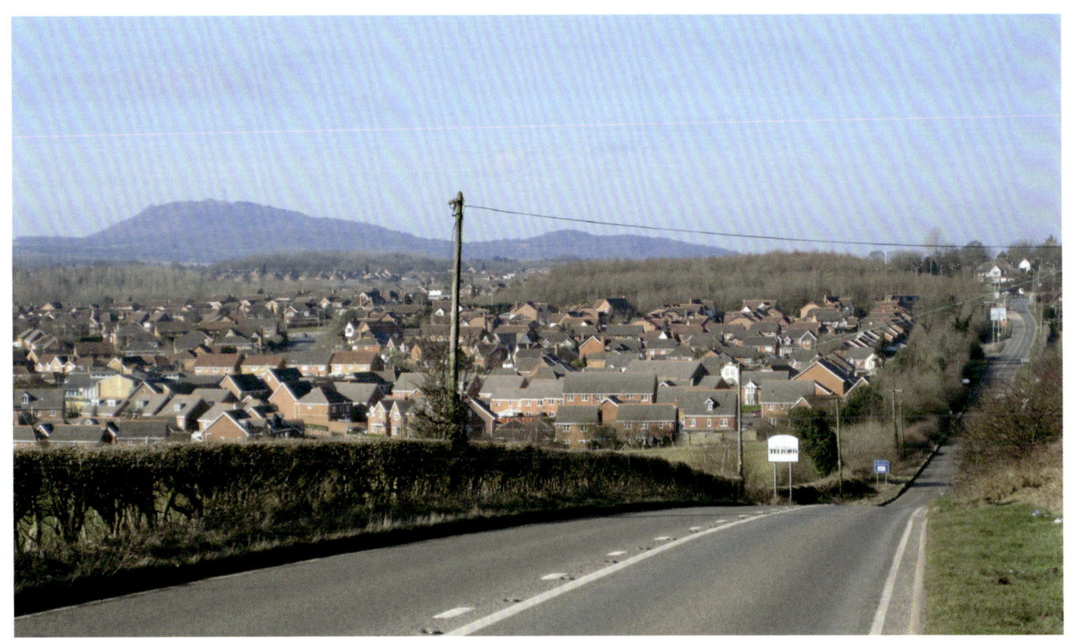

## Ancient Route

A stretch of the present A5 which was known as Watling Street provided an easy-to-travel route for ancient Britons and their subsequent Roman rulers. Above: Looking westwards over Priorslee from the Red Hill approach to Telford, with The Wrekin Hill in the distance. Below: The previous photograph was taken at the crest of Red Hill, where trees at left centre hide a modern reservoir ... and the remains of Uxacona, the last Roman staging camp on the way along Watling Street past The Wrekin Hill to Uriconium, the former legionary fort at Wroxeter which subsequently became the fourth largest city in Roman Britain.

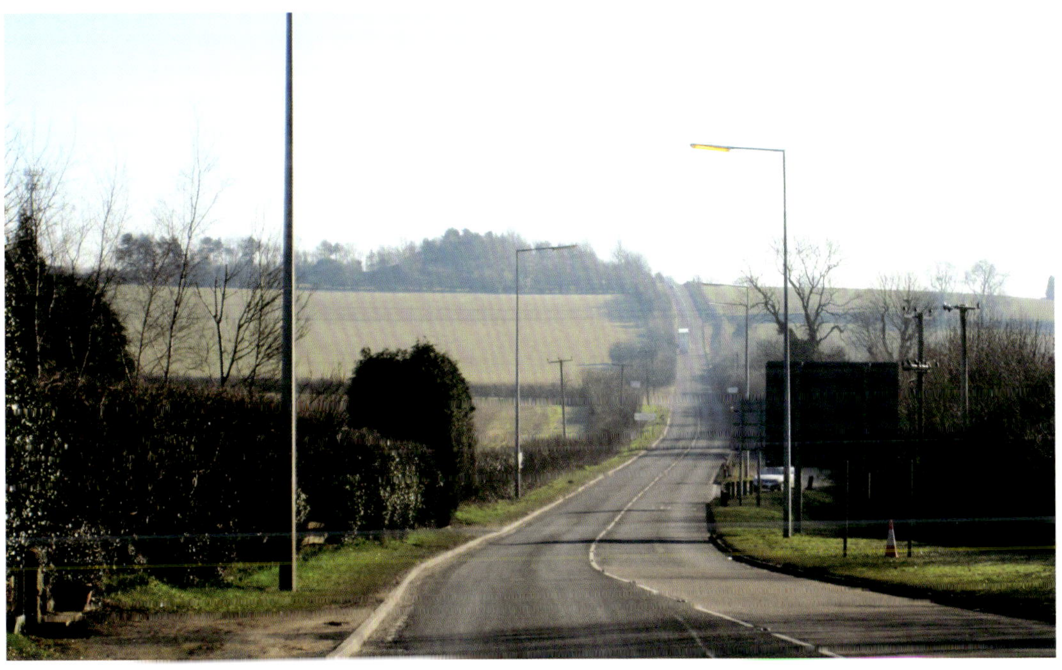

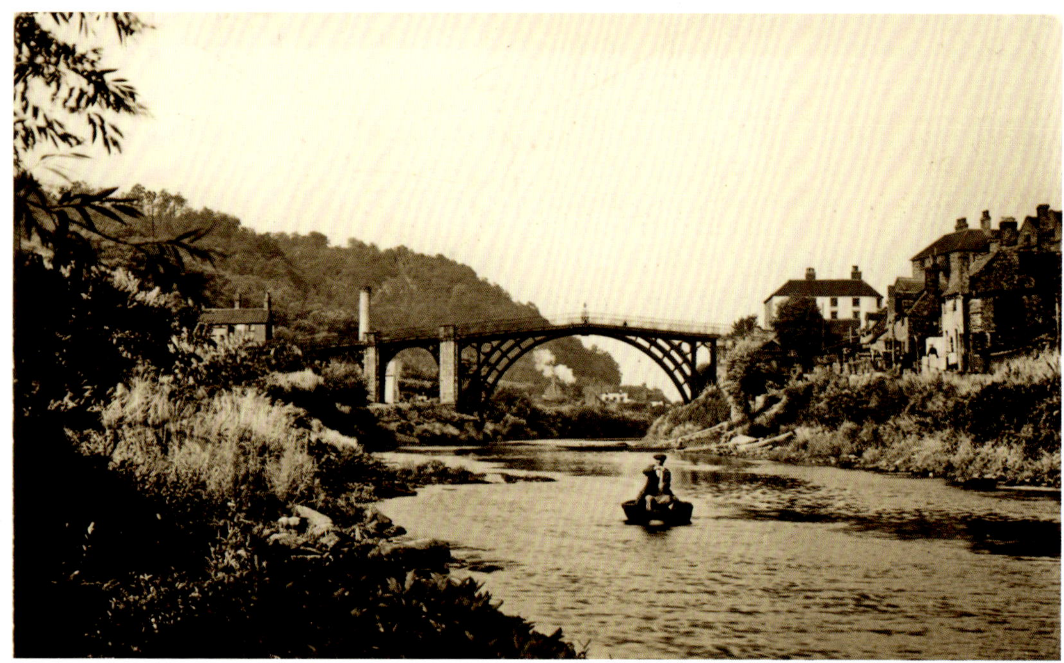

## Other Routes, Old and New

The River Severn flowing through the Ironbridge Gorge provided an alternative route for trade between the Bristol Channel and Shrewsbury. Coracles, such as that containing Tommy Rogers in this 1920s postcard, were in use on the river for over two thousand years, although larger craft were used to carry goods from Medieval times. Below: The M54 cuts through the centre of the Telford conurbation and provides the main link between the West Midlands and Wales. The Wrekin and Ercall Hills can be seen beneath the gantry.

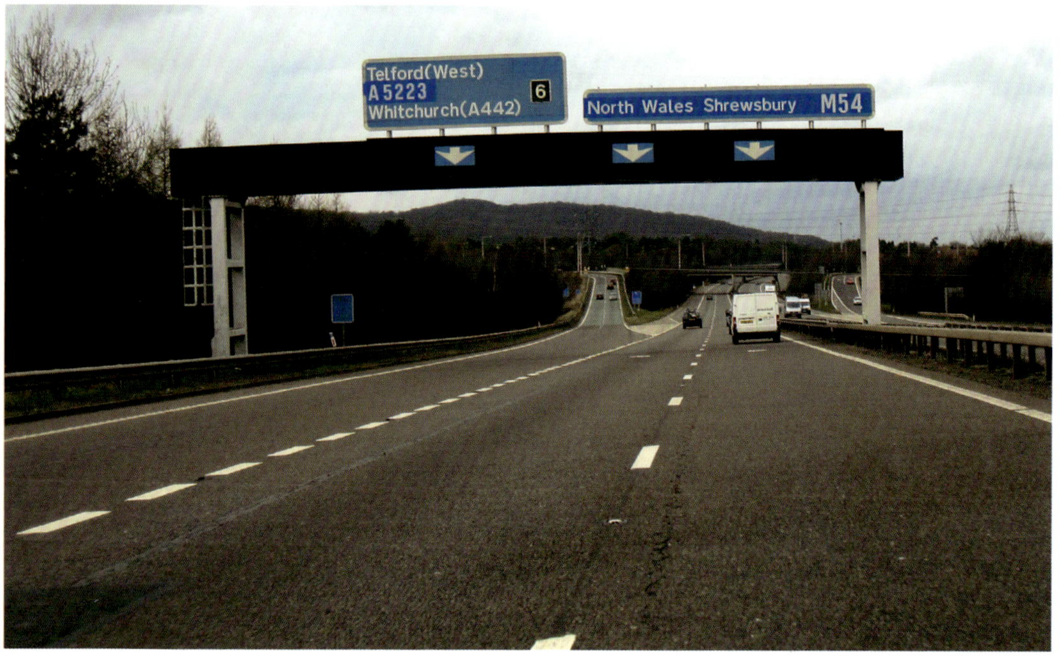

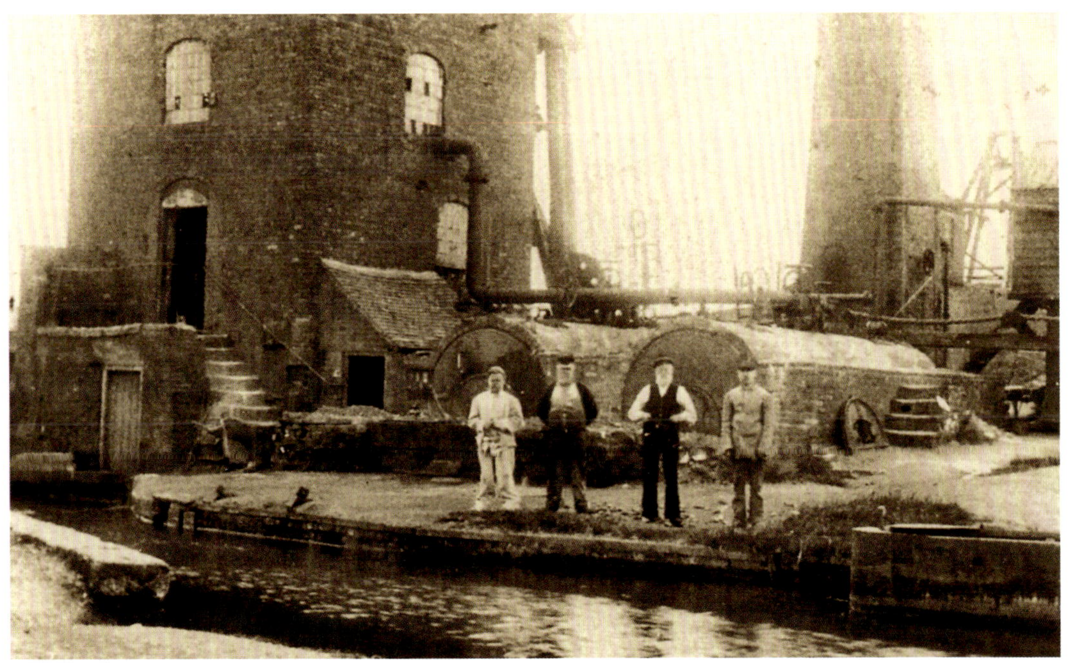

## Canals and Coaches

The Donnington Wood Canal, whose engine house is seen above, was the first to be constructed in Shropshire in 1767 and linked limestone pits at Lilleshall to the coal mines and iron furnaces at Donnington Wood. Tub boats, like that floating on the right, carried minerals as well as Sunday School children on their annual 'treats'. Stage coach travel during the 1820s to 1840s improved communications; The Wonder boasted a speedy journey from Shrewsbury via Wellington to London in a mere four days. Such long distance travel was superseded by a new form of travel: the steam railway.

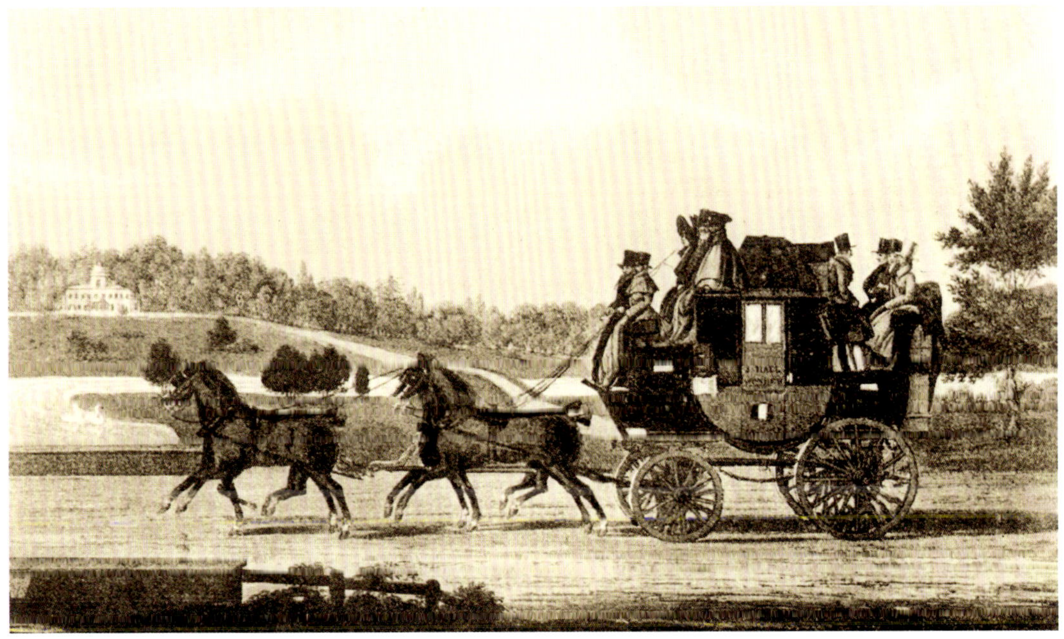

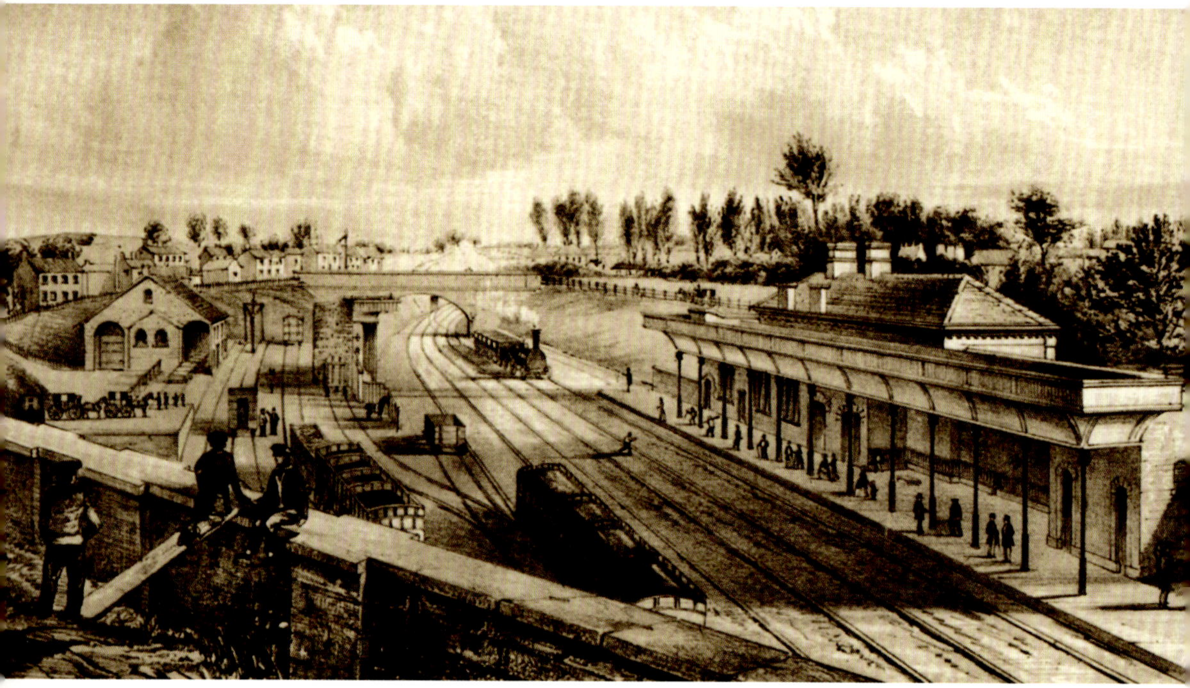

### Passenger Railway Stations

Wellington station opened in June 1849 and became a busy junction until Dr. Richard Beeching's 1960s rail reorganisation reduced the number of passenger and goods trains. The station is still open. Telford Central station, with its large car park and nearby 'Town Centre' offices, opened for passengers in 1986.

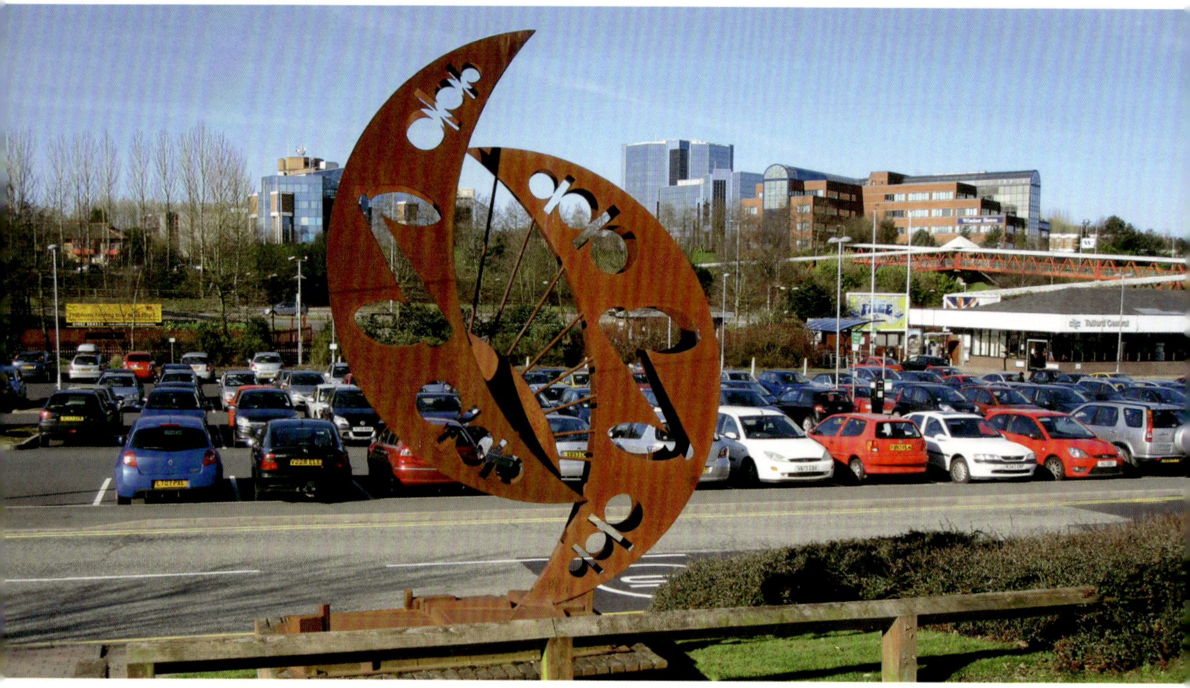

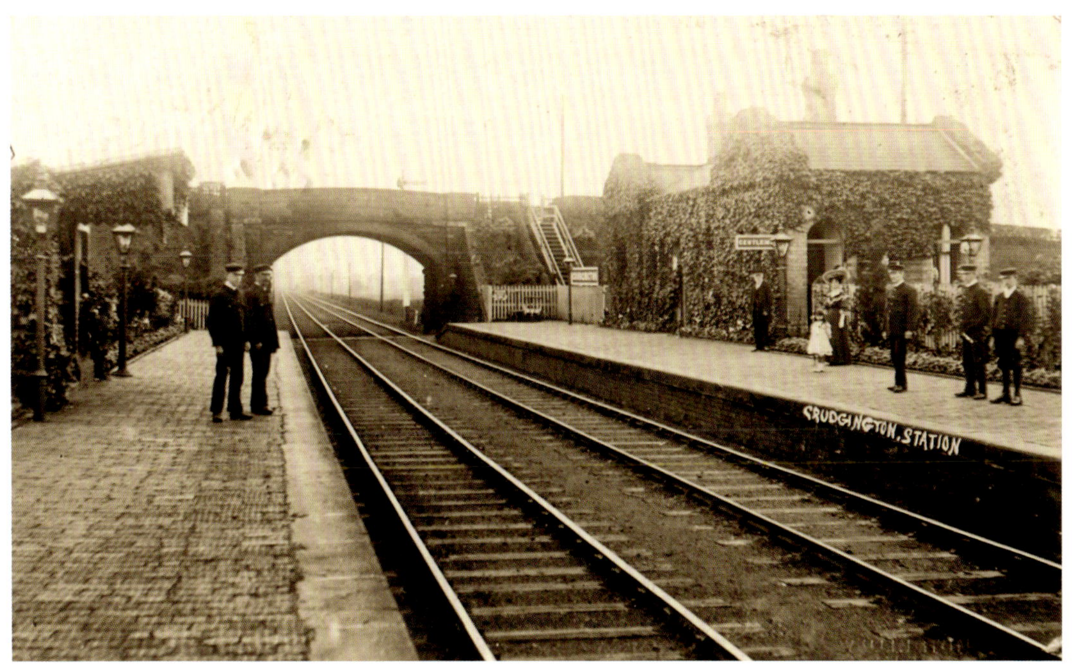



## Terminated Services

The overall effect of Transport Minister Dr. Beeching's 'axe' was to cut out what he regarded as inessential rail services, much to the detriment of the travelling public; it was an ill-conceived idea designed to reduce rail subsidies and promote road transport in general and the motor industry in particular. The Telford area lost almost all of its branch lines along with their town and village stations, like those at Crudgington (above) and Newport (below), both seen as they were about 100 years ago.

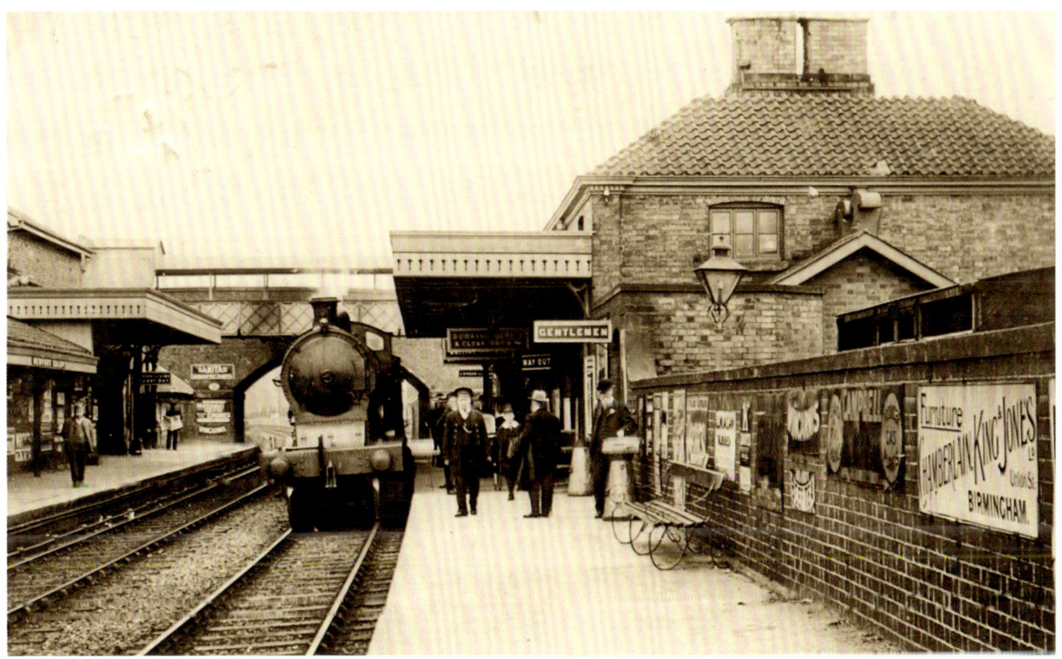

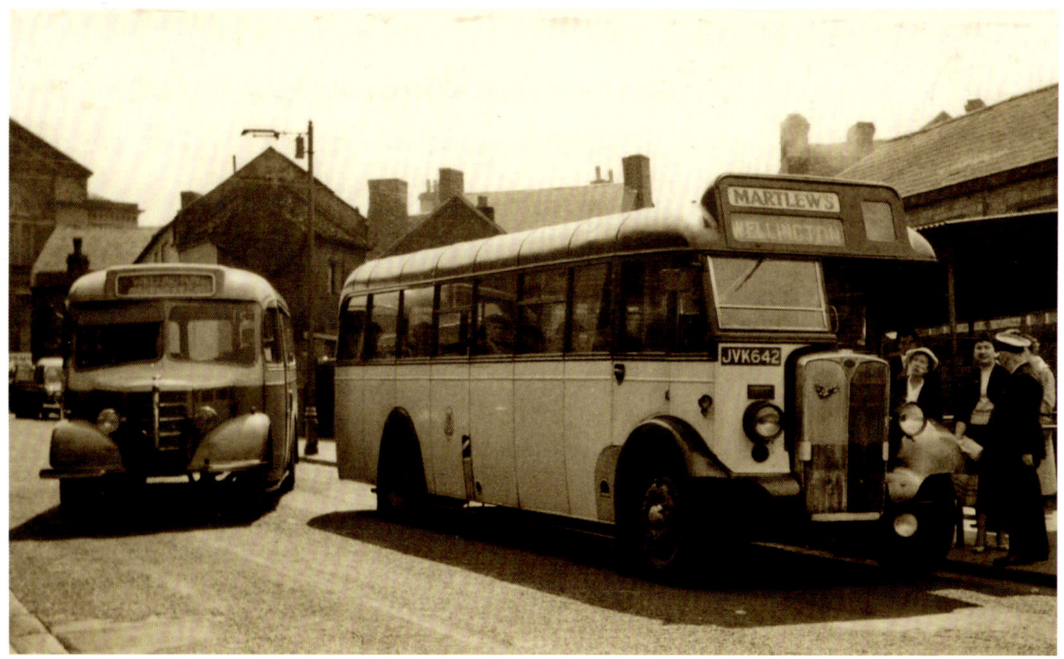

## On the Buses

Bus services throughout the district were operated by the numerous bus companies from the 1930s until 1978 when their historic rival, the Midland Red Omnibus Company, acquired monopoly status over all Telford services under its subsidiary trading name Tellus. Above: Wellington's Victoria Street provided the main bus terminus for the district until the one attached to Telford Town Centre (below) opened during the year that trading began there: 1973. This is how it looks today, with Arriva as the main bus operator.

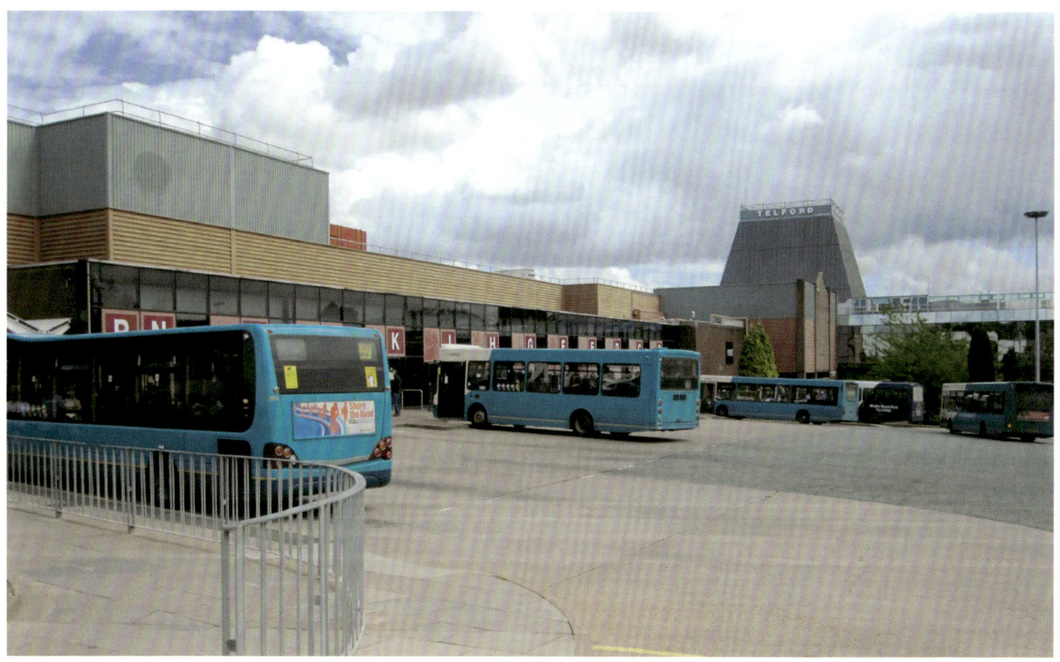

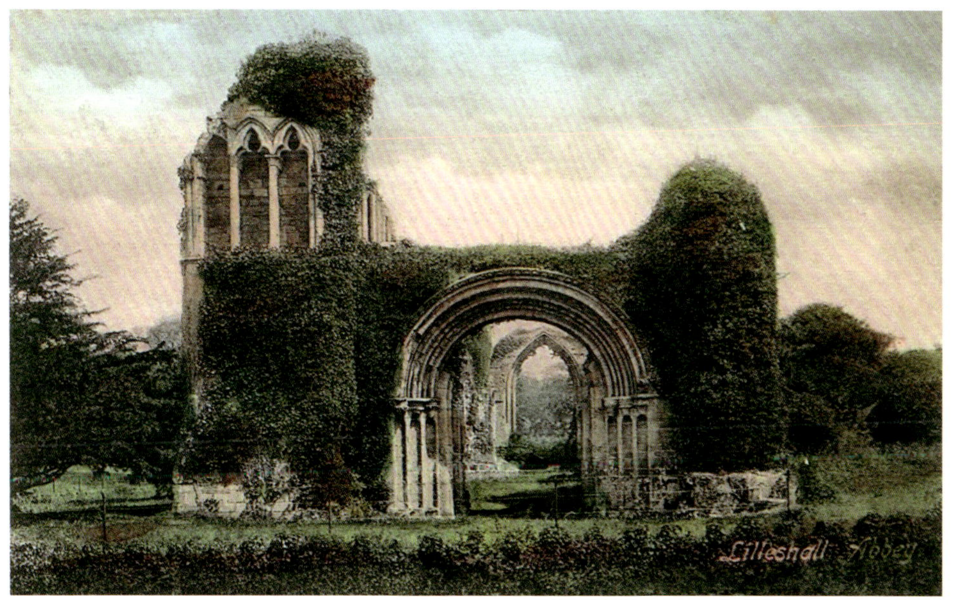



## Old Buildings

Unlike Wombridge Priory, substantial ruins remain of Lilleshall Abbey, founded in 1148. It was dissolved by King Henry VIII and sold in 1543 to James Leveson, a Wolverhampton wool merchant whose successors became Dukes of Sutherland. The buildings suffered considerable damage during the English Civil War. English Heritage now tends the ruins. The Levesons seldom lived in the abbey, preferring to stay when in the area at their hunting lodge (below) in the deer park at Donnington Wood, which was demolished in 1818.

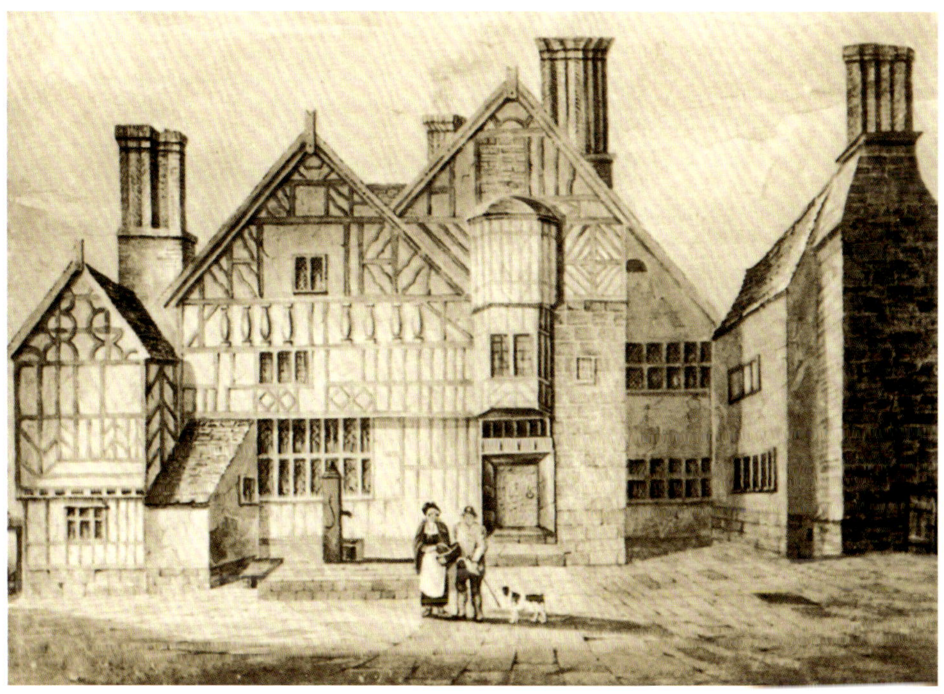

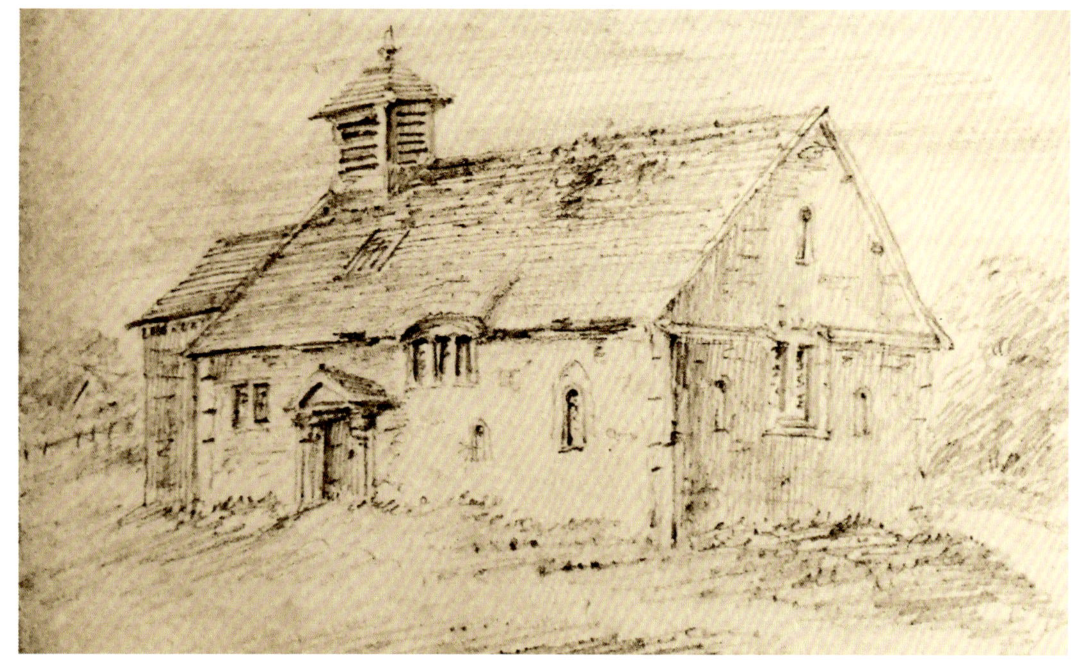

## Old Chapels and New Churches: Priorslee

Although the Domesday survey of 1086 lists several Saxon chapels in the area, it's unlikely many survived beyond the twelfth century. A few 'new' ones, like that at Priorslee in this 1816 sketch by Shrewsbury schoolteacher David Parkes, were built during that period. Most had been replaced by the time this one was demolished in favour of a new church dedicated to St. Peter (below), which opened in 1836 during a period when the Anglican church erected a number of new chapels to combat popular Methodism.

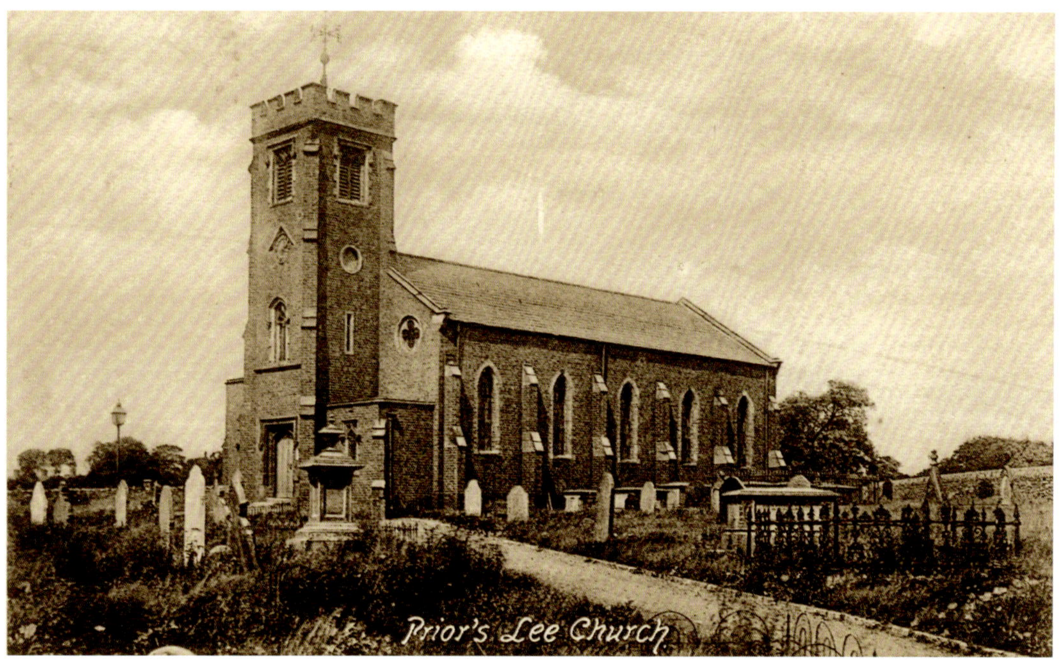

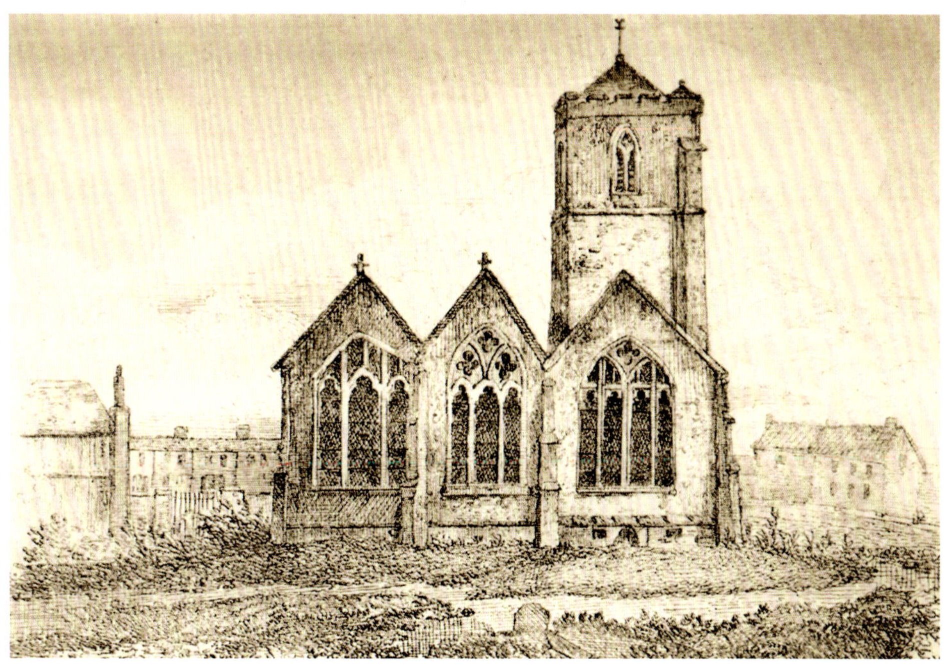

## All Saints Parish Church, Wellington

The twelfth century church (above) was belatedly demolished in 1789 following considerable damage done by Parliamentarian troops who occupied it during the English Civil War and used its windows and statuettes for target practice. The present church (below) designed by George Steuart was erected in 1790. The churchyard, which once accommodated an even earlier Saxon chapel, was levelled and converted into a Garden of Rest in 1952 as part of the town's celebrations for Queen Elizabeth II's coronation.

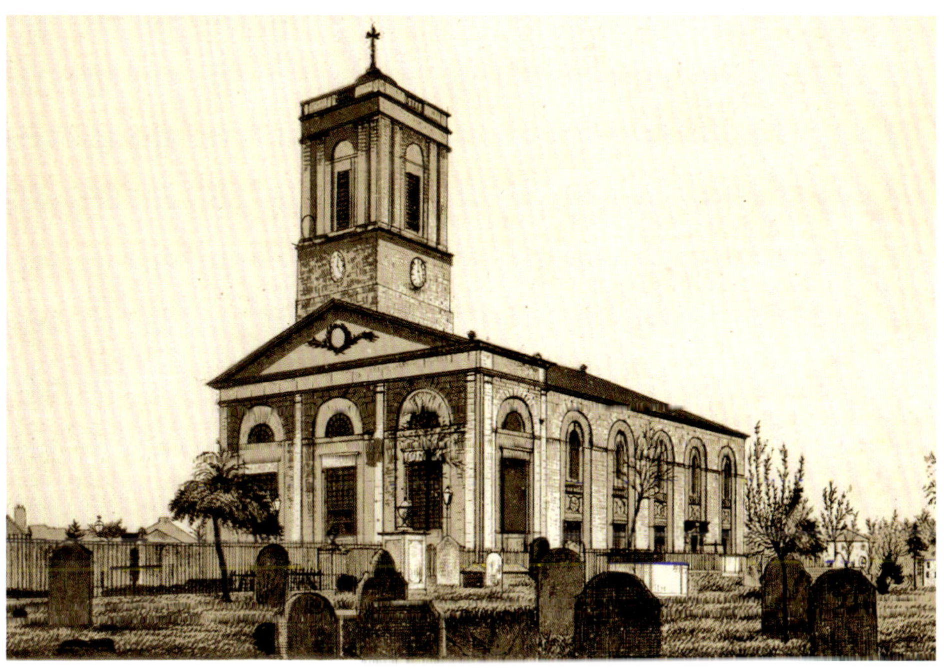

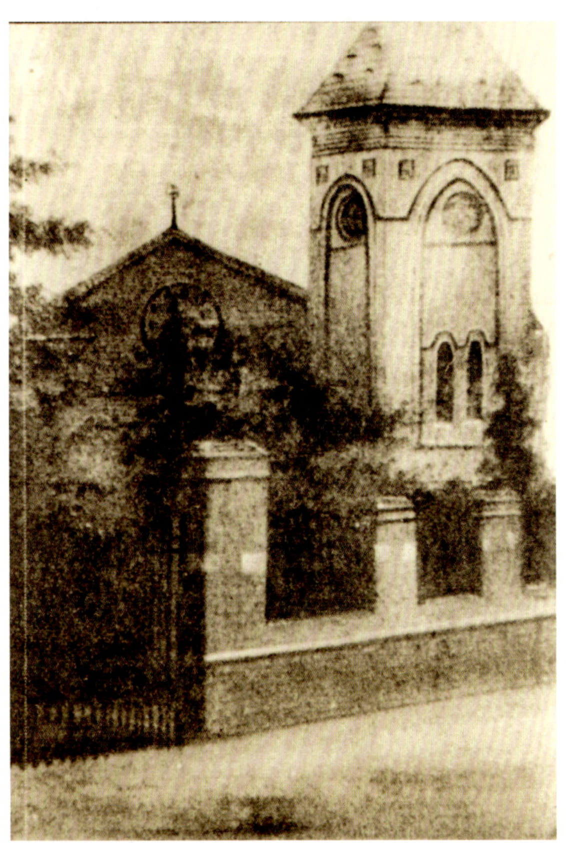

## Replacement for Roman Catholics

*Left:* A rare photograph of the former Roman Catholic church on Mill Bank, Wellington, now demolished. Erected in 1838, it was the only Roman Catholic church in the area. The present church (below) was erected in 1906 on the corner of King Street and Plough Road, as seen in this unusual postcard produced by newsagent and stationer Tom Austin. From then until its demolition *c.* 1971, the old church was used as a parish hall, a roller-skating rink, the Picture Pavilion (the first cinema in the area, showing silent films between 1911 and March 1927 as well as providing live performances by travelling companies accompanied by the Pavilion Orchestra), a training centre for unemployed people and a Catholic schoolroom.

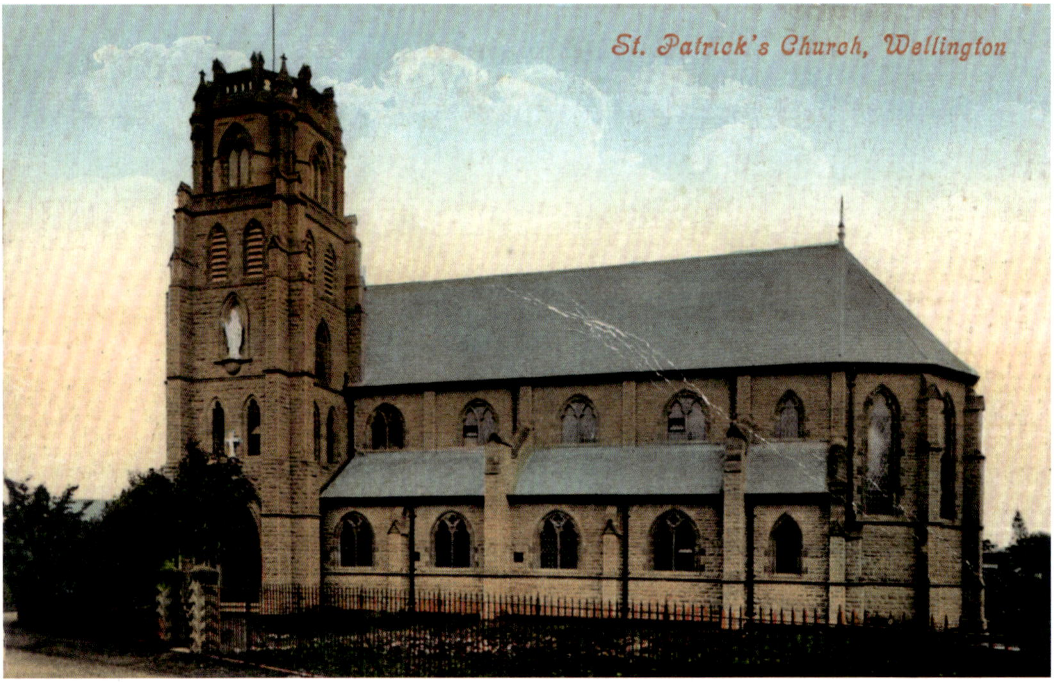

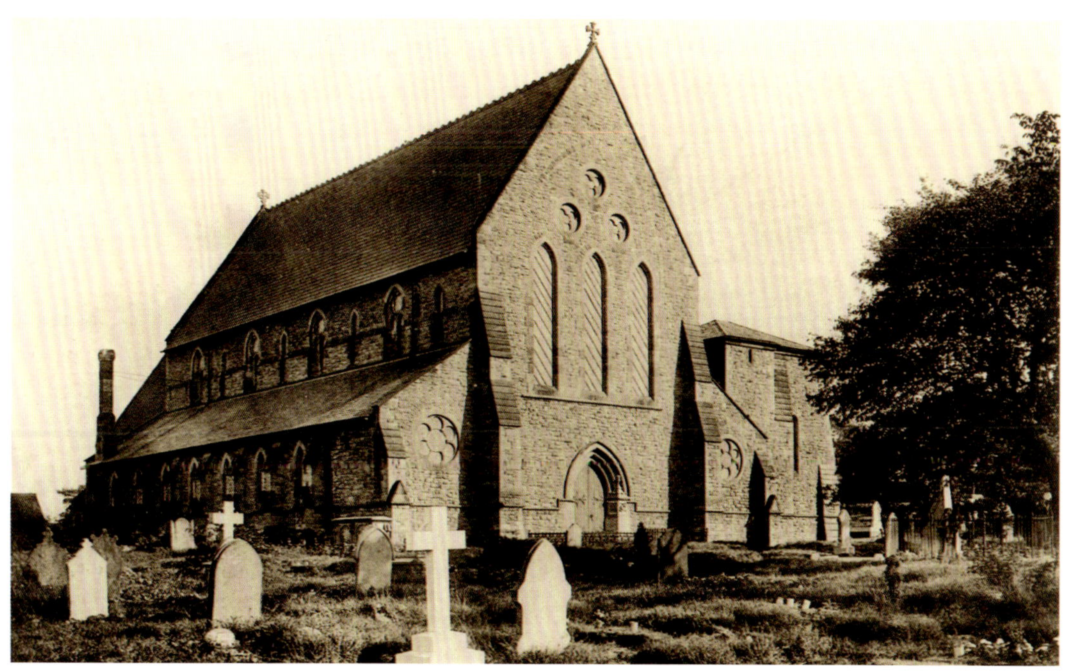

## St. Georges Church extended

Two views of the same church. The present church dedicated to St. George replaced an earlier chapel of ease erected in 1806 in Pains Lane (the former name for St. Georges township) and seems to have taken its dedication name from St. George Leveson-Gower, the Marquis of Stafford's dead son. Subsequently inadequate for a growing congregation, the church was rebuilt in 1860 and the new parish of St. Georges created a year later. The tower was added in 1929.

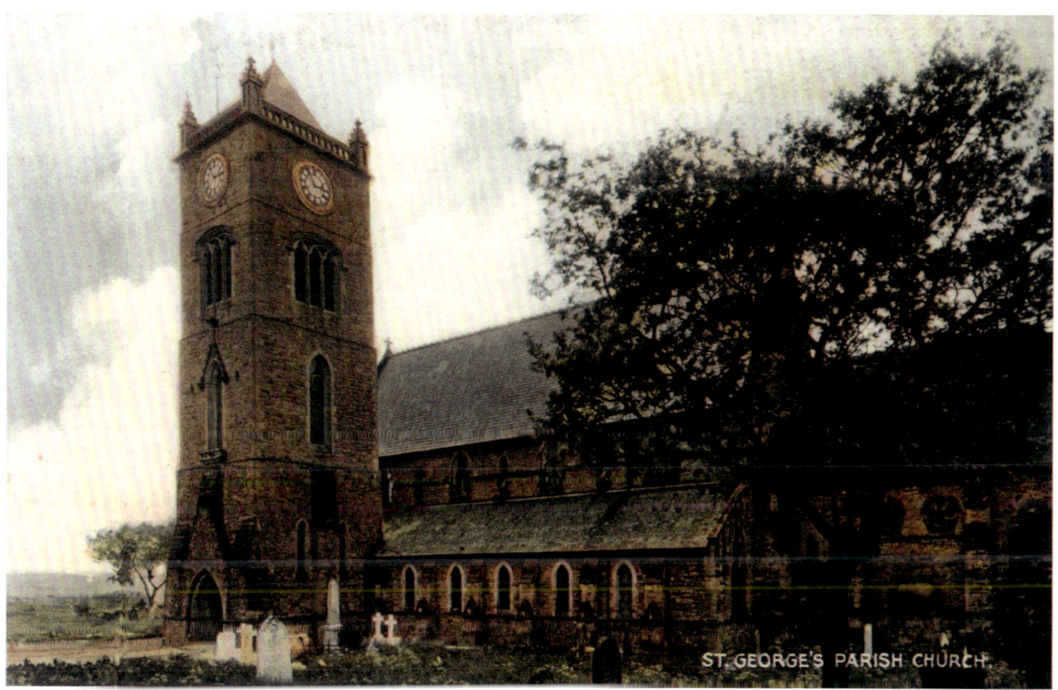

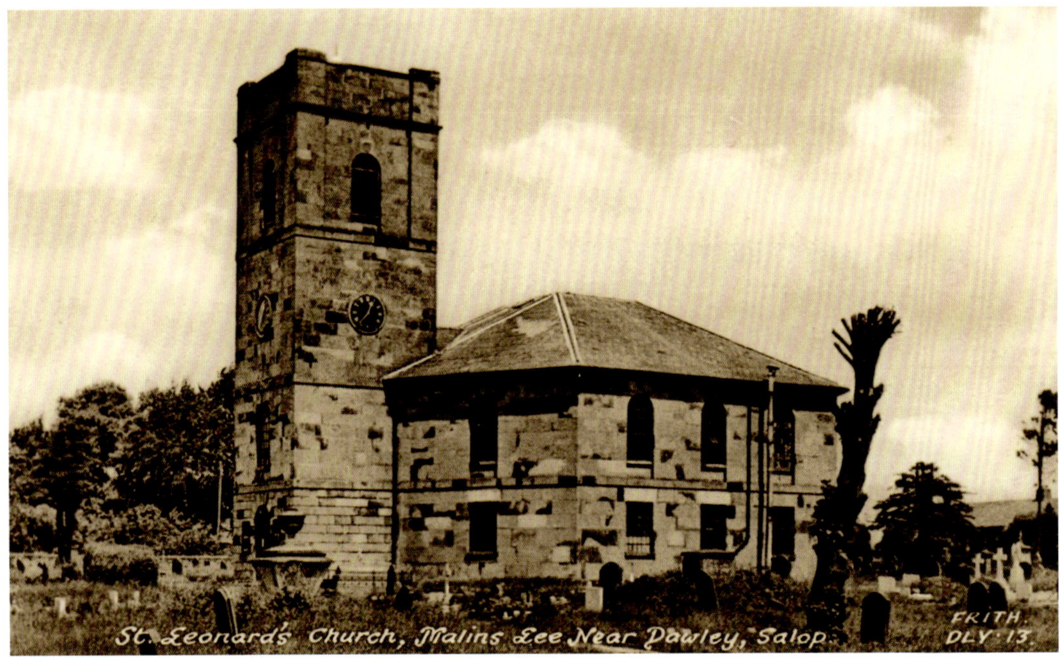



## Telford's Designs

St. Leonard's church at Malinslee, constructed in 1805, was the last Shropshire church designed by Thomas Telford. It follows a similar, albeit smaller, octagonal design used by Telford when his other church in the area, St. Michael's at Madeley (below), was erected in 1797 on the site of a more ancient church. Both churches look very similar in these old photographs. The churchyard at Madeley contains a number of cast iron family vaults, a reflection of the importance of the iron industry in the area, as well as the communal grave of nine coal miners killed in the 1864 Lane Pits disaster. For more details of this tragic event, see *Death and Disaster in Victorian Telford* by this author.

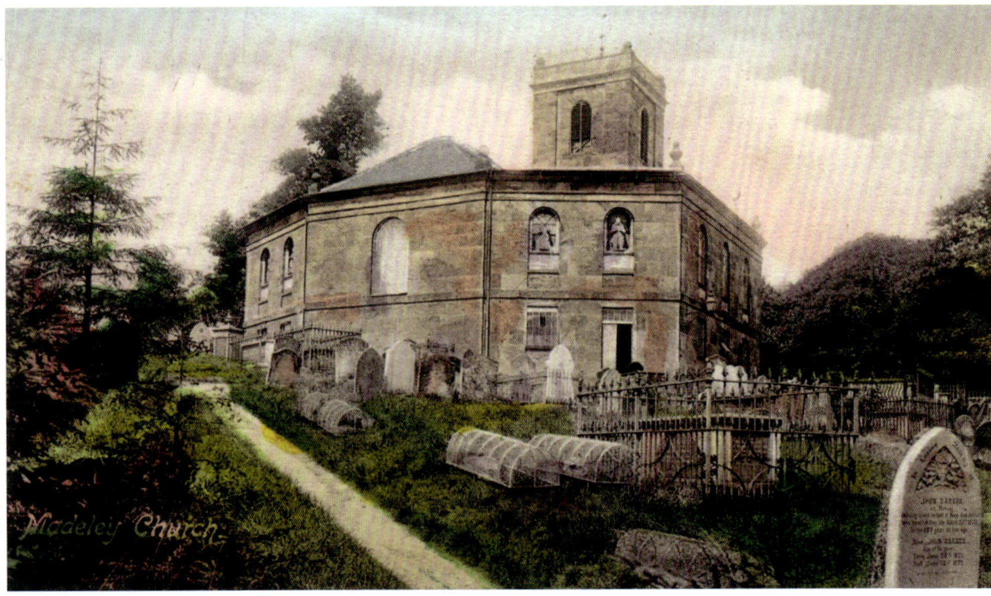

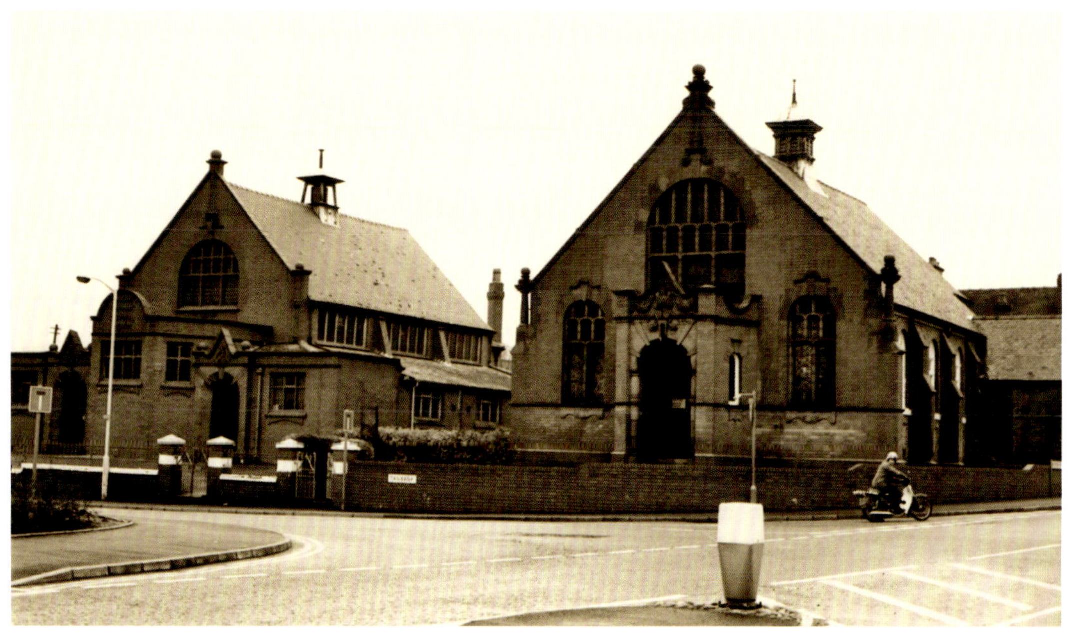

## New Worshippers

Tan Bank Primitive Methodist Chapel, Wellington, was erected in 1898, replacing an old 1826 predecessor which stood on the opposite side of the road. Upon merging with Wesleyan Methodists in New Street in 1966, it became home to Wellington Methodist Youth Club until 1978 when it became a Muslim mosque. Its Sunday schoolroom, built to a complimentary design in 1906, is now a place for worship by the First United Church of Jesus Christ (Apostolic), primarily a West Indian church whose congregation had previously met at Belmont Hall, New Street. Other former church buildings in the district have not been so fortunate in retaining a religious purpose.

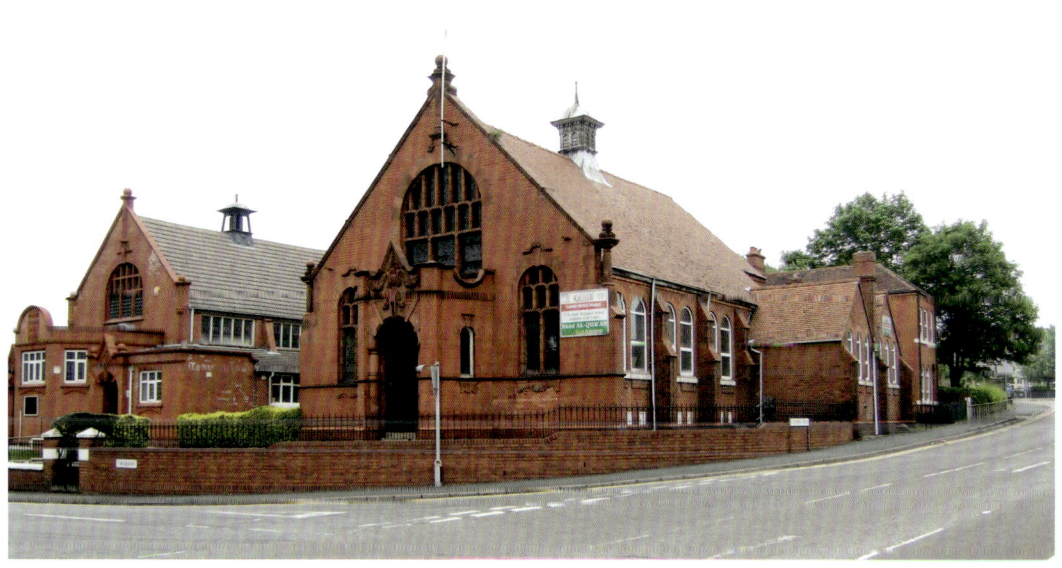

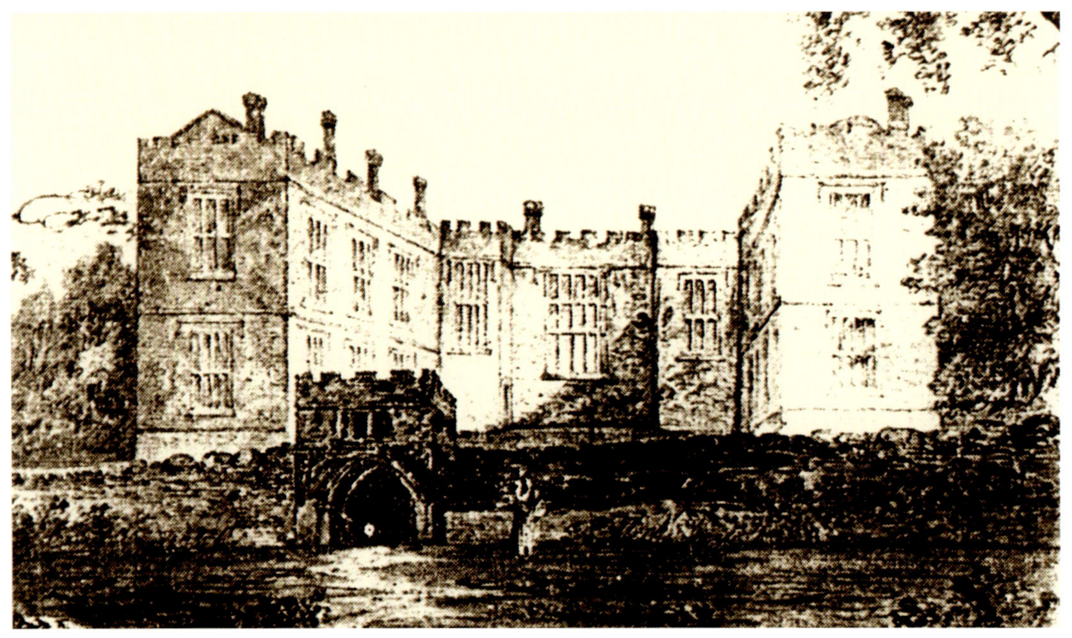

## Apley Castle(s)

The Telford area has provided homes for important families for centuries. There have been three Apley Castles near Wellington, the first formed in 1327 when Alan de Charlton crenelated his manor house. The second castle (above) was built nearby between 1567 and 1620 by other members of the Charlton family and suffered damage during the English Civil War; a restored stable block, converted into private accommodation, remains. The third castle (below, as it appeared a century ago) was built between 1792 and 1794. It was demolished *c.* 1955, although its lake and most of its overgrown grounds survive. Property developers hope to build houses on some of the land, despite local opposition.

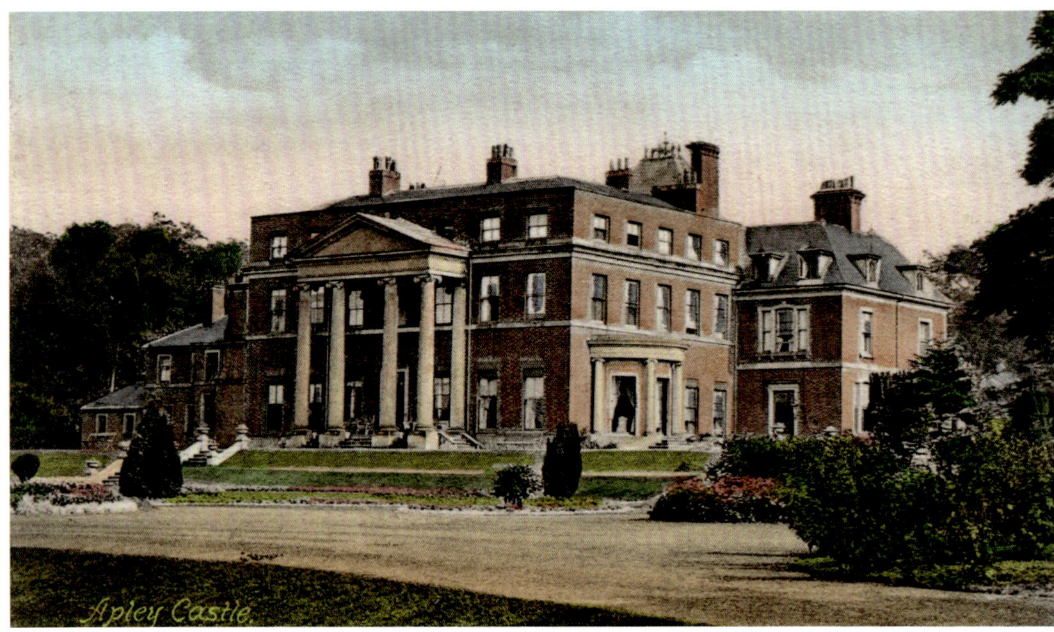

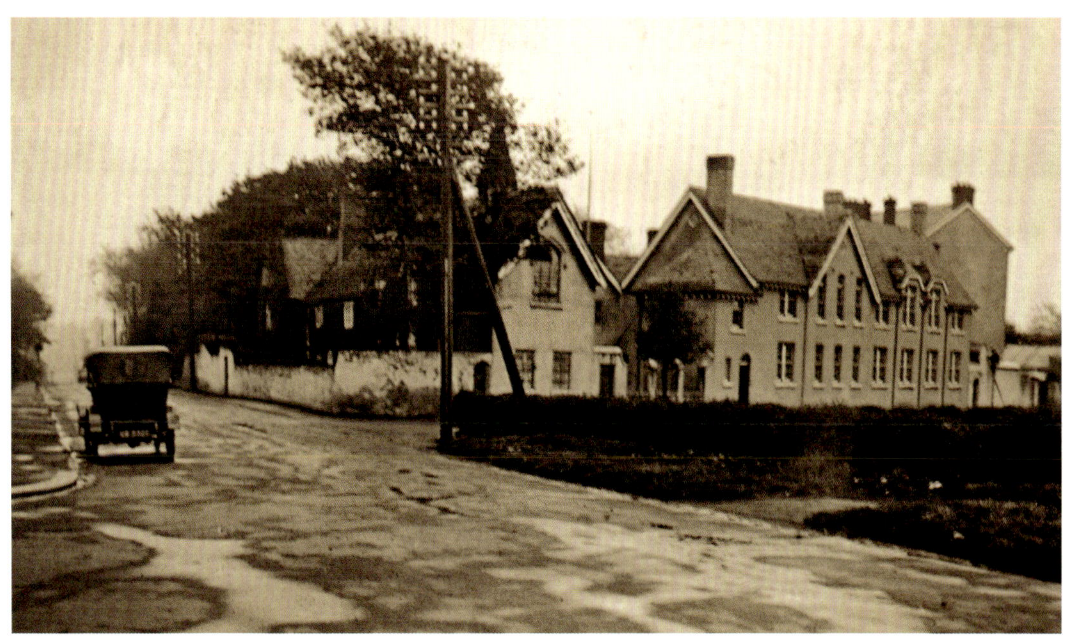

## Old Hall, Wellington

A timber-framed  hall (originally called Watling Street Hall) was built in 1480 for the Forester family, traditional keepers of the Royal Forest of The Wrekin who later became The Lords Forester and subsequently lived at Dothill, Wellington before moving to Willey, Broseley. Before 1835, Old Hall had become a school under the Cranages and developed into a boys' boarding school (by 1851), a preparatory school (1894) and accepted girls from 1976. The school moved into new premises off Stanley Road, Wellington, in 2006 and the Old Hall buildings and grounds have been developed into a small housing estate (below) at the corner of Holyhead Road and Lime Kiln Lane (whose earlier name was Woodward's Shute).

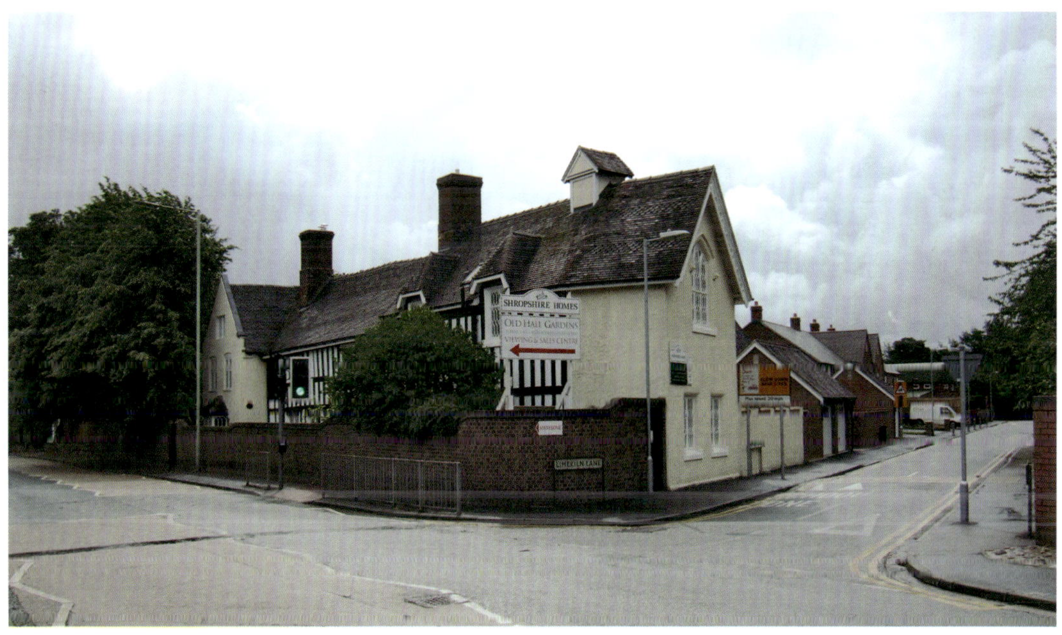

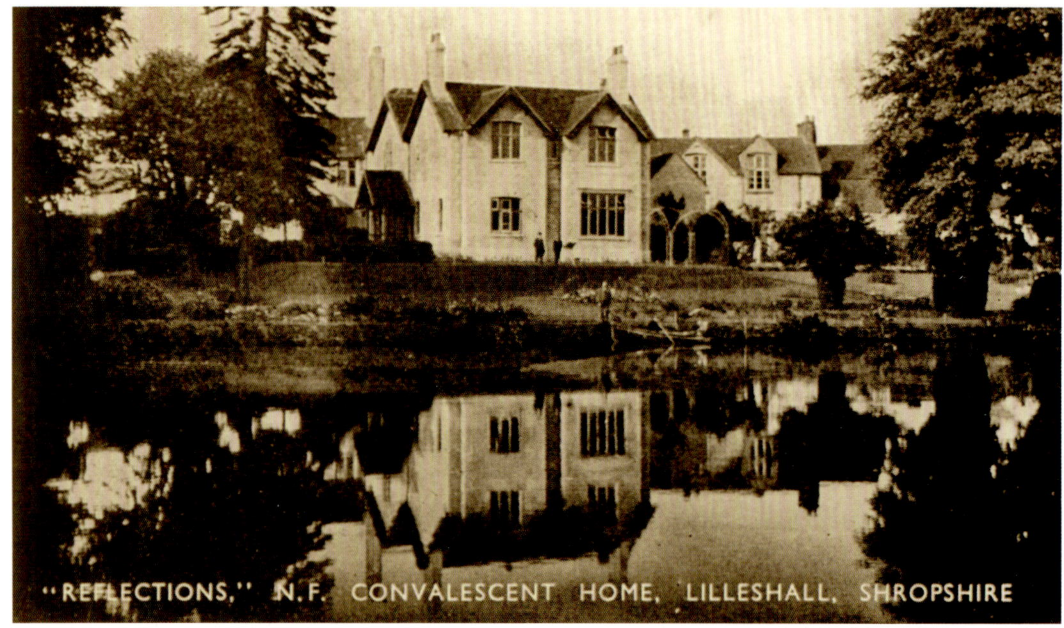



### Old Hall, Lilleshall

Apparently built in the late 1750 as a more desirable residence for the Leveson-Gowers than their hunting lodge at Donnington Wood, this former farmhouse was the main Shropshire seat of the family until it was regarded as insufficiently grand for Lord Gower who had Lilleshall Hall built. It was retained as a dower house until 1917 when C. & W. Walker of Donnington bought it. The firm then sold it to the National Federation of Retail Newsagents, Booksellers and Stationers as a convalescent home which closed in 1972. In 1977, Old Ben Homes reopened and redeveloped it as retirement flats for newsvendors.

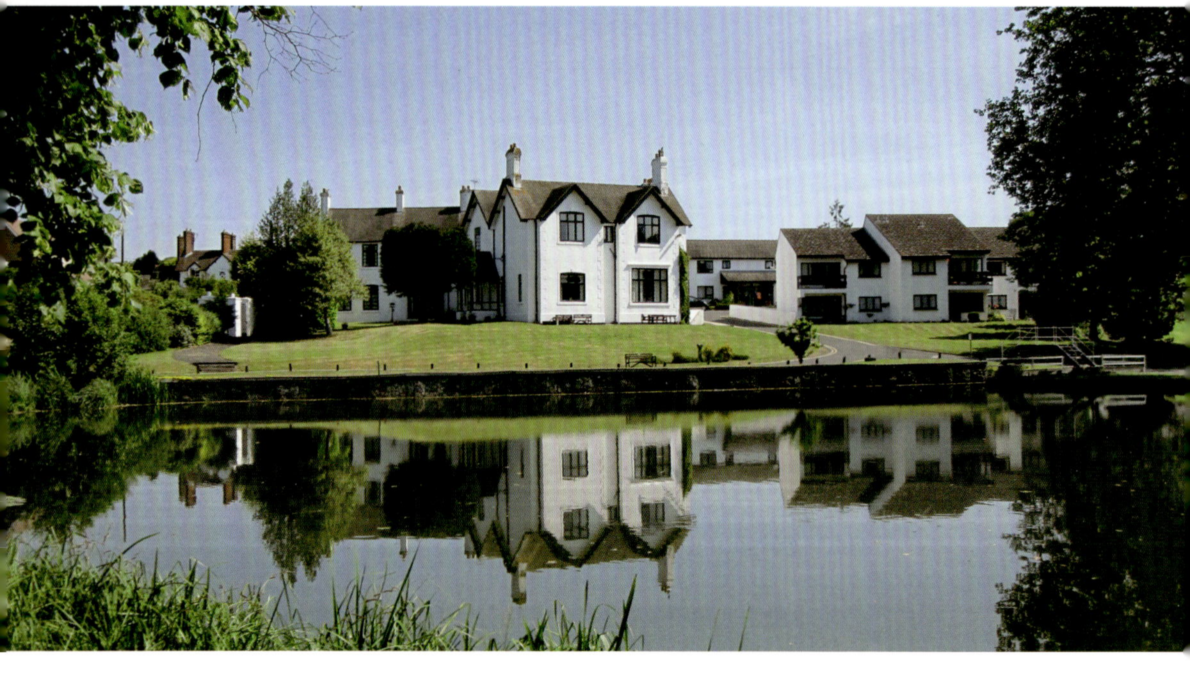

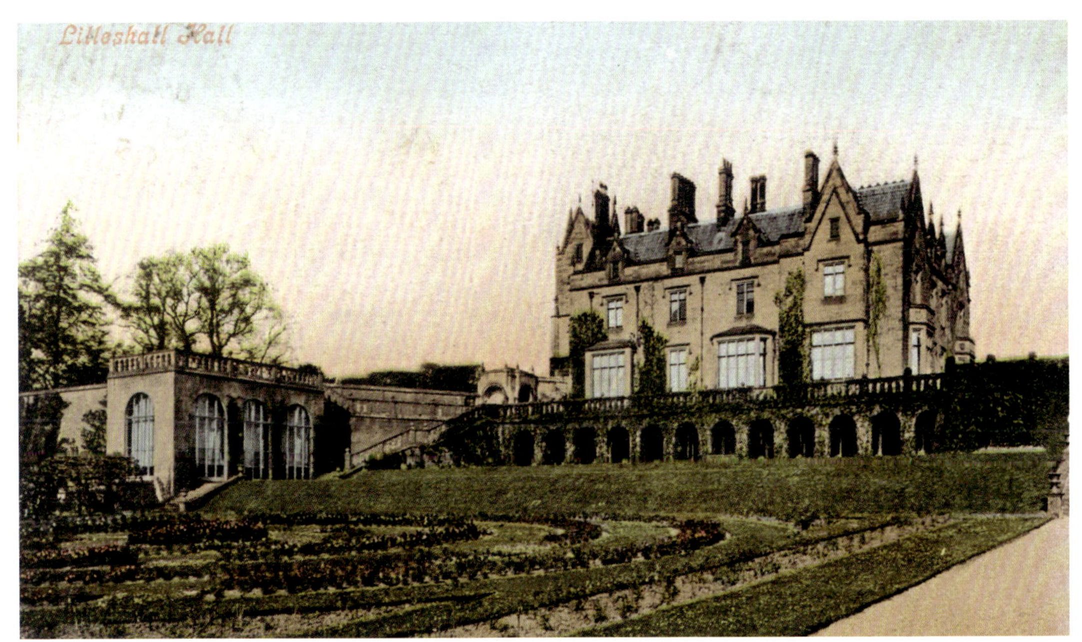


## Lilleshall Hall

Taking several years to build, the Hall became the main Shropshire residence of the Leveson-Gowers in 1831, two years before their principal member became the first Duke of Sutherland. It was sold first to Sir John Lee in 1917, then to Herbert Ford, an Ironbridge industrialist who opened it as a stately home (complete with narrow gauge railway) open to the public throughout the 1930s. During the Second World War, wooden huts were used by Cheltenham Ladies' College and Dr. Barnardo's. In 1951 Princess Elizabeth opened it as a sports centre. It is now run by Leisure Connection on behalf of Sport England.

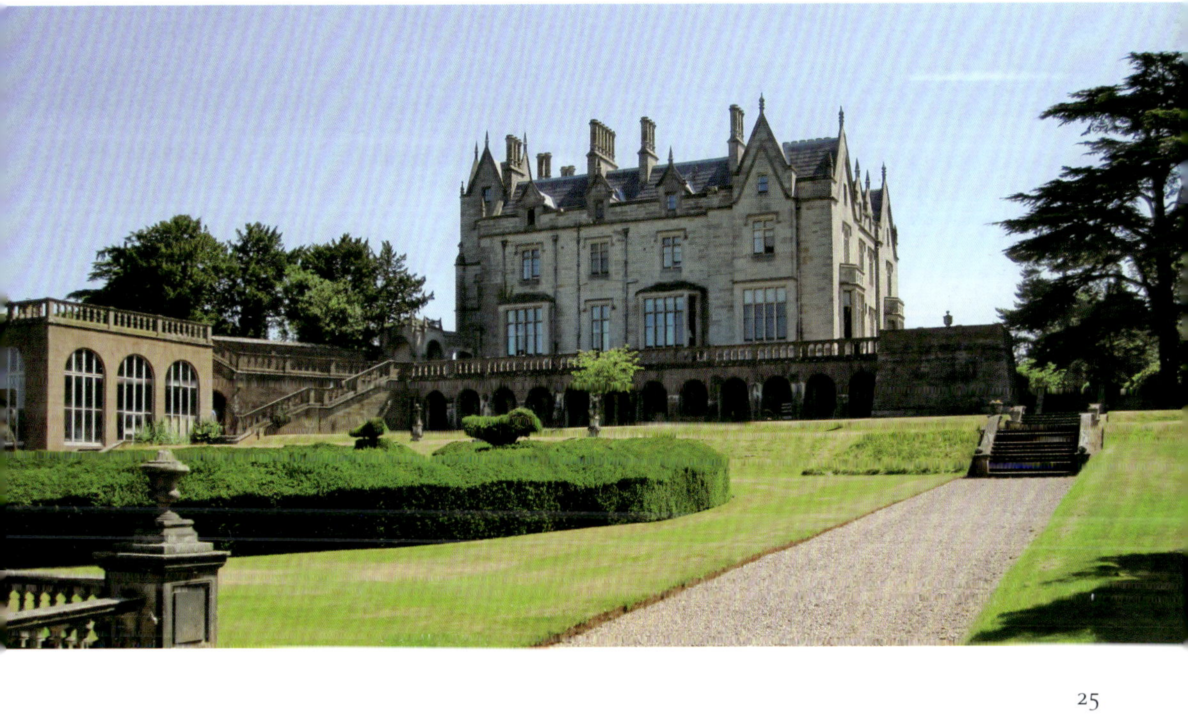

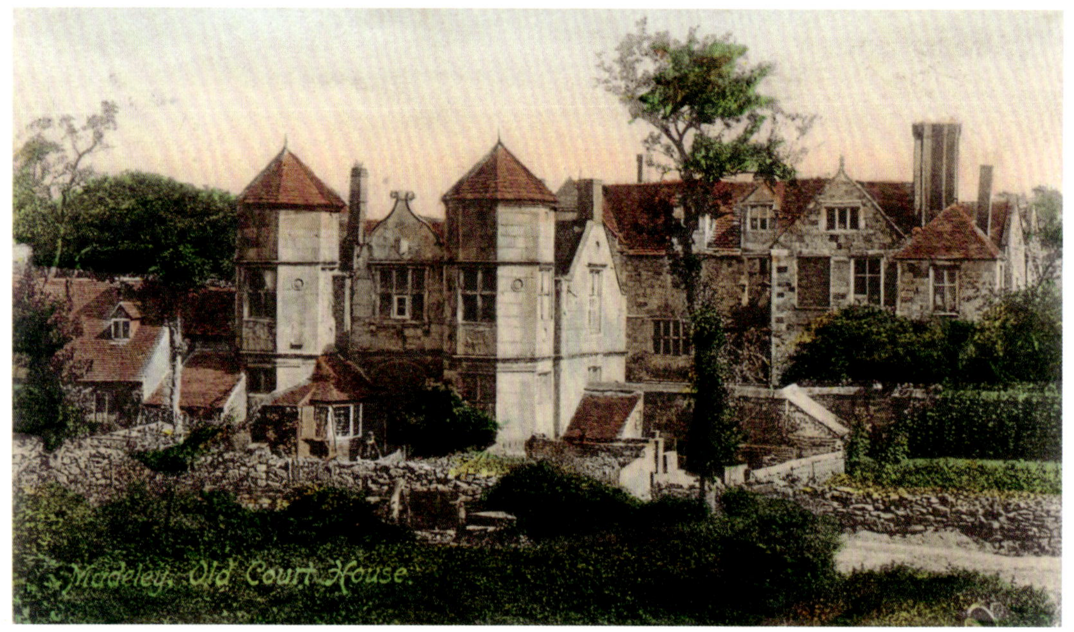



## Madeley Court

With parts dating back to the thirteenth century on the site of a former monastic grange, Madeley Court was home to the Brooke family, Lords of the manor of Madeley, of which Robert Brooke was Speaker in the House of Commons during the reign of Bloody Mary. His successors were enthusiastic Catholics, which led to the temporary loss of ownership during the English Civil War. The prominent gate house mainly dates back to the 1500s. The last lord of the manor to reside there was Basil Brooke. From his death in 1699, the property fell into a long, almost unhindered decline with a succession of tenants (including Abraham Darby I) and farmers. It was sold to Dawley Development Corporation by the Barnett family in 1964 and has since taken on the role of a luxury hotel.

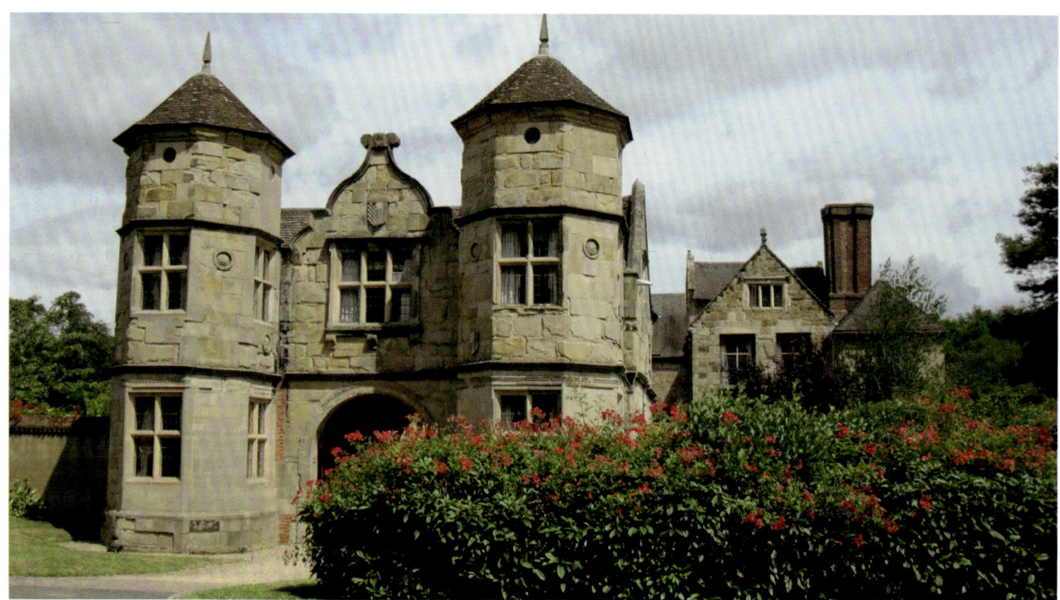

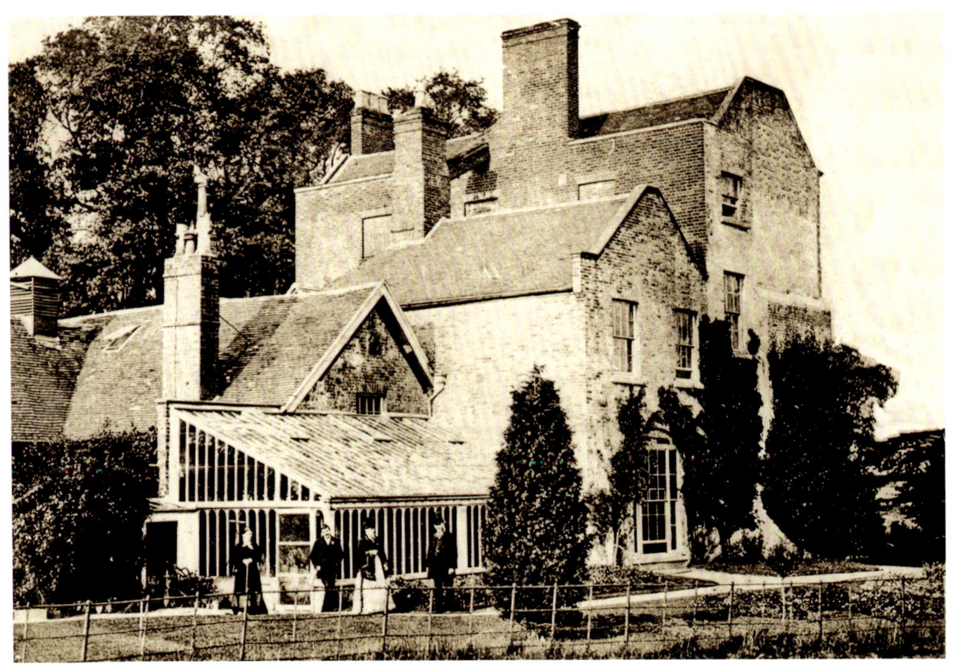

## Dothill and Orleton

Both estates are on the outskirts of Wellington. The manor of Dothill dated from Medieval times and was home to a succession of notable families, from Praeres to Horton to Streventon and thence by marriage to Lord Forester of Old Hall, Wellington. The Groom family (above), wealthy Victorian timber merchants, acquired part of the estate before H. F. Hodgson sold much of its park to Wellington Urban District Council for building a housing estate and schools. Orleton Hall (below, 1891), originally part of the manor of Wrockwardine, was occupied by the Cludde family, who built the present Hall during the eighteenth century. It then passed by marriage to the Herberts (Earls of Powis) and is now owned by descendant Peter Holt.

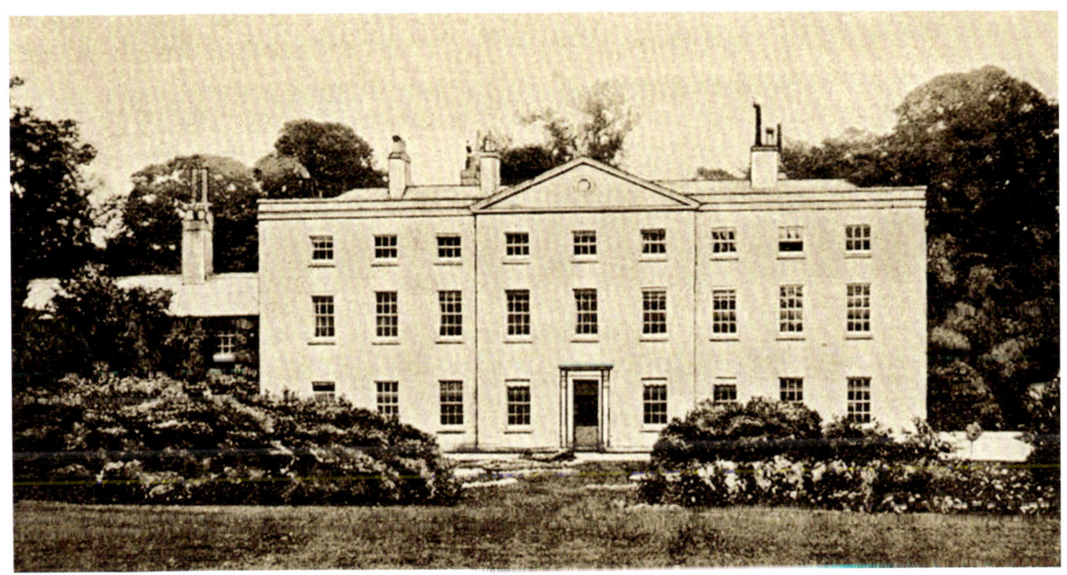

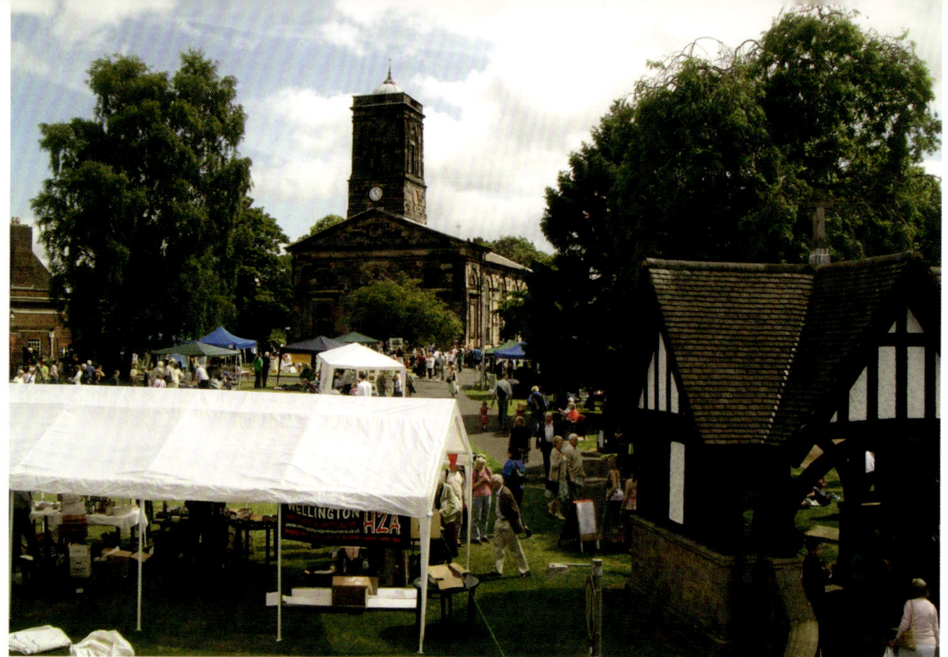

## Telford's Towns: Wellington

Telford comprises many townships, the most important of which, historically, economically and socially, is Wellington, whose continued survival can be traced back to its Medieval markets and fairs, which originally took place in the parish churchyard, where Midsummer Fayres like that above have been reintroduced in recent years. After King Edward I banned all such events taking place in churchyards from 1285 onwards, Wellington's weekly markets and periodic fayres spread from The Green (which stands next to the building  at the left of the photo), down Church Street and eventually formed Market Square (below), seen here 100 years ago.  Between the 1500s and 1805, a Market House on pillars stood here.

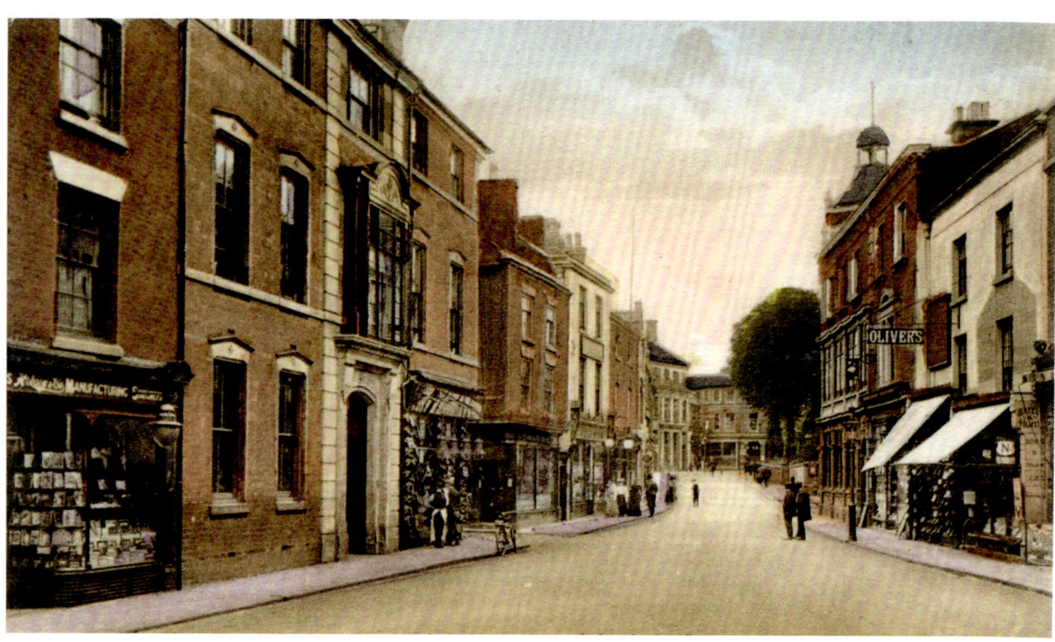

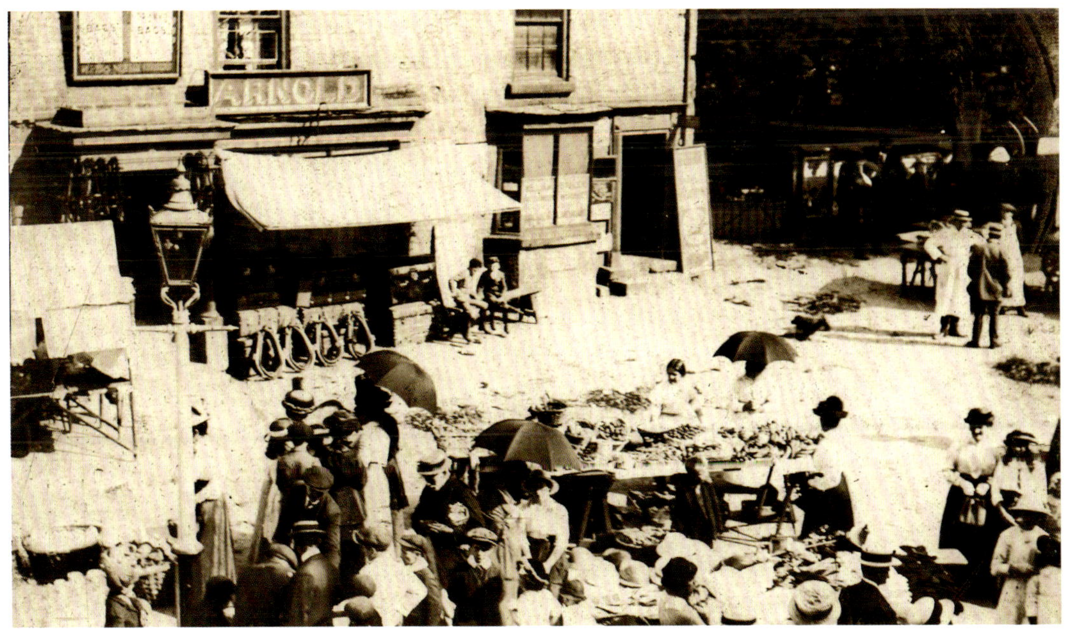

## Wellington's General Markets

Since 1864, when the present Market Hall was built (below, as seen in 1960; little has changed apart from the introduction of new facades to the shops fronting the Hall and other properties in Market Street.), general markets have taken place every week and now occur on Tuesdays, Thursday, Fridays and Saturdays. The one notable exception was in August 1914 after war had been declared on Germany. Because soldiers from the Cheshire Regiment occupied the market on their way to northern France, stall holders had to revive the old practice of setting up stall on The Green and along Church Street into Market Square (above).

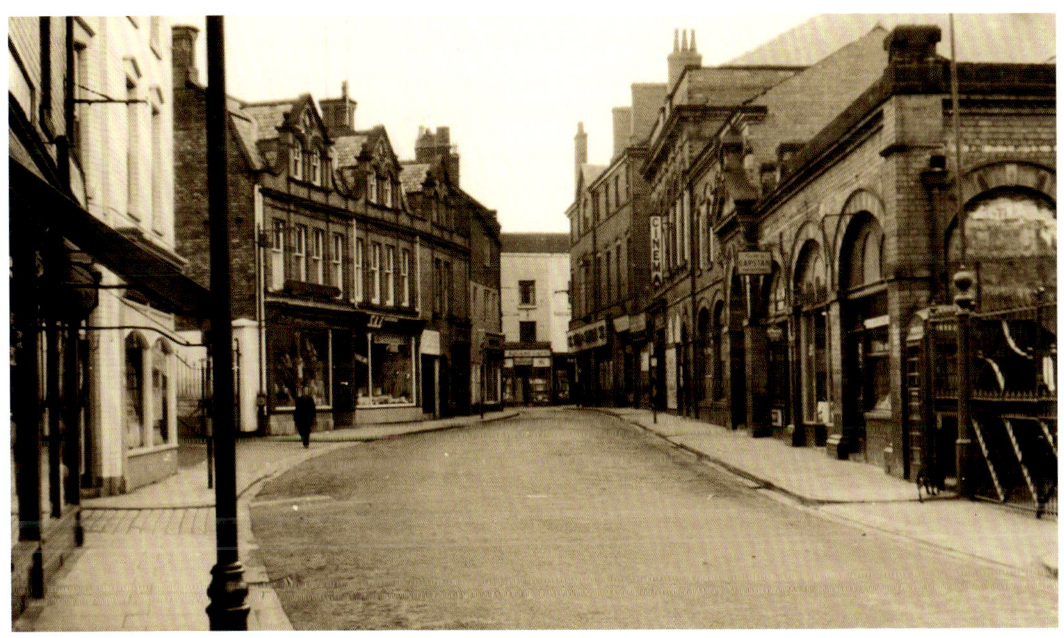

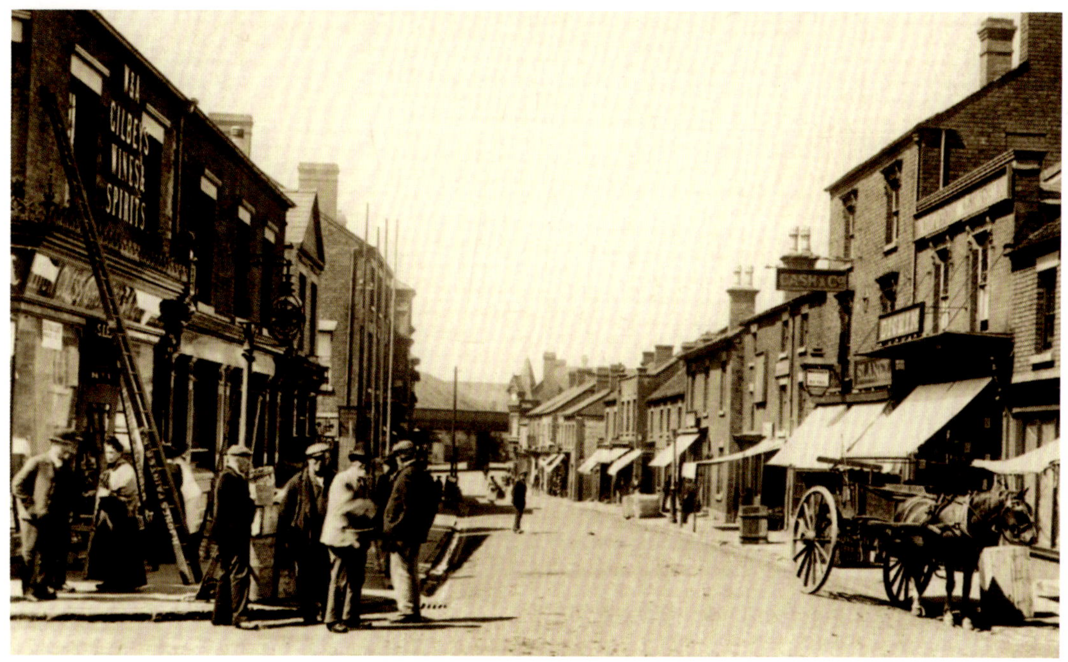

## Market Street, Oakengates

Originating as a late Medieval village, Oakengates grew into a town during the mid nineteenth century, largely because of the arrival of the railway (1849) in conjunction with nearby mining, iron working and other industries; the then lord of the manor of Wombridge, William Charlton of Apley Castle, did much to encourage the settlement's development, including a market, from which this street takes its name. The railway bridge in the distance lies at the western end of Market Street.

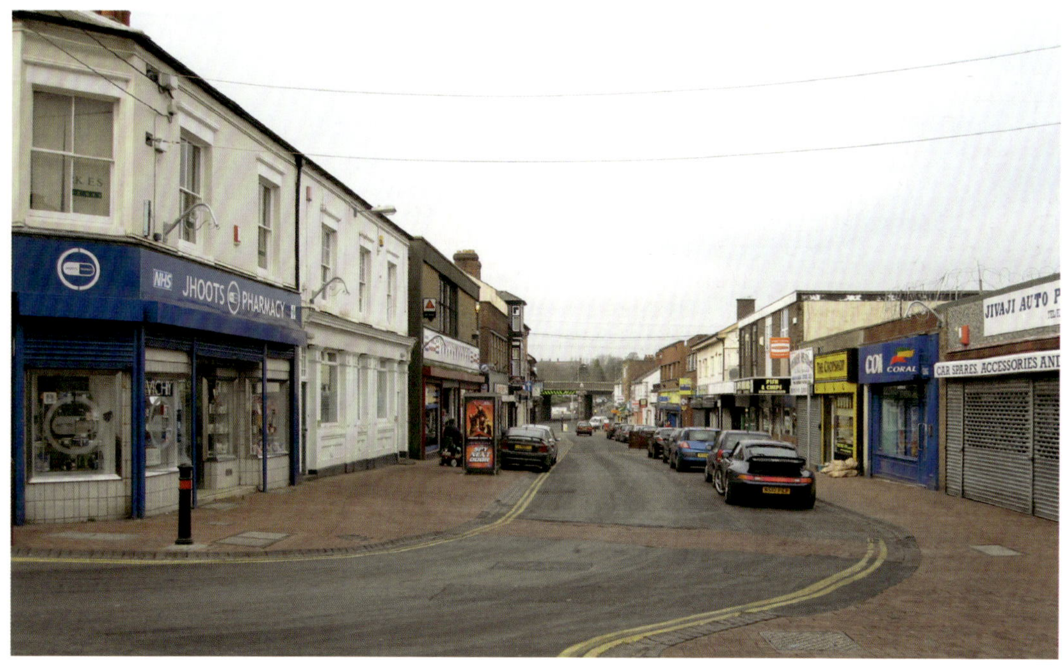

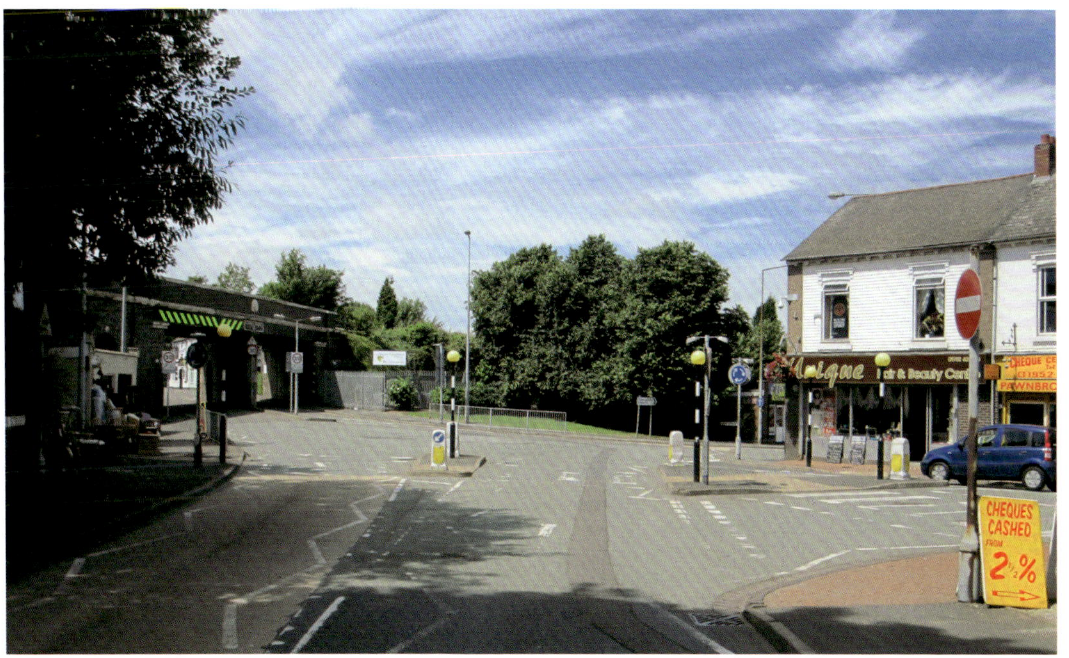

## The Green, Oakengates

Fairs were held on The Green during the town Wakes in early October until the railway bridge (built by the Lilleshall Company) cut through the grounds. They relocated to Owen's field until the 1980s and now take place at Donnington. The Coffee Palace in the centre was built in 1895, at which time The Green was still being used for occasional public entertainment, like the swing boats. The buildings to the right of the railway bridge had gone by the time a ring road around the town centre was completed in 1975.

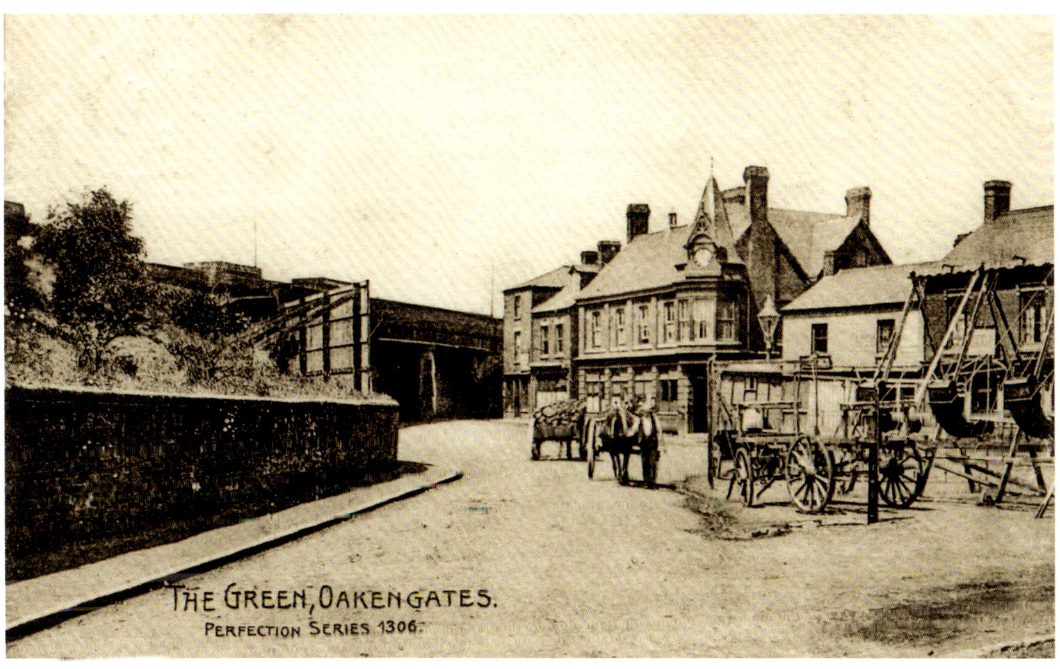

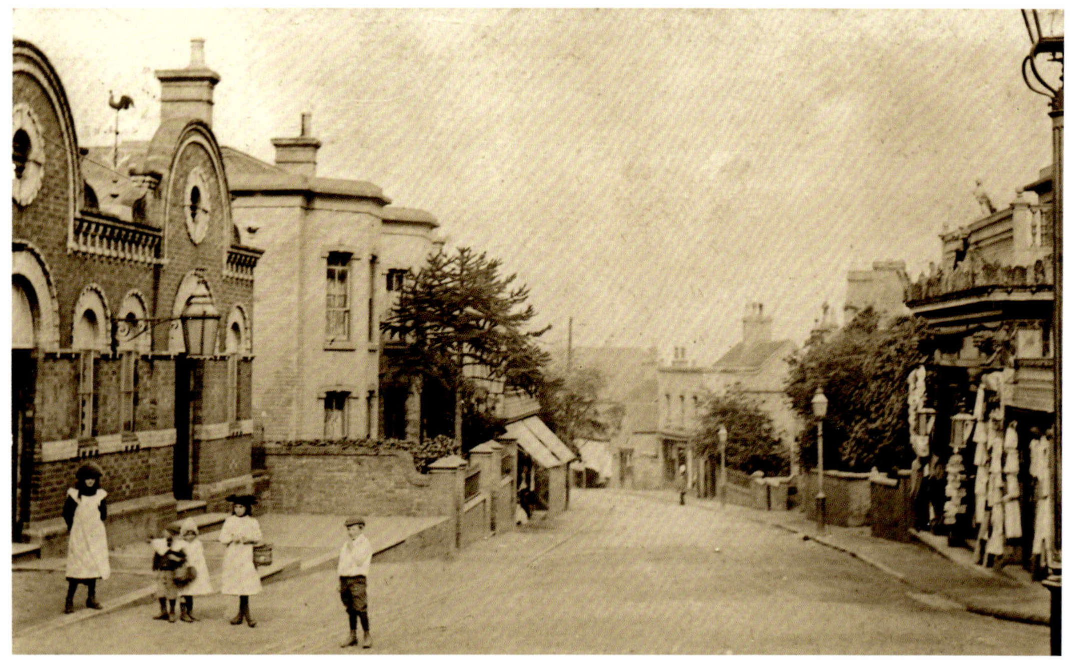

## Madeley High Street (West End)

Like Wellington, Madeley's origins seem to date back to the seventh century and the town's market charter dates to 1269. The building on the left was the town's Market Hall, built in 1870, the first permanent indoor market hall since an earlier one burnt down, possibly during the English Civil War. Madeley markets seem to have met with mixed fortunes for a variety of reasons (not least the building of an iron bridge in the parish in 1779) and appears to have ceased in 1903. (Wrekin district council revived a market in Russell Square in 1980.) Sometime before it was renamed Jubilee House and became home to Madeley Parish Council in 1998, this impressive building had served time as a nut and bolt factory.

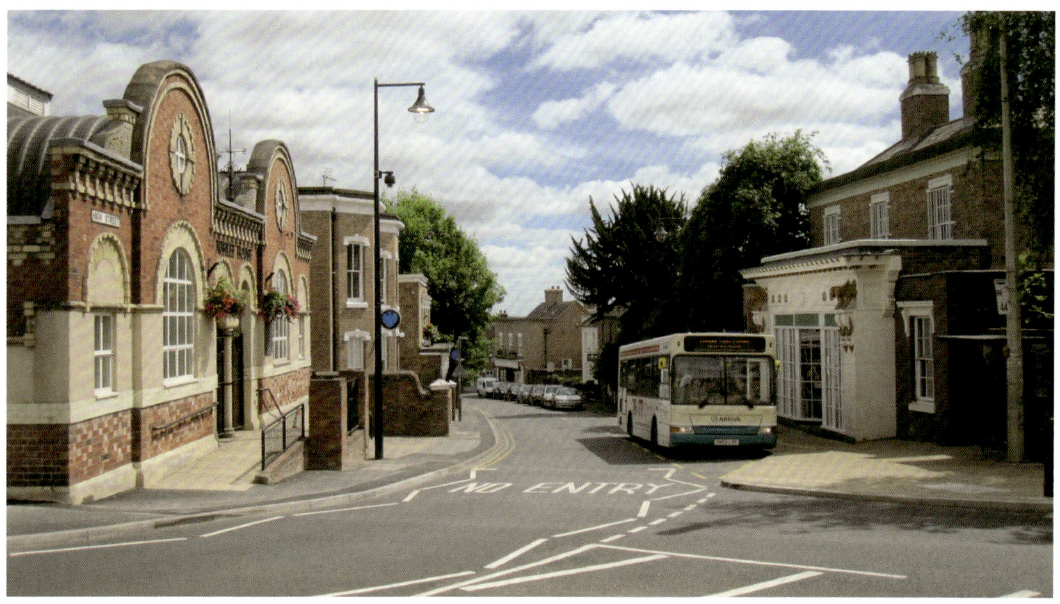

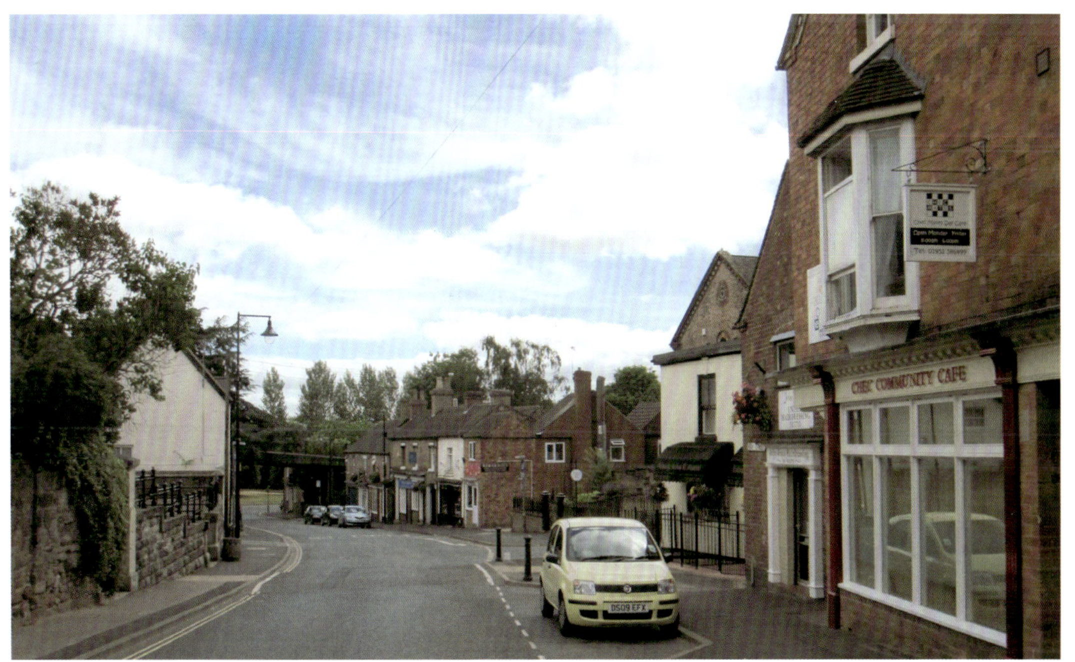

### Madeley High Street (East End)

The railway bridge in the 1938 photo has been replaced by a footbridge and cycle track as part of the 14-mile Silkin Way spanning the conurbation from Coalport to Admaston. Like the majority of public houses in Telford, the Royal Oak (then a Wem Ales house) is no longer a pub. Now an Indian restaurant, the building is thought to date back to the eighteenth century, an opinion reinforced by the belief that the Revd John Fletcher, Vicar of Madeley (whose impressive grave lies in St. Michael's churchyard) occasionally preached from a pulpit erected in a meeting room on the top floor (now removed) of the premises. Station Road runs off to the right behind the front car in both photographs.

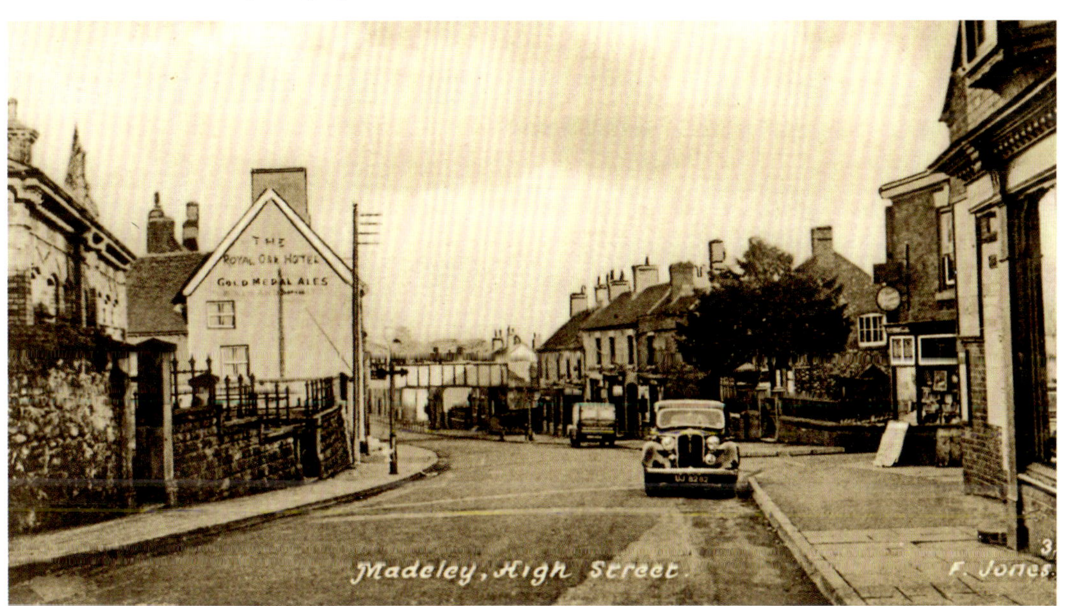

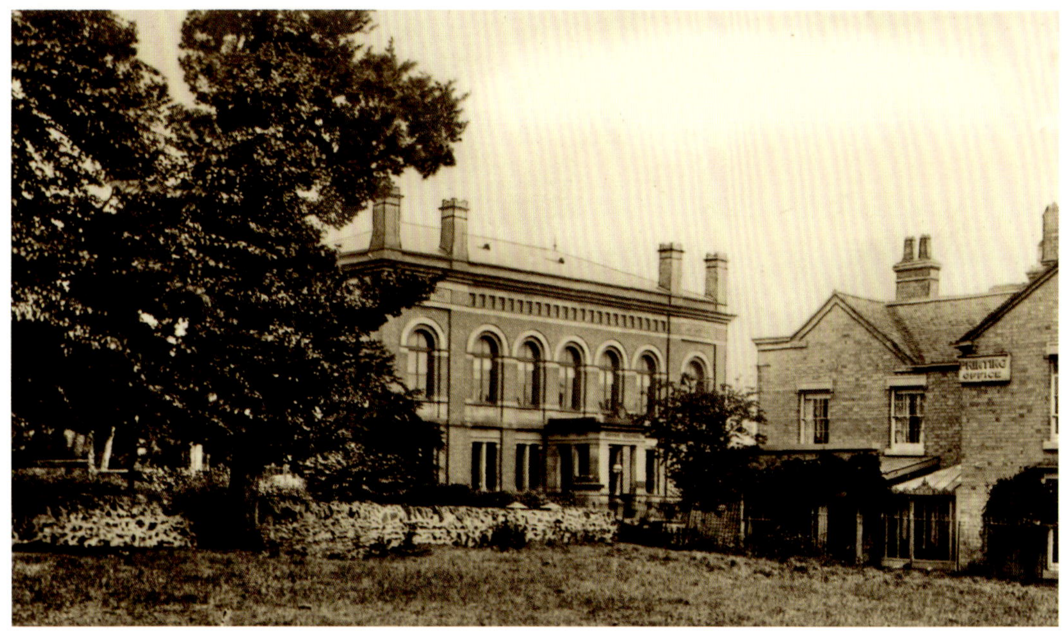

## Anstice Memorial Institute, Madeley

Now called The Anstice Club, this impressive building was built in 1869 in memory of ironmaster John Anstice who died in 1867. Anstice owned the Madeley Wood Company, for many years one of the most profitable industrial concerns in the district. Believed to be the world's oldest club created especially for working men, it initially provided public lectures, a library and rooms for reading, billiards and smoking. In time it also became a popular venue for dances and theatrical performances as well as other social functions. An ill-designed late 1960s concrete-and-glass shopping centre masked the building until recent improvements restored it to its former glory.

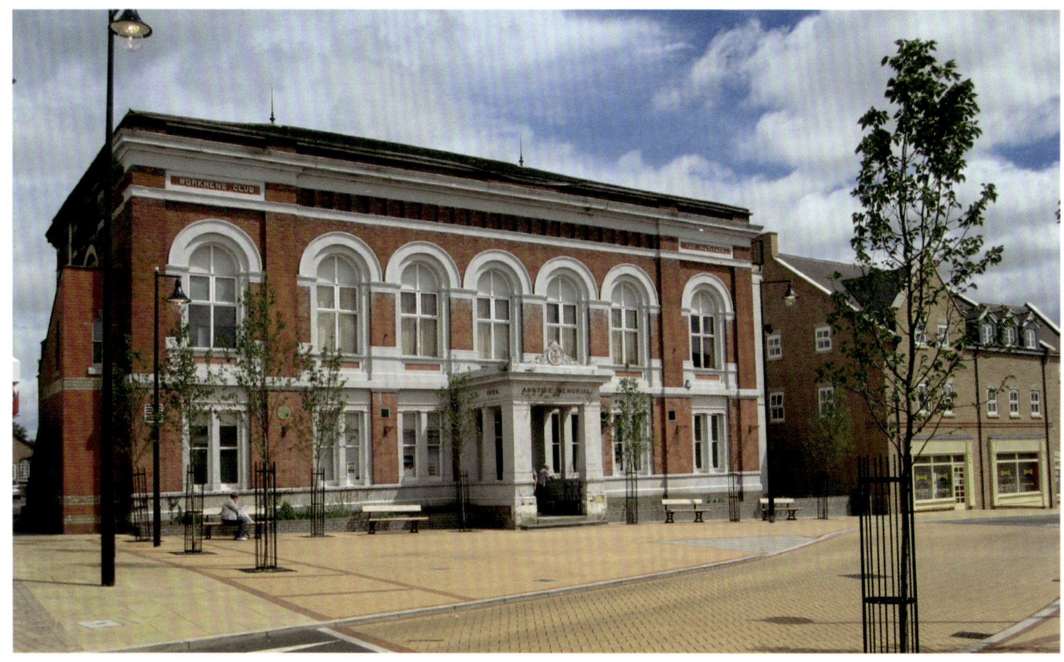

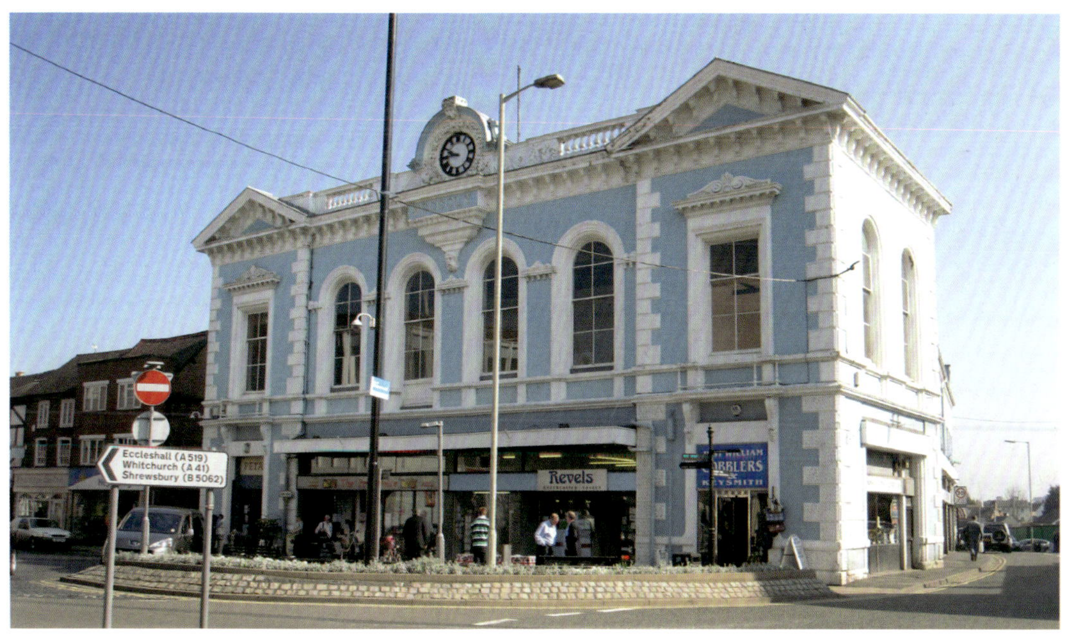

## Newport Markets

Telford was certainly not the first 'new town' in the area. Newport, in the manor of Edgmond, was created by the Normans. It began as a long S-shaped street lined with burgage plots (long, narrow strips of land with living quarters and shops facing the street and gardens and workshops behind). Early markets were held in a market hall, on the spot marked by the old butter cross (below, behind railings) until it burnt down. The present market hall (above) was erected in 1860 as a corn exchange with indoor and outdoor market facilities, together with an assembly room on the upper floor. Local government reorganisations in 1974 and 1998 brought the town within the Telford and Wrekin unitary authority.

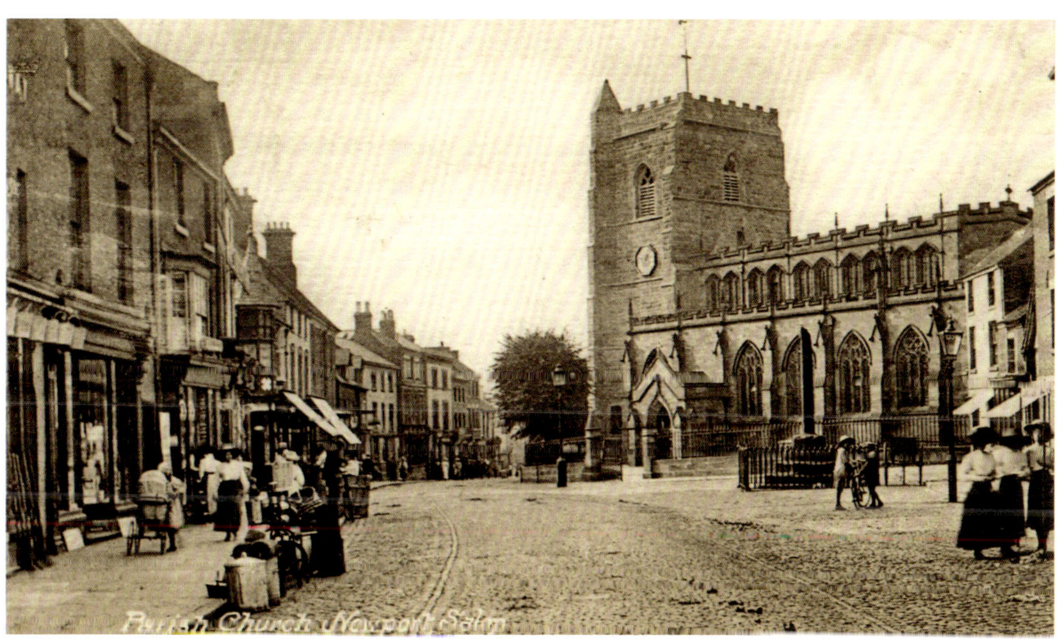

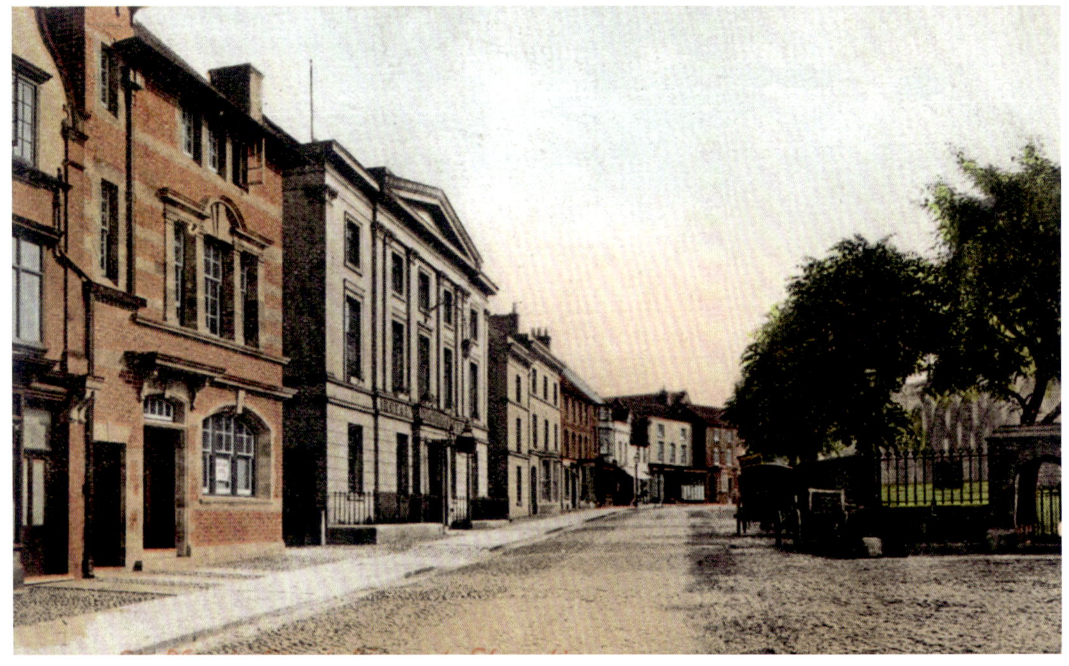

## Newport: St. Mary's Street looking South

This narrow street to the east of the parish church of St. Nicholas retains evidence of once being cobbled and is characterised by the premises of many small businesses. The most prominent building in the street is still the Royal Victoria Hotel, on the site of a pub called The Bear Inn which was renamed The Union and rebuilt. Princess Victoria stayed here in 1832; it was at her suggestion that it was given its present name. At one time it had a separate entrance at the rear specifically for patrons arriving by the nearby canal.

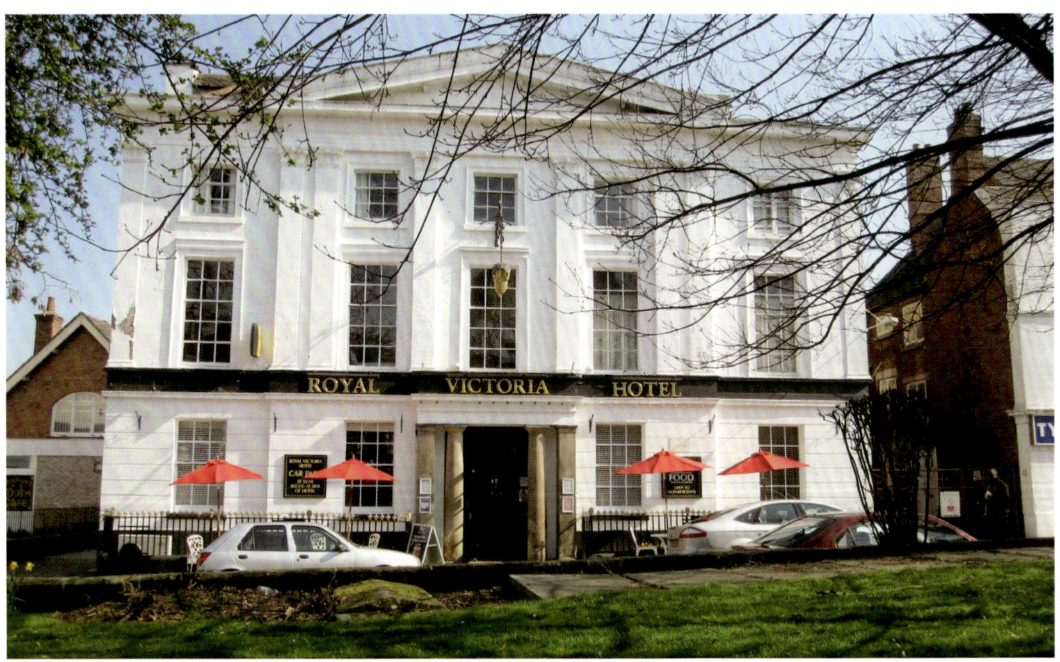

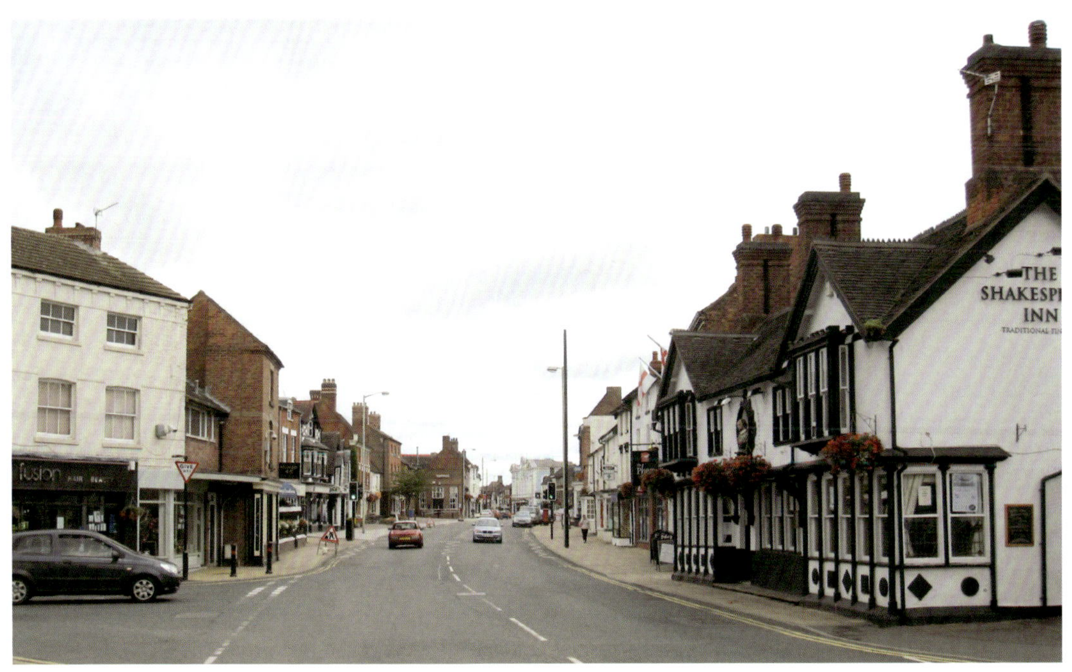

## Newport: High Street looking North

Regarded as the second most important town in the Borough after Wellington, Newport is justifiably proud of its main street although, in common with too many other towns in the prevailing economic climate, some of its business premises await new occupants. These views show the High Street curving to the right from Upper Bar before snaking to the left in the distance, past the church of St. Nicholas. The corner on the left is the entrance to Wellington Road.

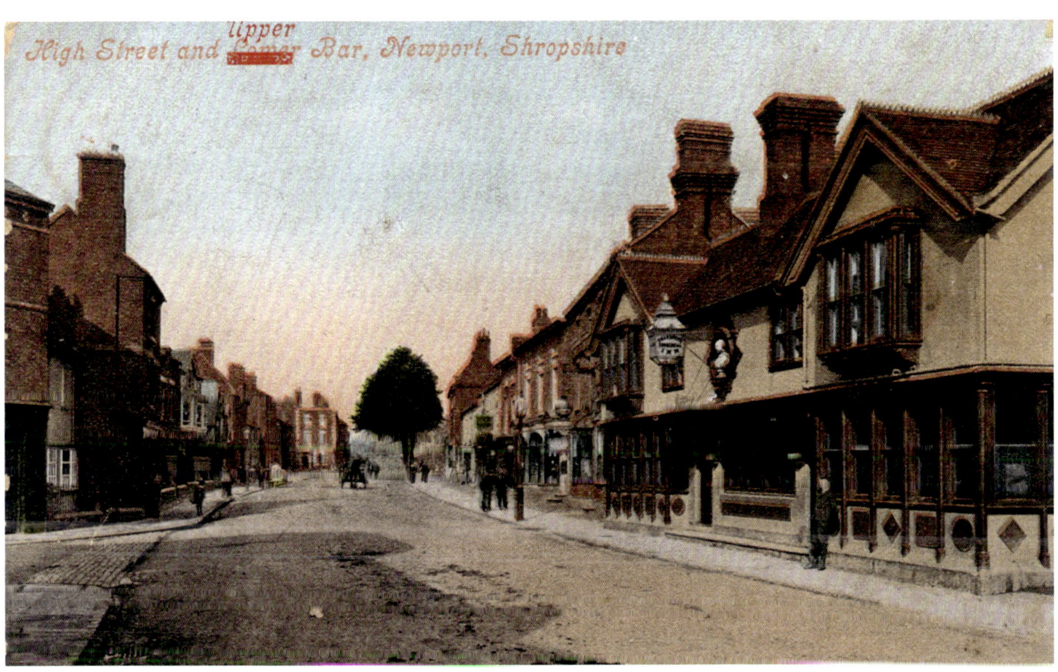

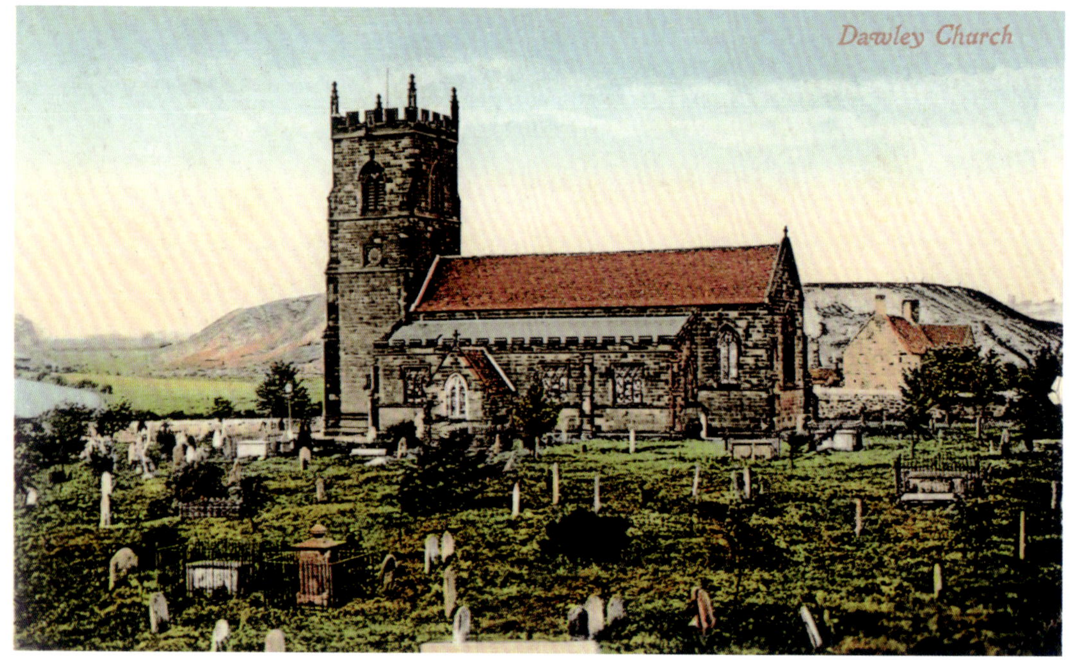



## Dawley

Dawley was once part of Wellington manor held by Grim before Domesday. Originally centred around the church, the settlement expanded considerably after coal mining and iron ore extraction led to innumerable pit mounds (sometimes called mounts) and blighted the landscape. In 1901, a public park and recreation ground was given to the town by W. S. Kenyon-Slaney and H. C. Simpson to alleviate the difficult lives and poor living conditions suffered by miners and their families.

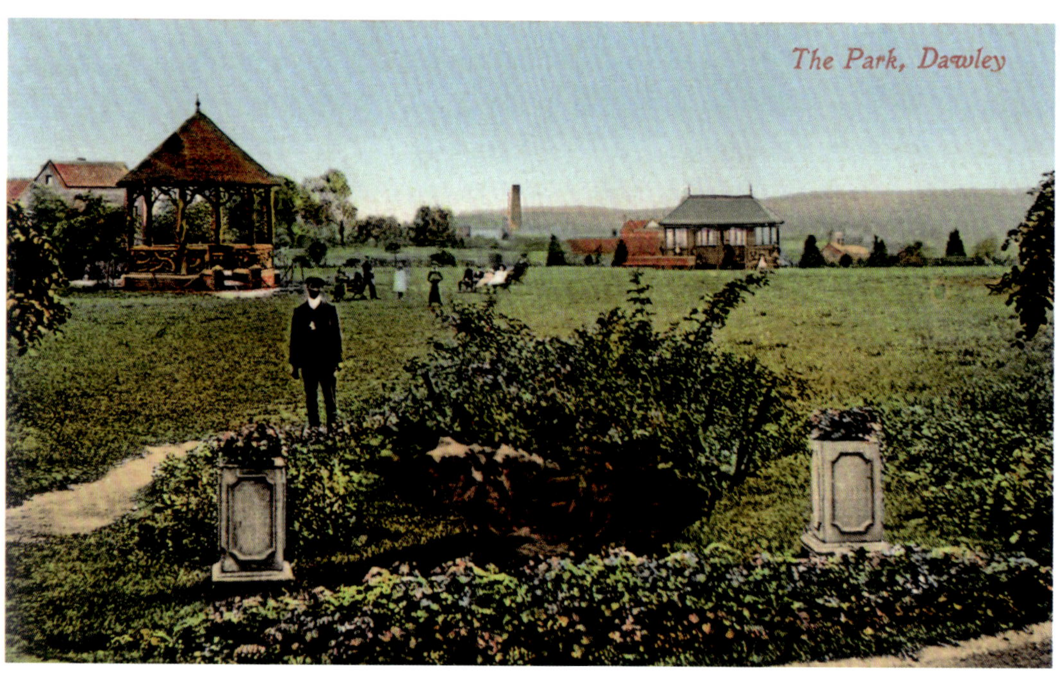

## Dawley: Captain Webb Memorial

'Nothing Great Is Easy.' Dawley's most famous son, Captain Matthew Webb became the first person to successfully swim across the English Channel, a feat he achieved at his second attempt on Tuesday, 24th August 1875. Covered in porpoise oil, his breast-stroke journey was hampered by jelly fish stings and strong currents, which made the journey from Dover to near Calais over 39 miles and took a gruelling 21 hours 45 minutes. Webb left the merchant navy to take advantage of his new-found fame, writing 'The Art of Swimming' and licensing his name and photograph on pottery souvenirs and boxes of matches. As a professional swimmer, he took part in exhibitions, but died when attempting to swim through the Whirlpool Rapids near Niagara Falls on Tuesday, 24th July 1883. Buried in Oakwood Cemetery, New York state, Matthew's brother Thomas unveiled the Captain Webb Memorial Fountain in High Street (below) in 1909. Although it has since been moved and damaged by a lorry in 2009, the memorial has been restored and returned close to its original location.

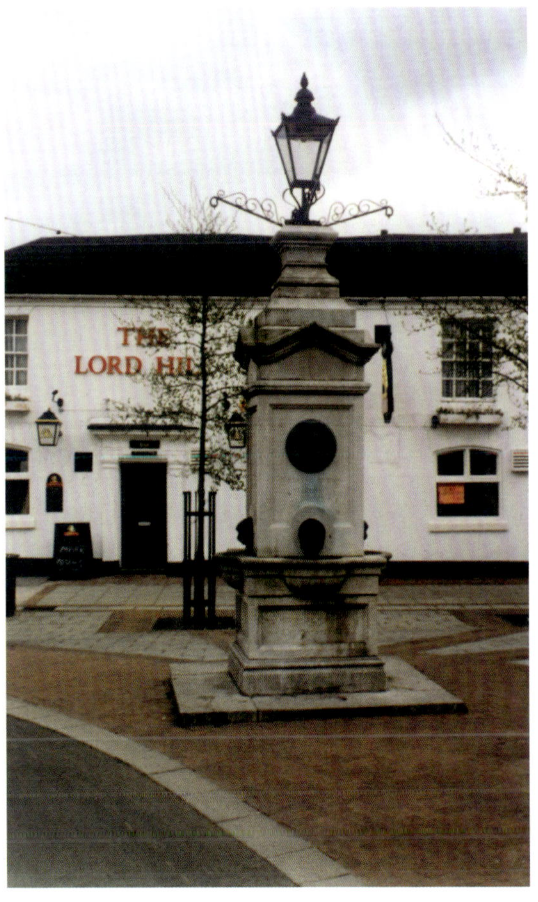


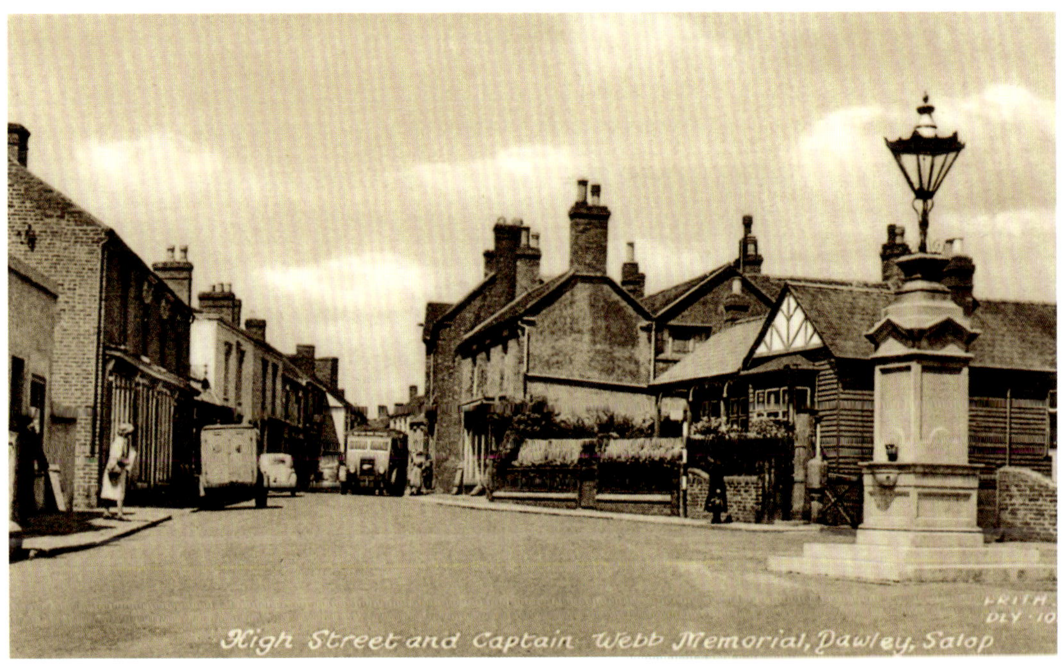

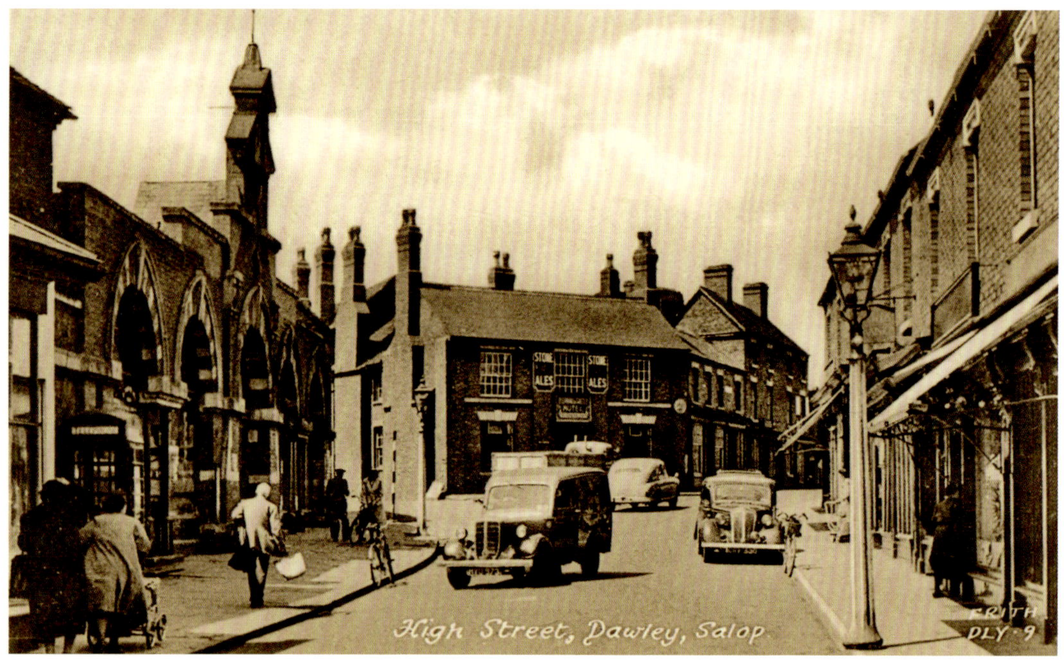



## Dawley High Street

From the Memorial to this northern end, High Street was plagued by decades of slow-moving traffic. Now largely pedestrianised, this once-thriving street is, like other borough towns, suffering from a lack of investment and over-promotion of Telford Town Centre. Steps are now being taken by current leaders of the borough council to revive the local economy and breathe new life and prosperity into the town.

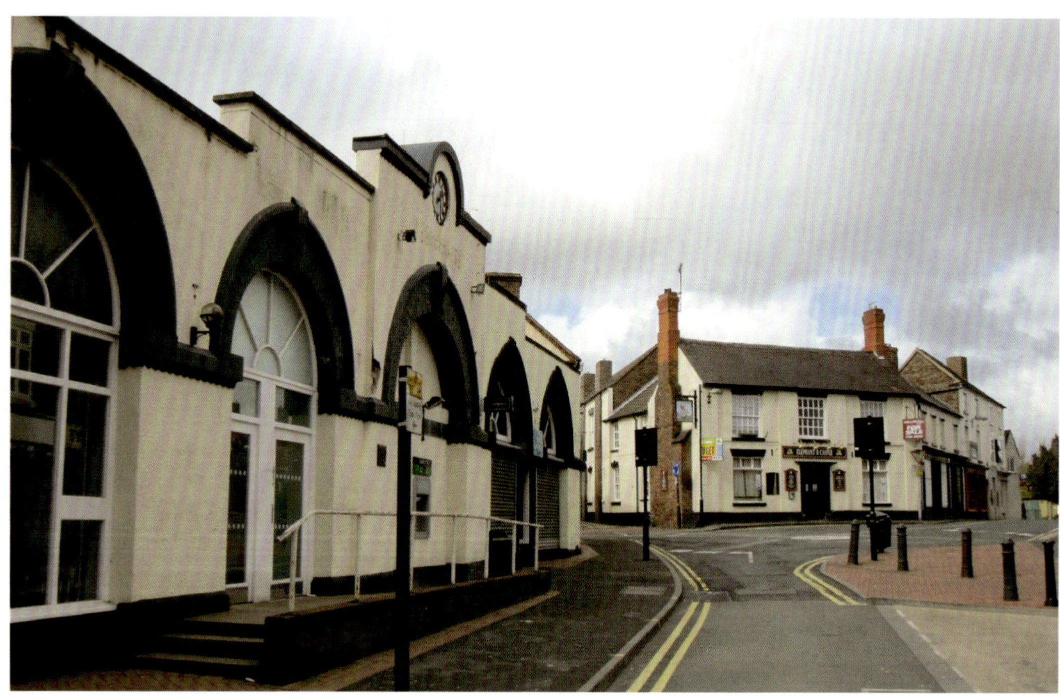

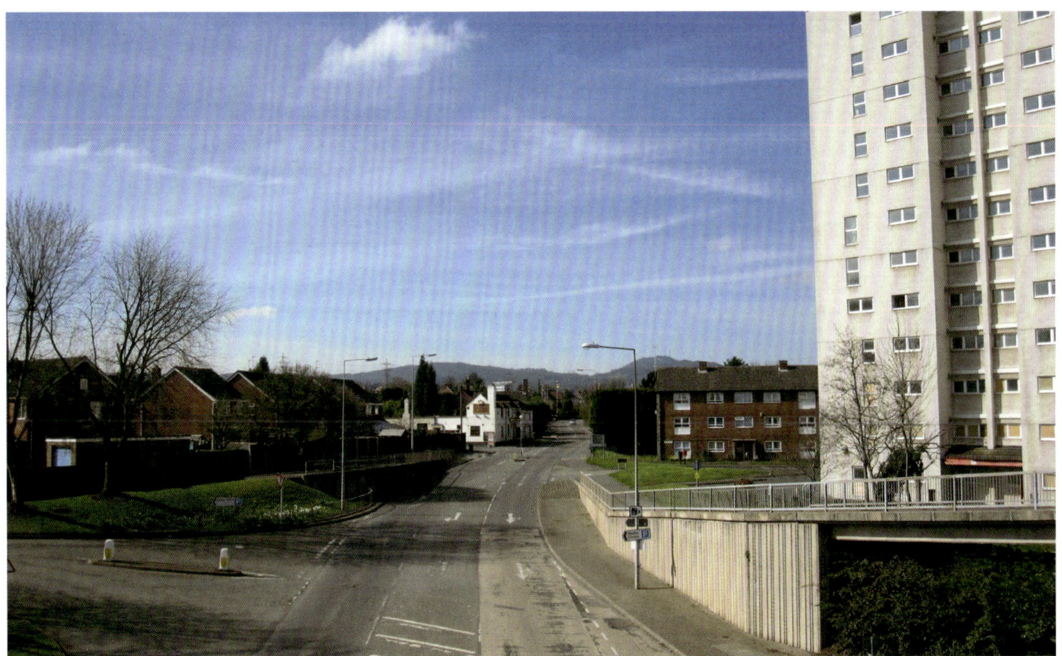

## Hadley

Looking eastwards from Hadley centre with Manor Heights on the right; the flats replaced long rows of rundown cottages. The main points of reference in both scenes are the Cross Keys Inn and The Wrekin Hill. Taken at the junction where the former road into Hadley curved left from Wellington (ahead) and Shawbirch/Wem (to the right), a new road with its own 'flyover' pedestrian bridge bypasses the centre.

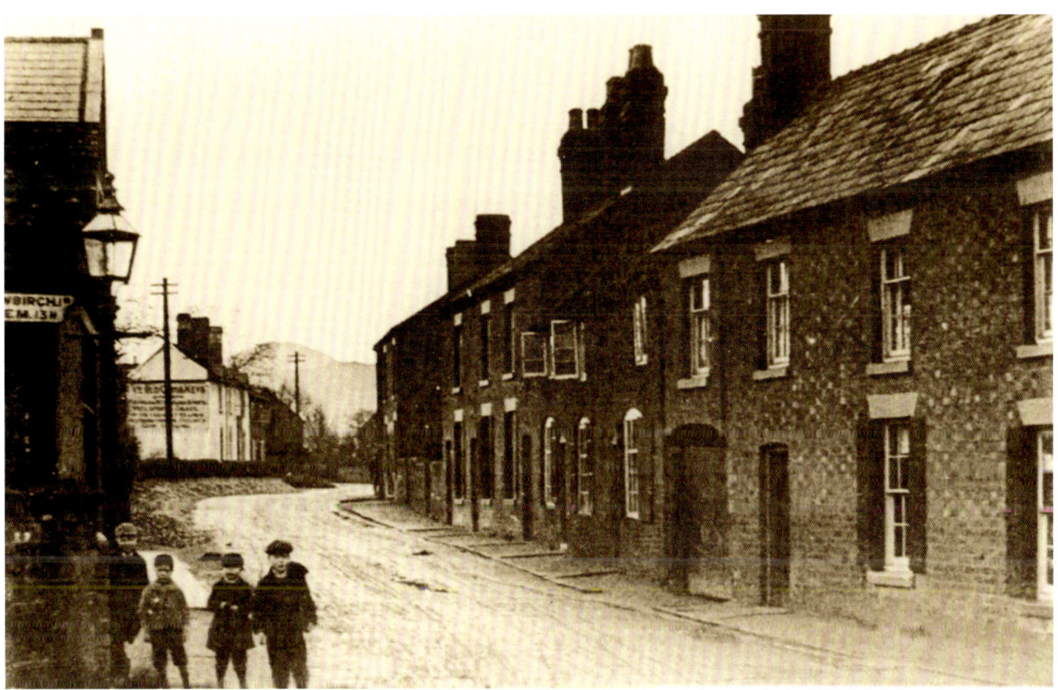

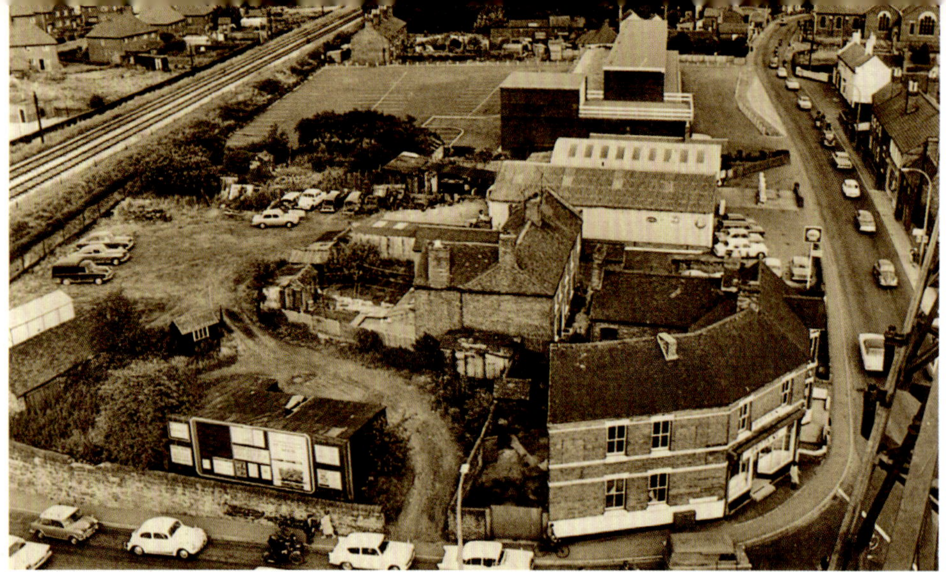

## Hadley Centre

Taken from the top of Manor Heights in 1966, the road from Wellington curved into High Street, now pedestrianised. The white building in the distance, right, is the King's Head Inn. The road to Shawbirch runs bottom left; this junction has been altered significantly by a bypass called Britannia Way in recognition of the Britannia ('The Brit') Inn which was demolished in the 1970s. Hadley was a small village which relied on the varying fortunes of agriculture for its livelihood. Industry was slow to develop; the Haybridge Iron Company, on the site now occupied by Furrows Ford dealership, began at Haybridge in 1864, and the manufacture of bricks became increasingly important from the early twentieth century when Blockleys opened. It was the Castle Iron Works which opened in 1871 and became home to various engineering firms, most notably Joseph Sankey & Sons, later GKN Sankey, that had the greatest impact on employment in the town. The scene below is today's opposite view, with Manor Heights in the distance.

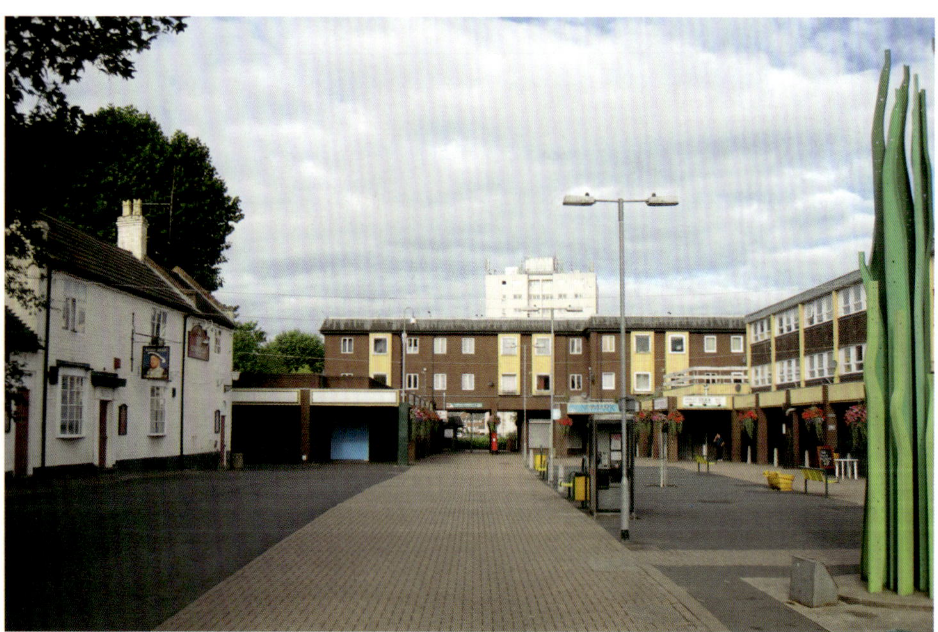

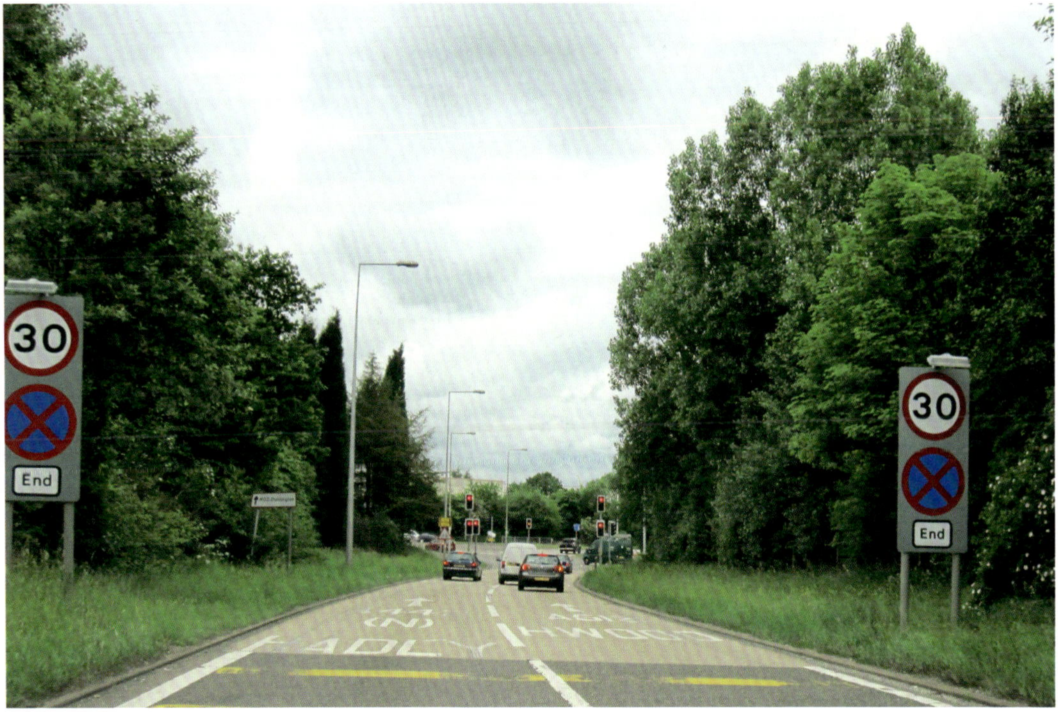

### Trench Lock

Several new roads in the district run along old railway lines and even canal structures. Trench Lock (below) stood at the northern end of an inclined plane which lifted (and lowered) tub boats from one canal to another using the Wombridge Pumping Engine. The bridge behind the lock mechanism carried the main Wellington to Newport road. The Trench Lock Interchange and A442 (above) now occupy the site.

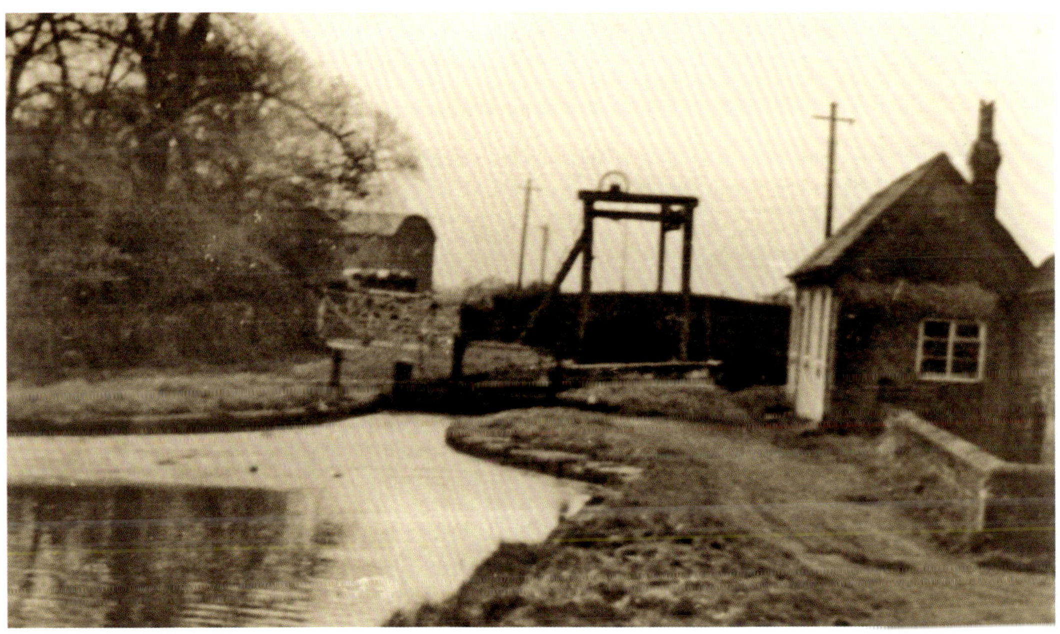

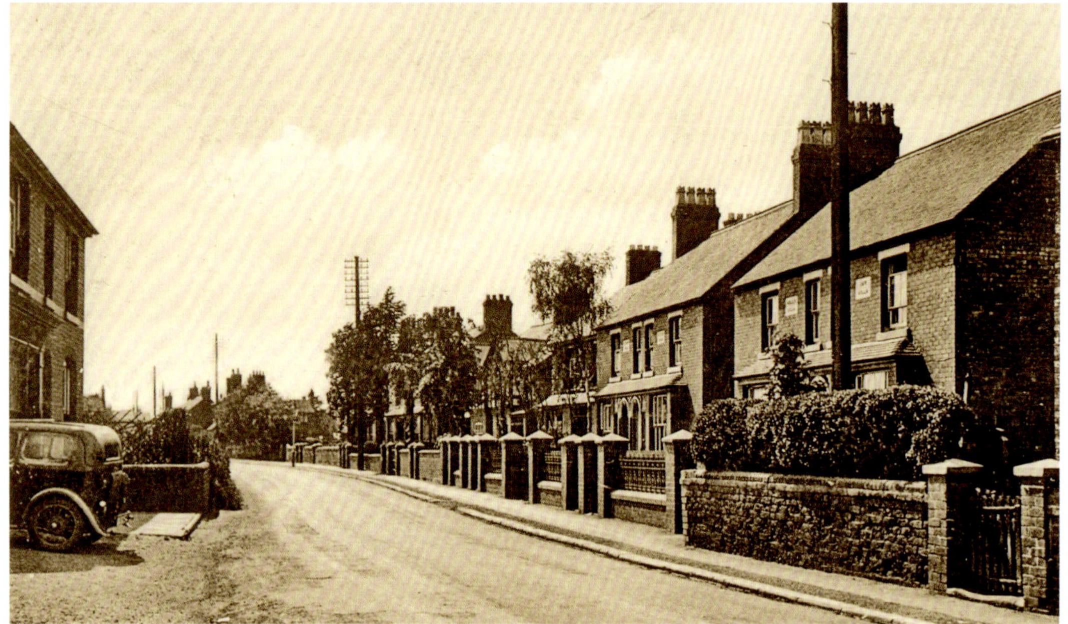

## Trench

Wellington Road, Trench as it was in the early 1940s (above) and now. Trench (formerly The Trench) is  thought to have received its name from the long channel, containing this section of the route from Newport to Wellington, which separated parts of the ancient  Royal Forest of The Wrekin which, on its eastern side, reached almost to Lilleshall. The Trench Tavern, originally called New Inn House, was renamed  several times before receiving its present name. Horton Road on the right is now blocked to vehicles.

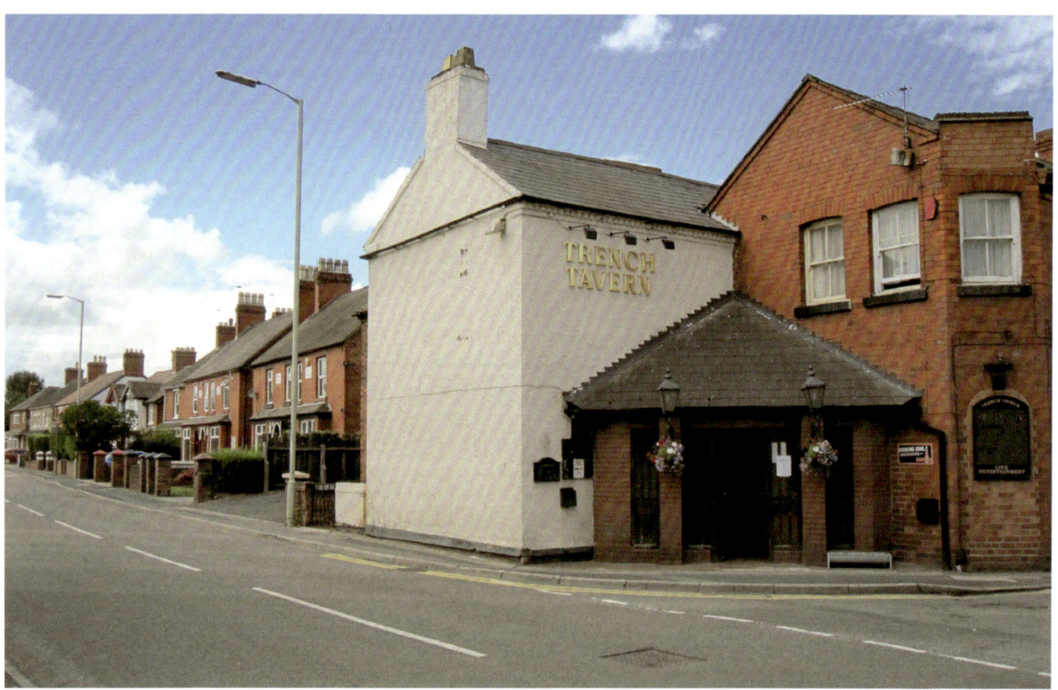

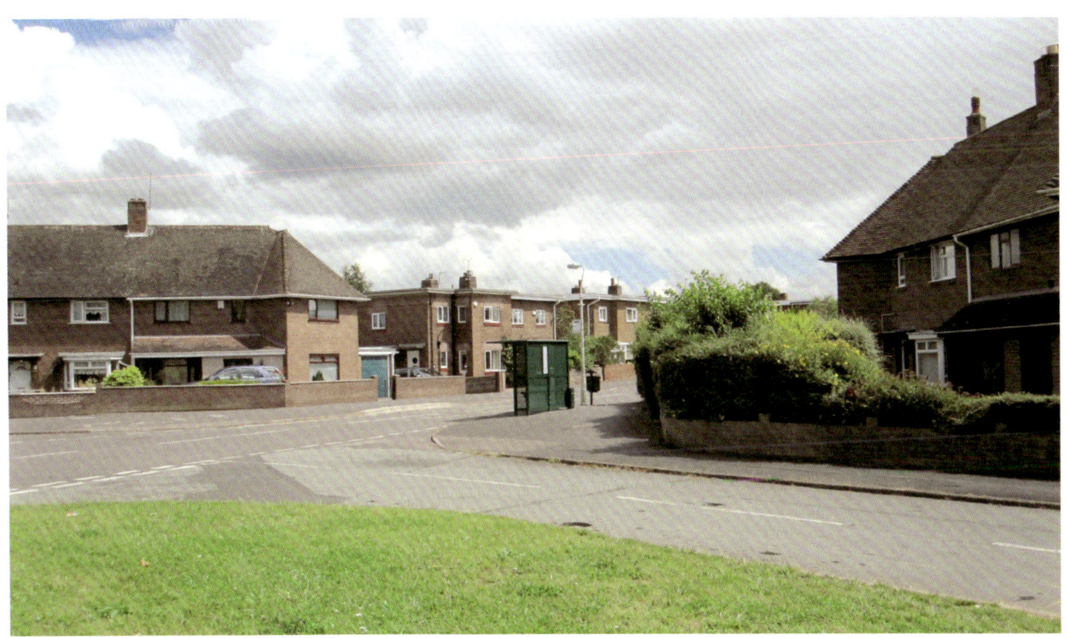

### New Donnington

New Donnington was the name of the new town created on farmland shortly before the outbreak of the Second World War to accommodate personnel transferred to the area when the Civilian Ordnance Deport was relocated to the edge of the Weald Moors near the ancient settlement of Donnington, which ran along Wellington Road. Shortage of building materials led to flat roofs for 'ordinary' workers and The Parade shopping centre, while senior civil service managers and army officers were allowed a little more timber: their homes had pitched roofs.

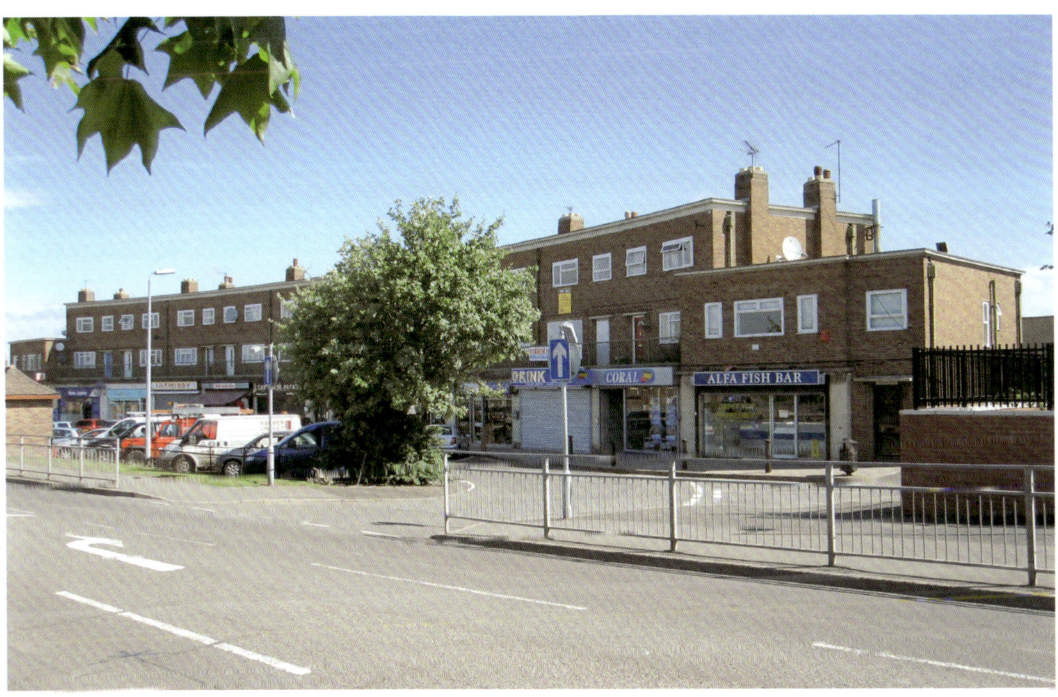

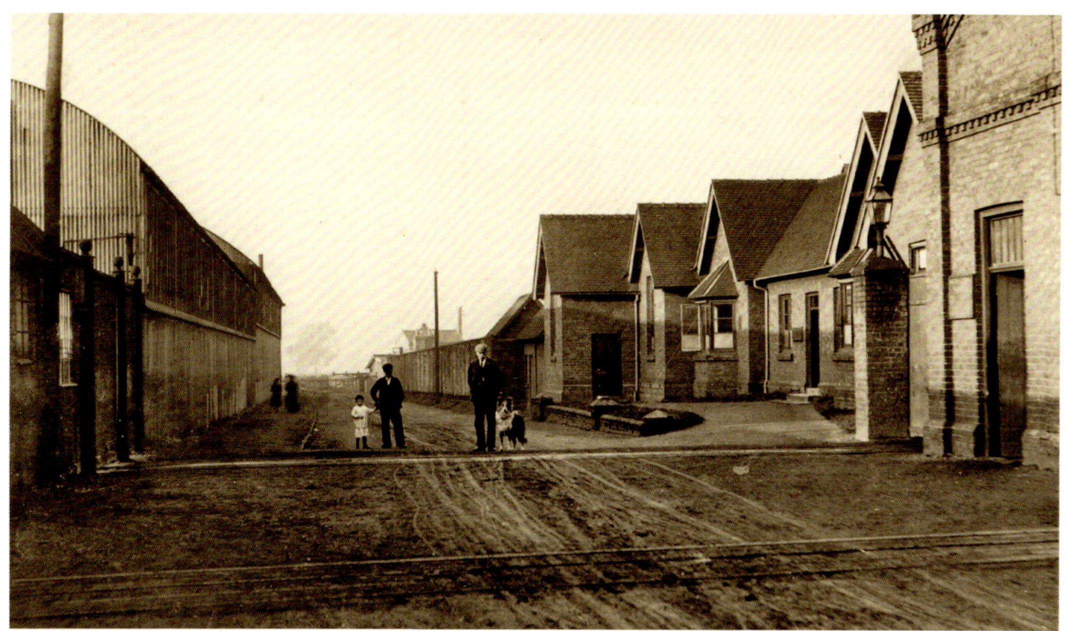

## Donnington

C. & W. Walker's Midland Iron Works, internationally famous for its enormous gas holders and which moved to this location from Clerkenwell, London, in 1857, straddled Station Road  and even had its own railway connecting factory buildings. The road actually takes its name from Donnington railway station on the Wellington-Stafford line, the crossing gates to which are just visible in the distance. After the factory closed in the late 1970s it became a trading estate; finally, the buildings were demolished to make way for a small housing estate. The former factory clock has been placed on top of a column on a traffic island marking the approximate location of Donnington station.

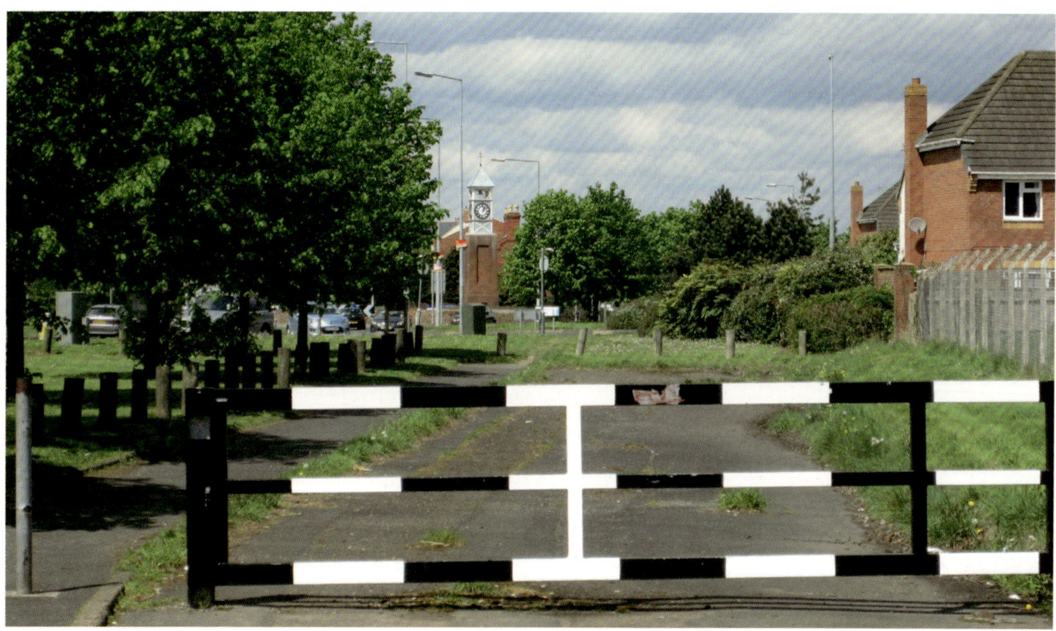

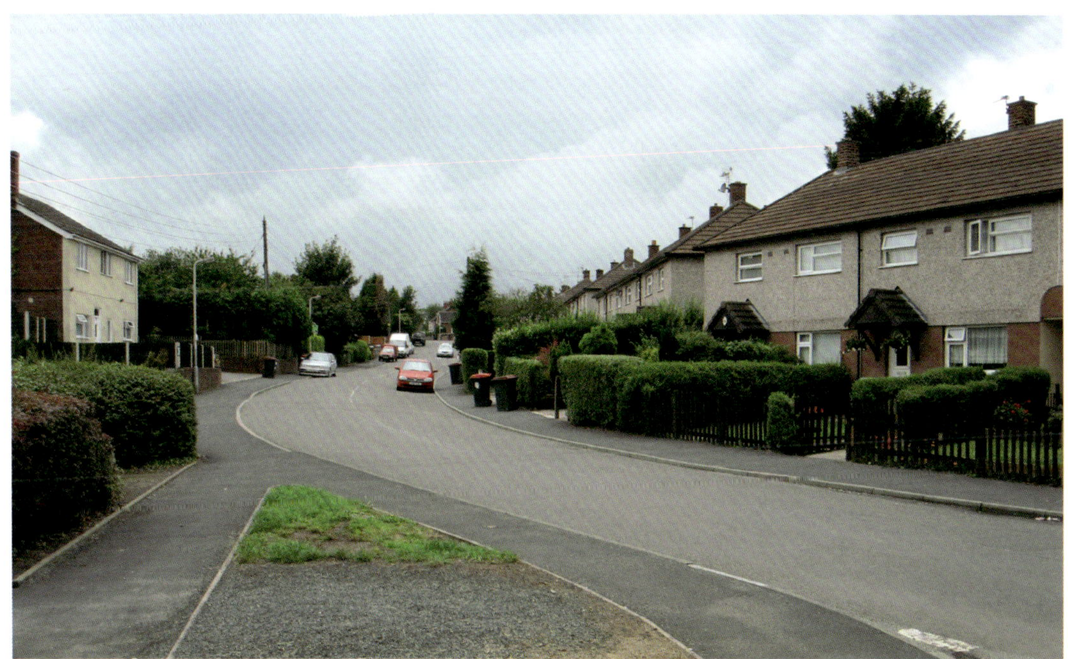

### Donnington Wood

This 'Donnington' completes the trilogy. Until mining activity got under way during the eighteenth century, this area south of the original Donnington was essentially farmland. After 1768, the Donnington Wood canal not only gave a boost to industrial activity but also turned the area into a series of isolated shanty rows, or 'barrack houses', like those on School Road (aside, *c* .1930), each small two-roomed house accommodating a mine- or furnace worker's family of up to a dozen members. In time, small pockets of Wellington Rural District Council housing (as in Jubilee Avenue) were expanded from the late 1940s to include all three Donningtons. Terraces of precast concrete houses, like those on the right of Queens Road (above) were built, and caused a major headache for subsequent councils who were obliged to carry out remedial repairs and structural reinforcements from the 1980s, even to the point of buying back properties sold under the Right To Buy scheme. Further council (nowadays 'social') housing has taken place since the 1960s, most notably on The Common (again part of Donnington Wood).

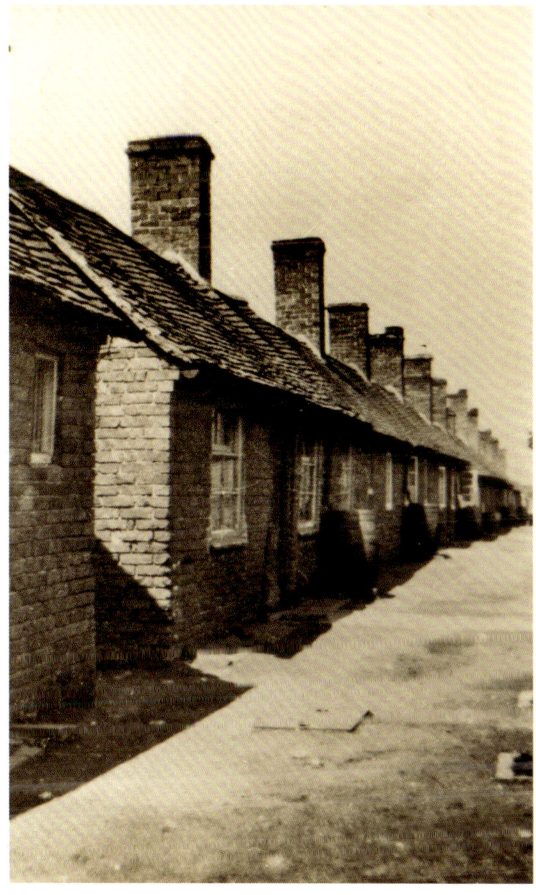

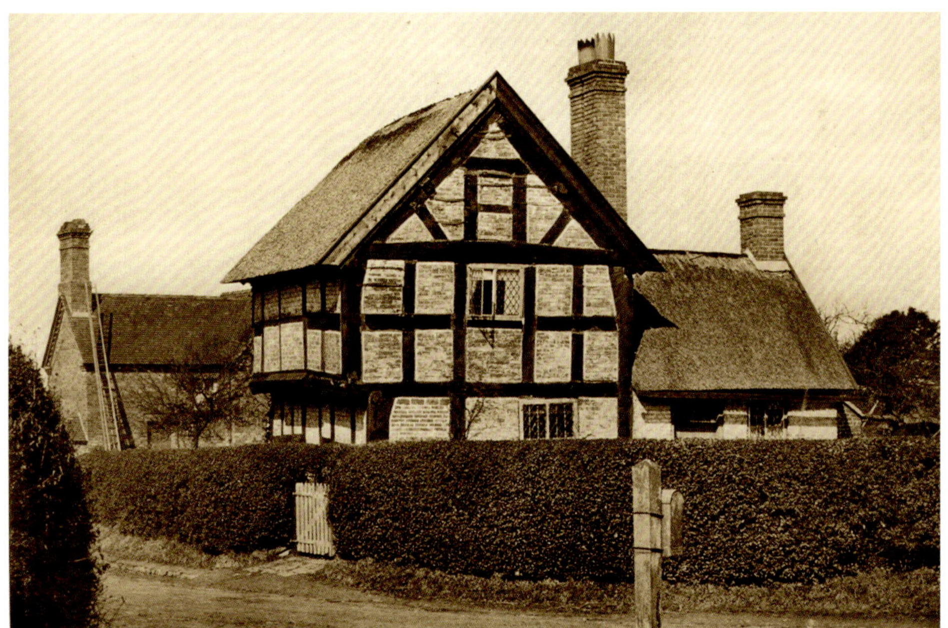

## Muxton

Until Wrekin District Council realigned several settlement boundaries, Muxton was almost entirely confined to Muxton Lane (above) with a little land on either side and bounded at its northern end by the Sutherland Arms public house on Wellington Road. Perhaps because newly defined boundaries have been extended into areas that historically belonged to Donnington, New Donnington and Donnington Wood, Muxton now includes several private housing estates erected on former industrial, mining and marshland sites. For example Marshbrook Way hints at the fact that the ground here, just north of the former Freehold Colliery which was the lowest-lying mine on the east Shropshire coalfield, was prone to saturation.

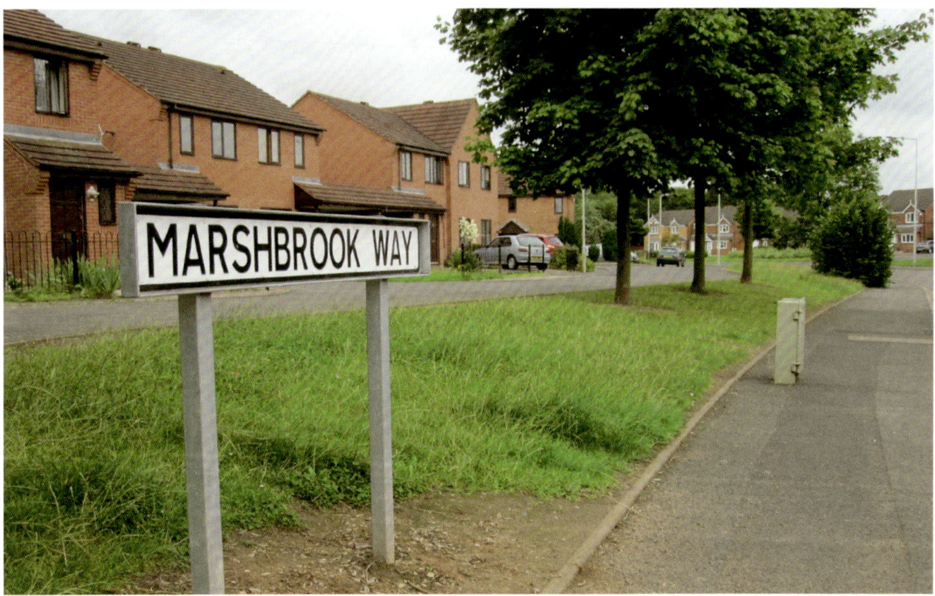

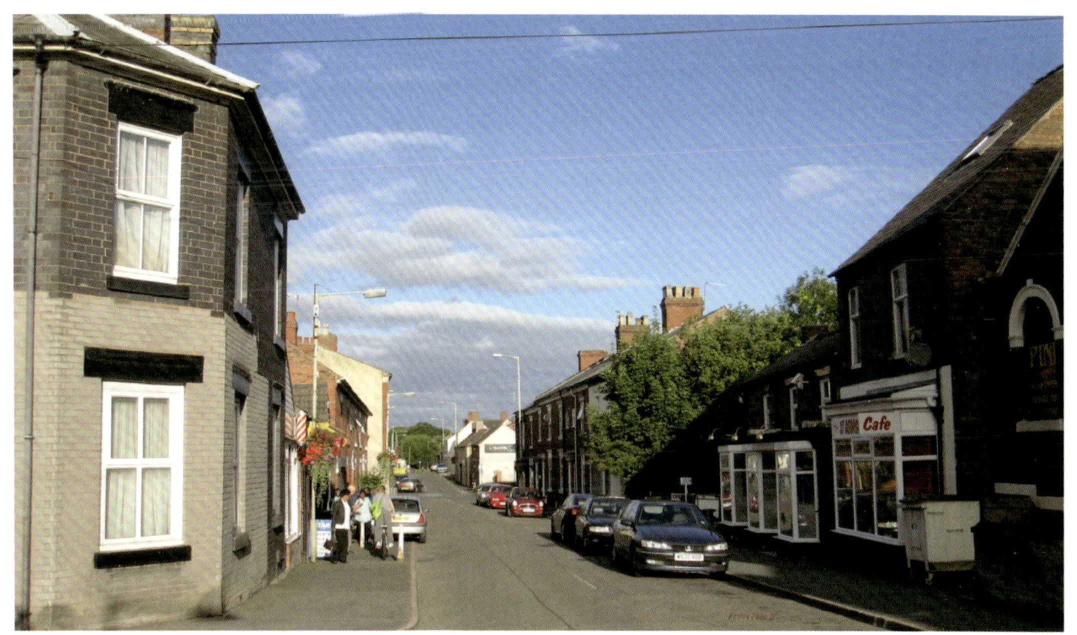

## Church Street, St. Georges, looking West

Originally a settlement spread sparsely along the ancient Watling Street, St. Georges was, until a little over 100 years ago, still called Pain's Lane by locals. Church Street forms part of the old road leading from Red Hill in the east towards Oakengates and onwards to the Roman town of Uriconium in the west. In the 1920s scene, Holleyhead's was a butchers with a slaughterhouse at the rear. On the same side of the road, men stand outside Leonard Tranter's motor repair and charabanc hire premises; directly opposite was Ernest Tranter's grocery shop, while William Tranter's hardware store is next door to the Methodist Jubilee Sunday school building on the extreme right. The entrance to Grove Street is on the extreme left.

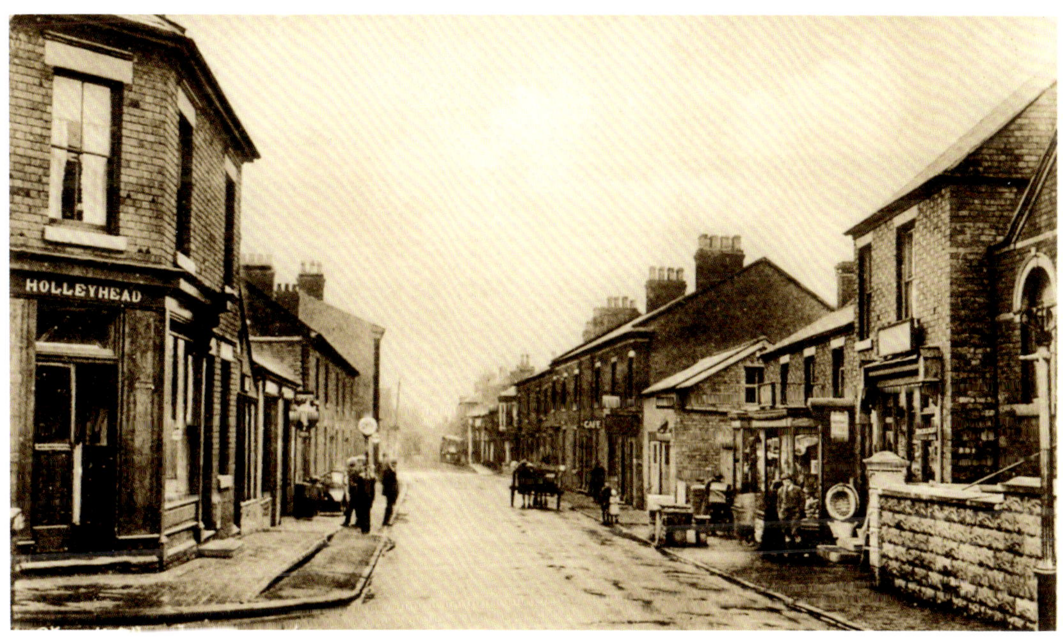

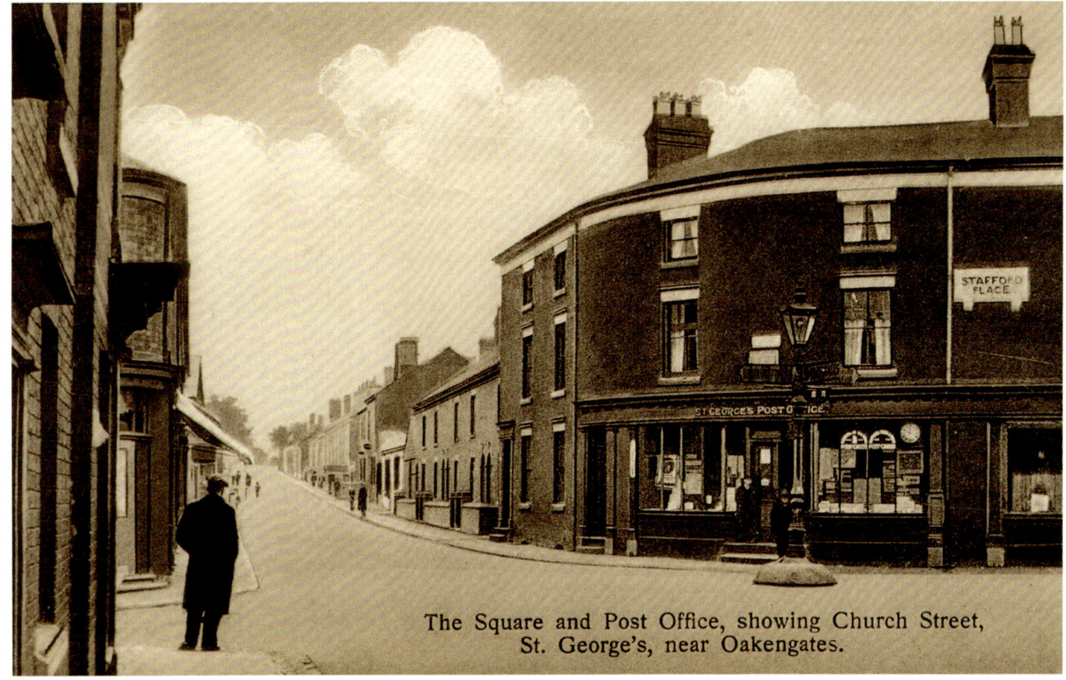

The Square and Post Office, showing Church Street, St. George's, near Oakengates.

### The Square, St. Georges

Looking eastwards from West Street across The Square into Church Street beyond, the curved building in Stafford Place has changed use from a Post Office to Lifestyle Express, a grocery store. The Post Office last occupied premises in Church Street until cuts led to its closure a few years ago. The lamppost was also a signpost pointing to Donnington, Oakengates and Priorslee; now a 'pimple' roundabout controls traffic.

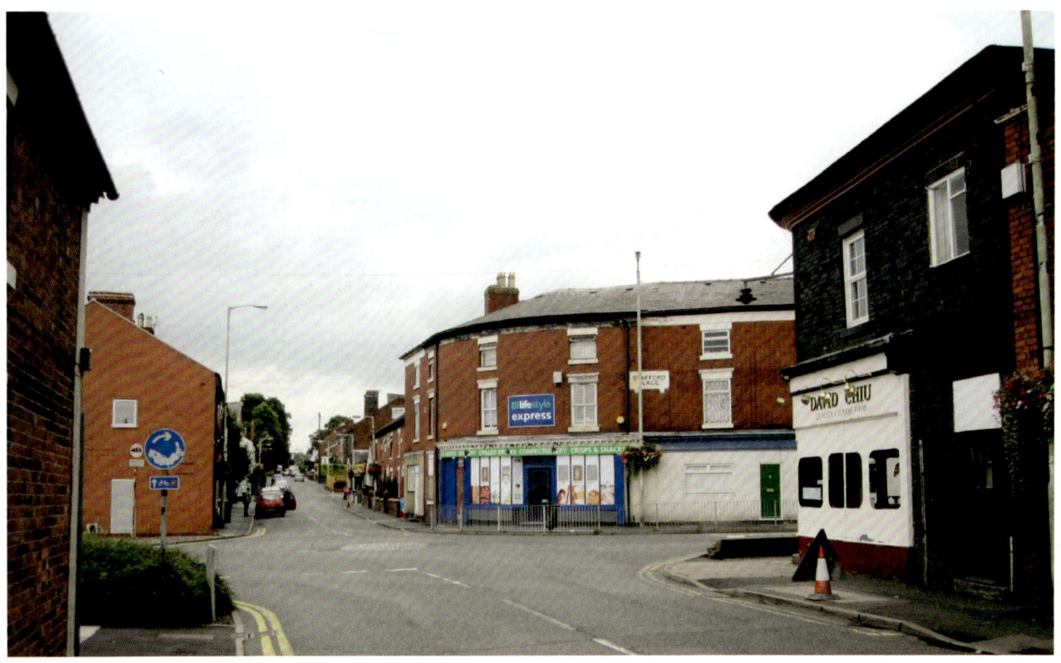

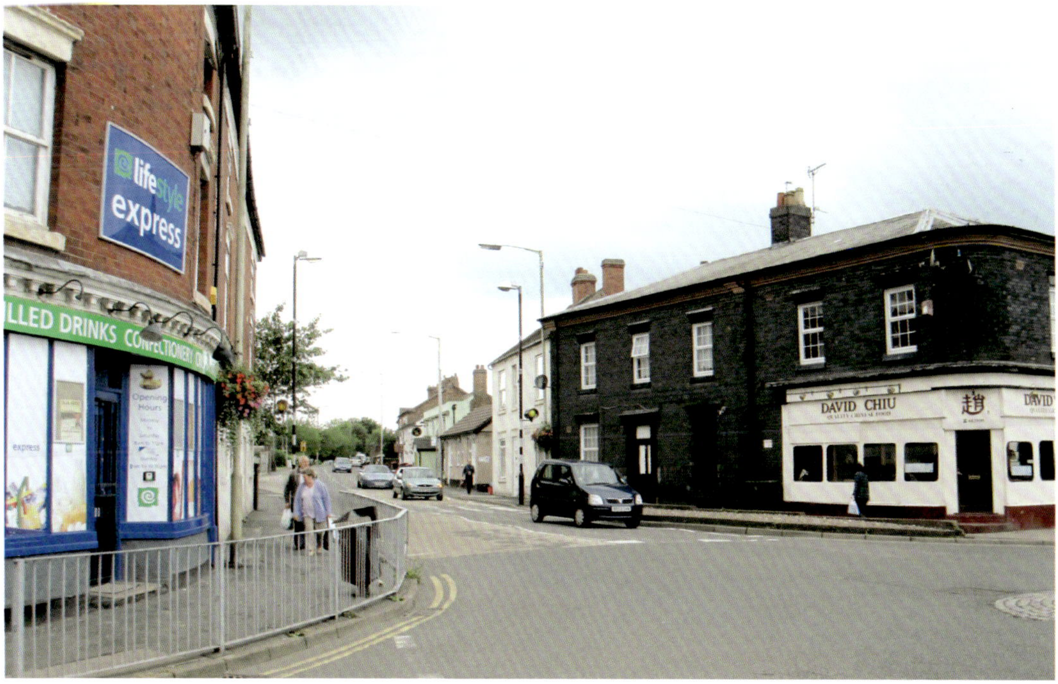

## Stafford Street, St. Georges

By the 1920s, the Post Office had became a printer's run by Herbert Price after Mr. Edkins died. Next door was J. C. Owen's motor bike and cycle shop. Opposite, a grocery store occupied the premises now acting as David Chiu's popular Chinese takeaway. St. Georges has seen many housing developments on its periphery in recent years which have helped revive the local economy.

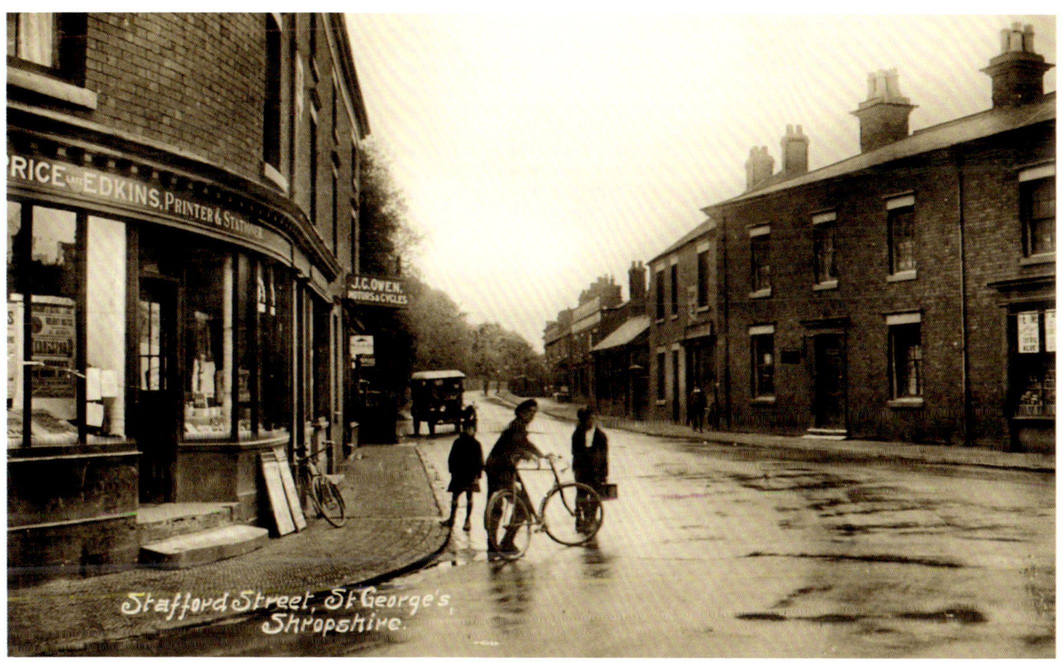

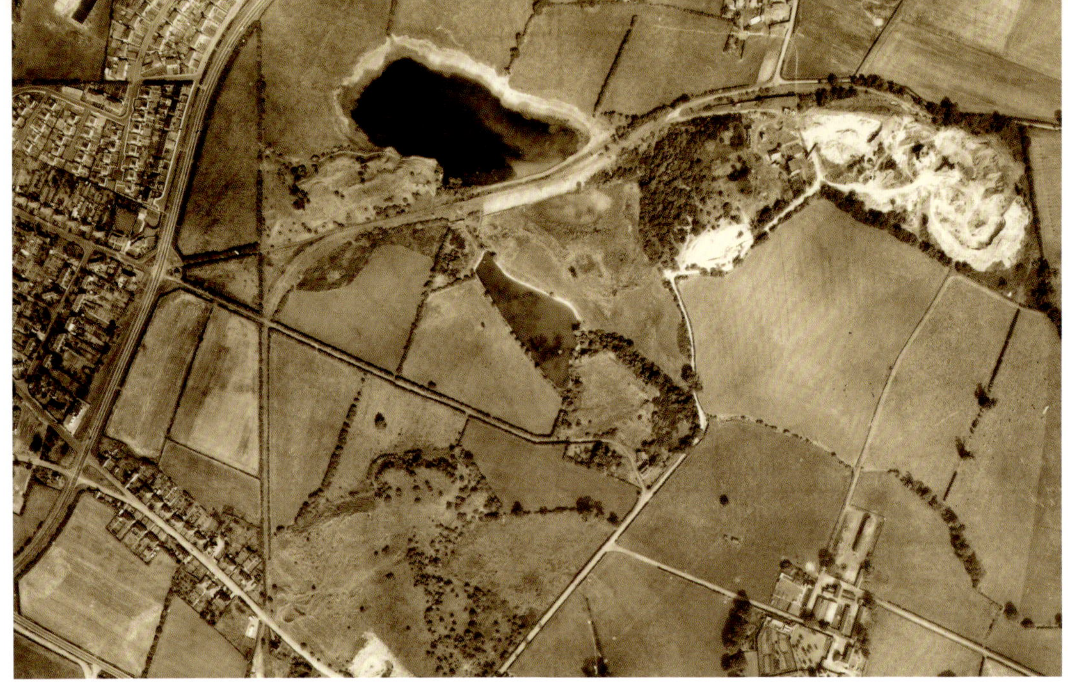

## The Flash, Priorslee

Coal mining at the Woodhouse Colliery caused severe subsidence and the creation of three pools. The colliery had its own mineral railway whose line curved southwards between them and terminated at the Lilleshall Company's nearby Snedshill works. Surrounded by farmland (and several pit mounds), the area became a prime location when the Telford Development Corporation sought to build 'desirable executive private housing' in the area. Two of the pools were conjoined and remodelled to form The Flash.

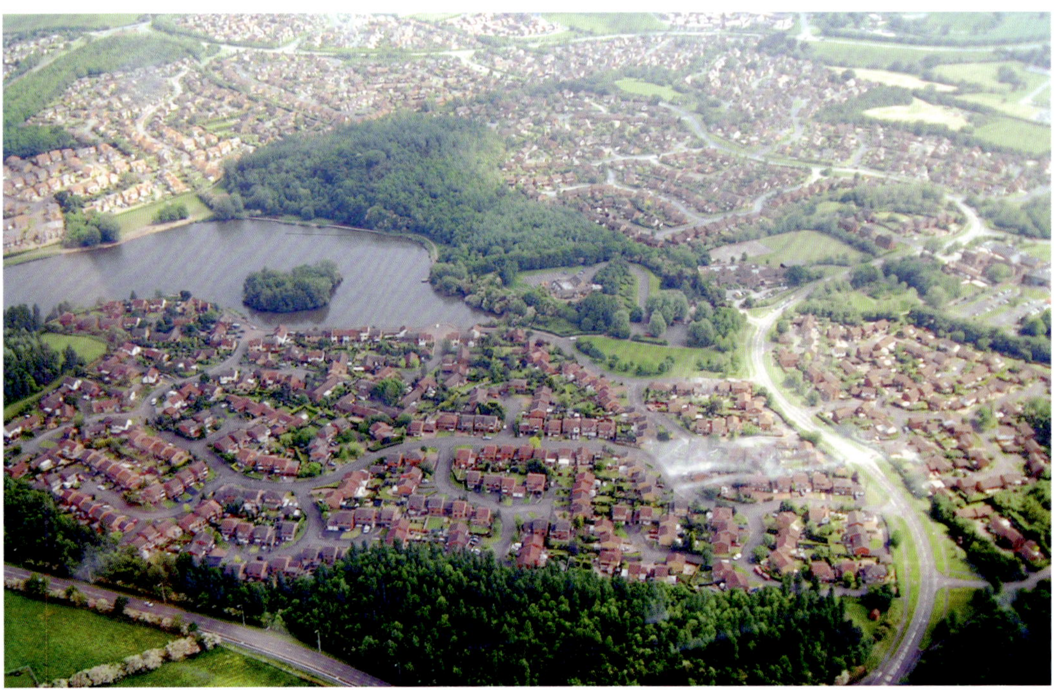

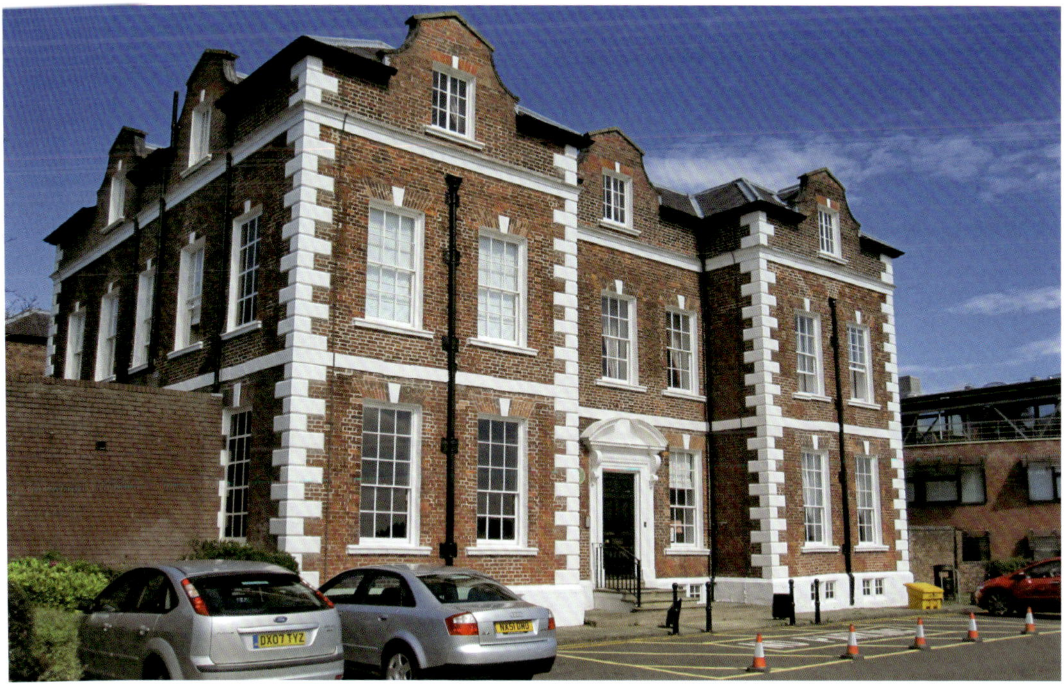

### Priorslee Hall

Originally built before 1729, the hall became the headquarters of the Lilleshall Company, formed in 1802. From 1819, when ironmaster John Horton occupied the building (after which several enlargements were made), the hall was regarded as the official residence of the managing partner (and, later, managing directors) of the company's expanding empire. Dawley (and hence Telford) Development Corporation bought it as their own HQ. It is now a campus, including halls of residence, for Wolverhampton University.

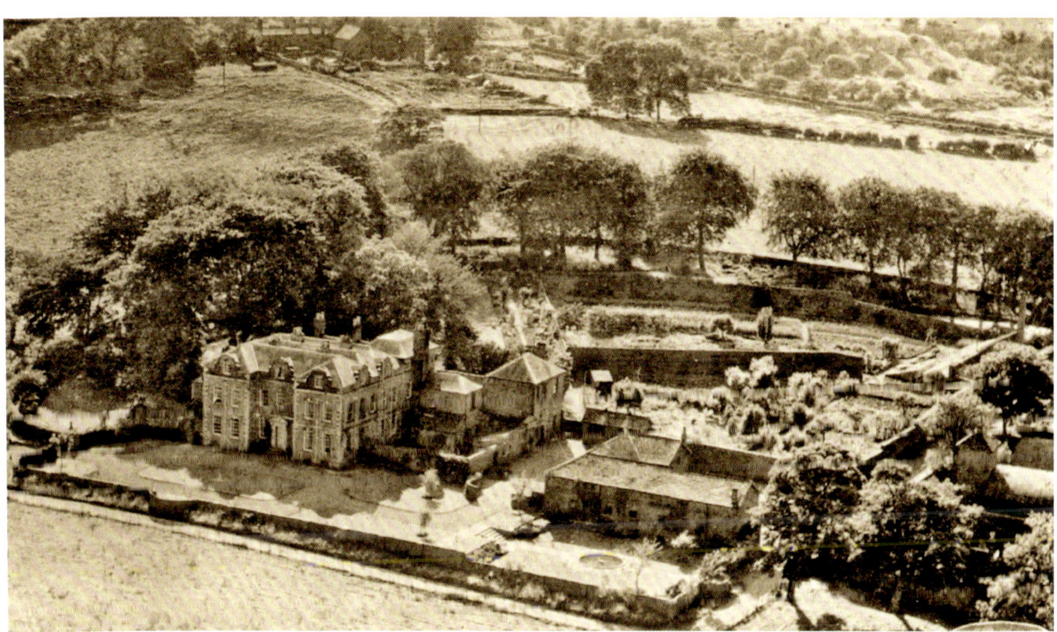

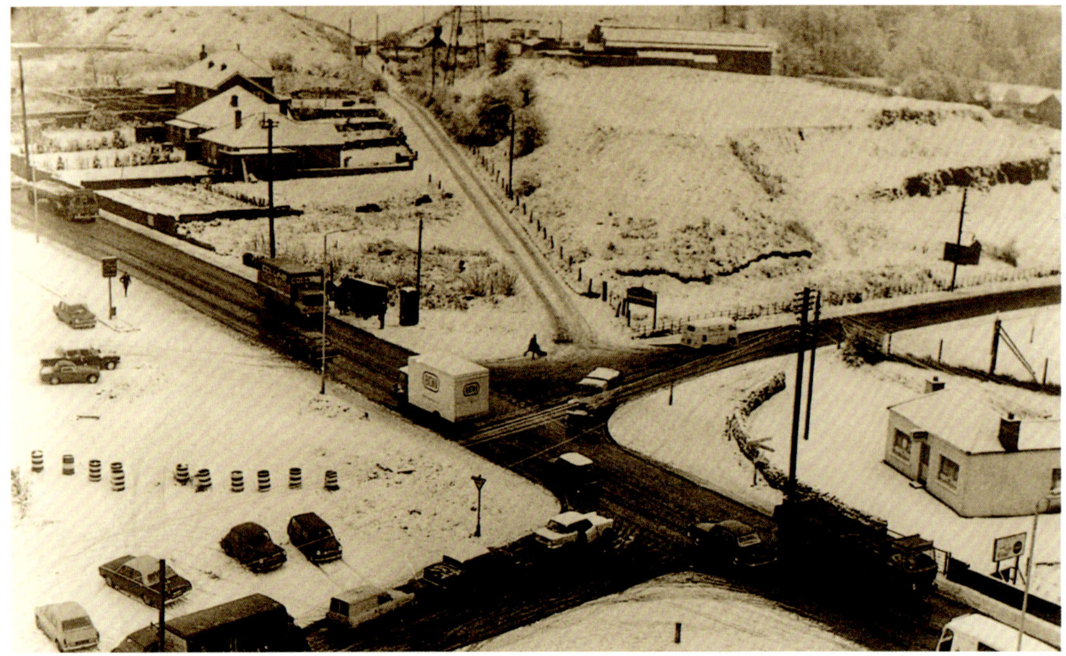

## Ketley Crossroads

One of the most notable features of Telford's development was the way roads were improved to allow easier movement of traffic. Not all have been immediately successful, such as the 'Seven Stars' crossroads at Ketley (named after nearby former pubs built roughly on the same site, the last of which was unaccountably called the Elephant and Castle and is now an Indian restaurant). In 1968, the stretch running left to right was part of the congested A5, now the B5061. The layout of the crossroads has been altered several times. At least the chip shop bottom right, now called Ketley Cod, remains a constant feature.

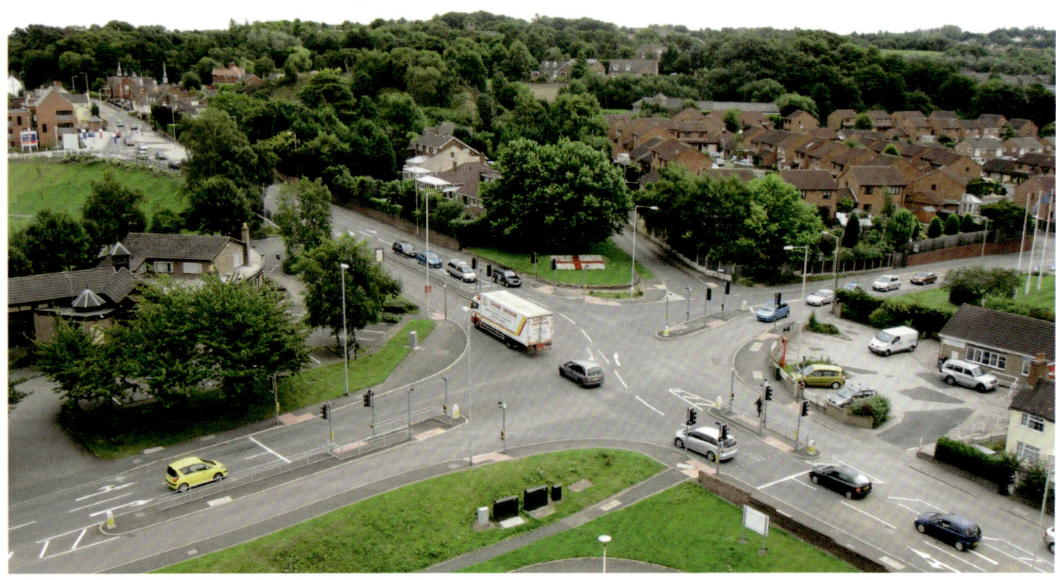

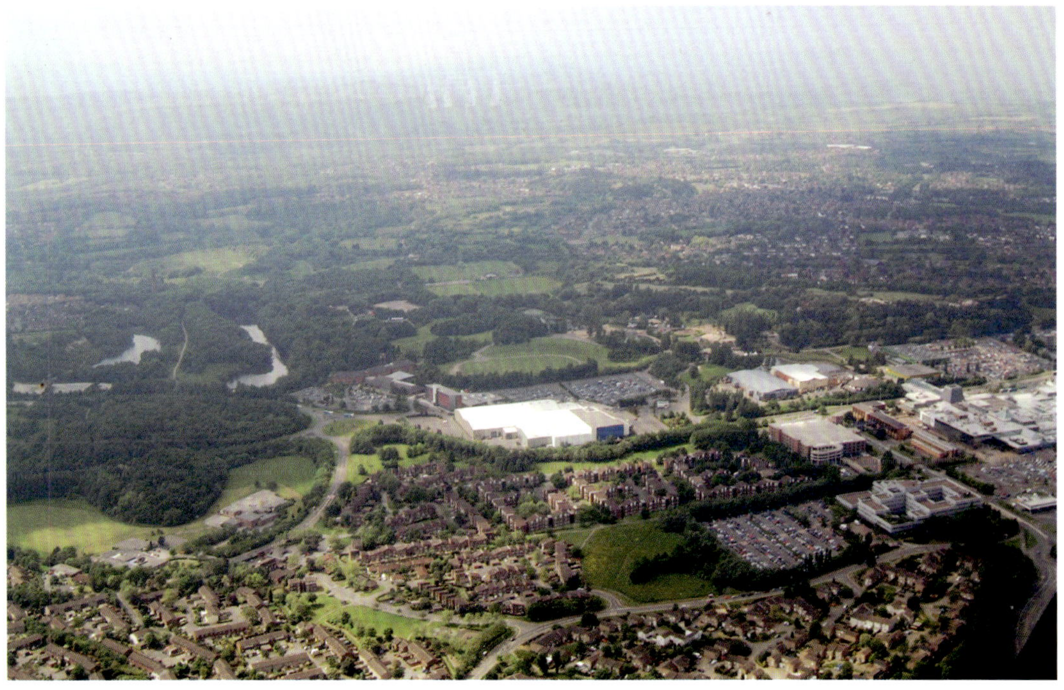

## Brand New Estates

Expansion of the Telford conurbation has led to the construction of new housing and industrial estates on a massive scale. These scenes are of Hollinswood and the Town Centre in 1960 (with north at top) and 2006 looking south towards Buildwas power station. Not all developments were entirely successful. 1960s planners were criticised for the style of 'social' housing they promoted, such as those at Sutton Hill, Woodside and Brookside, which were thought to be of very poor quality, leaving something of a maintenance headache for the Wrekin council which inherited them from the Development Corporation.

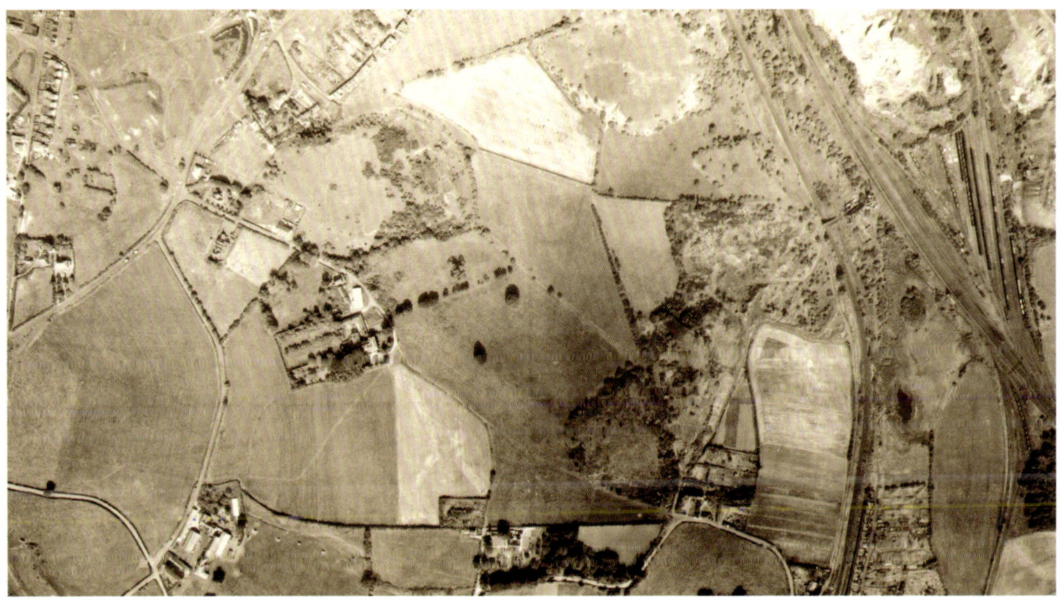

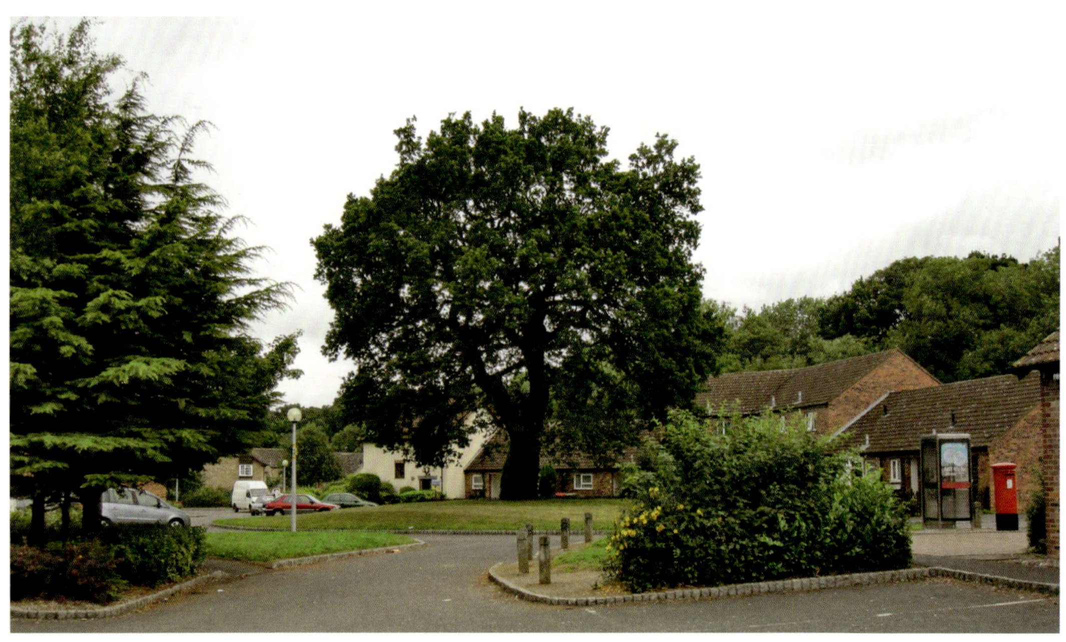

## Building on Former Productive Farmland

Partly as a result of the late Labour government's edicts and partly because of other economic pressures (not least the need to generate more council taxes), other housing developments have taken place. Some, like those at Shawbirch (above) and Leegomery (below, with the Princess Royal Hospital complex in the centre), are on former prime farmland. Like public houses, more than a few farms have disappeared from the Telford landscape over the last four decades.

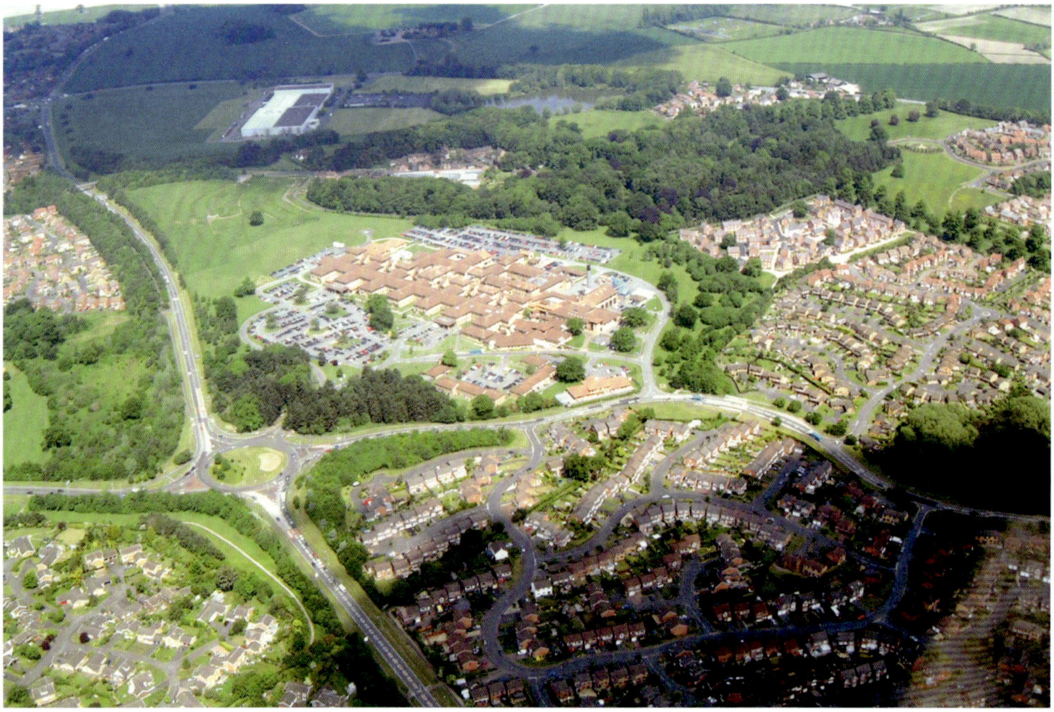

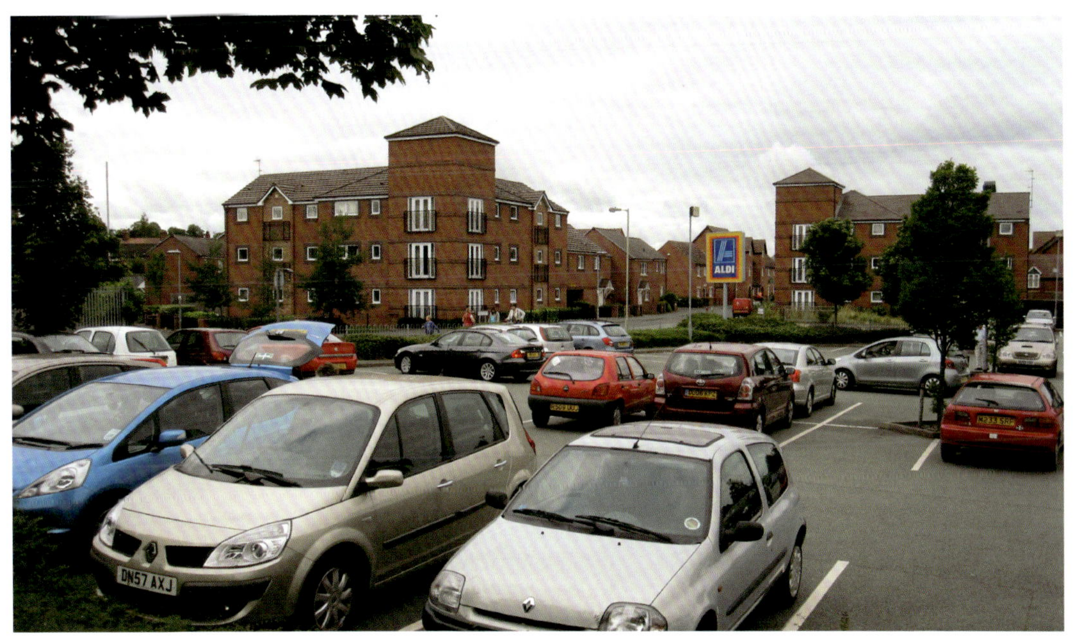



## Housing on Former Brownfield Sites

Private housing developments have naturally taken place on disused industrial locations, such as the mini-estate on the former gas works and Groom's timber yard sites in Wellington which also incorporates an ALDI supermarket. Despite doubts raised about the advisability of building residential properties on potentially toxic land (the gas works created many by-products as a result of processing coal to produce town gas), planners have issued assurances that there is no cause for concern.

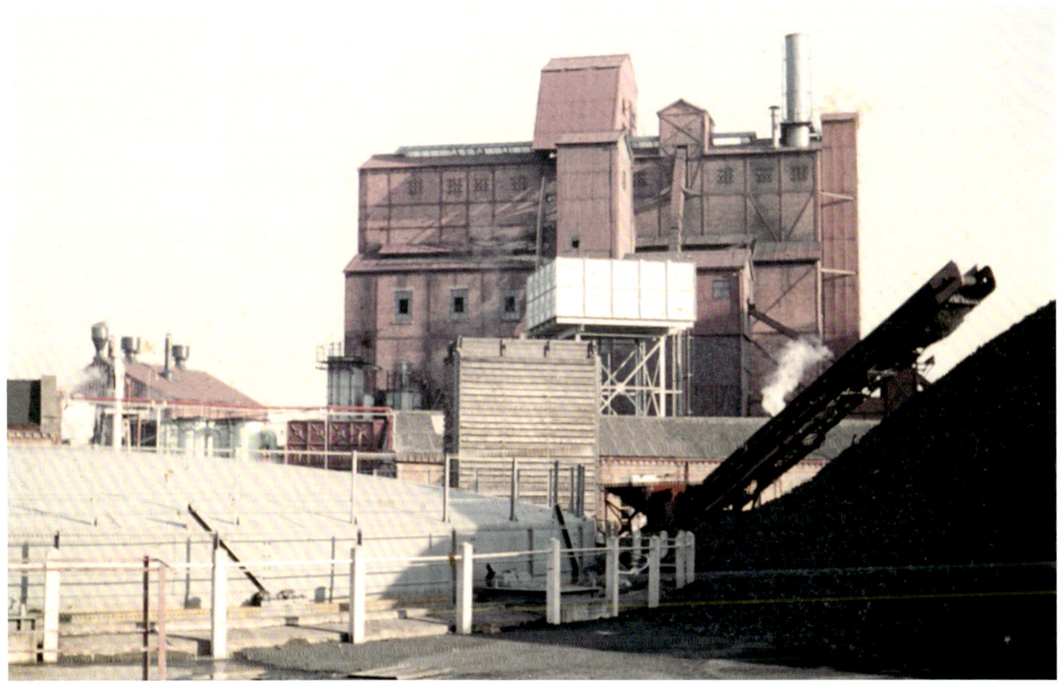

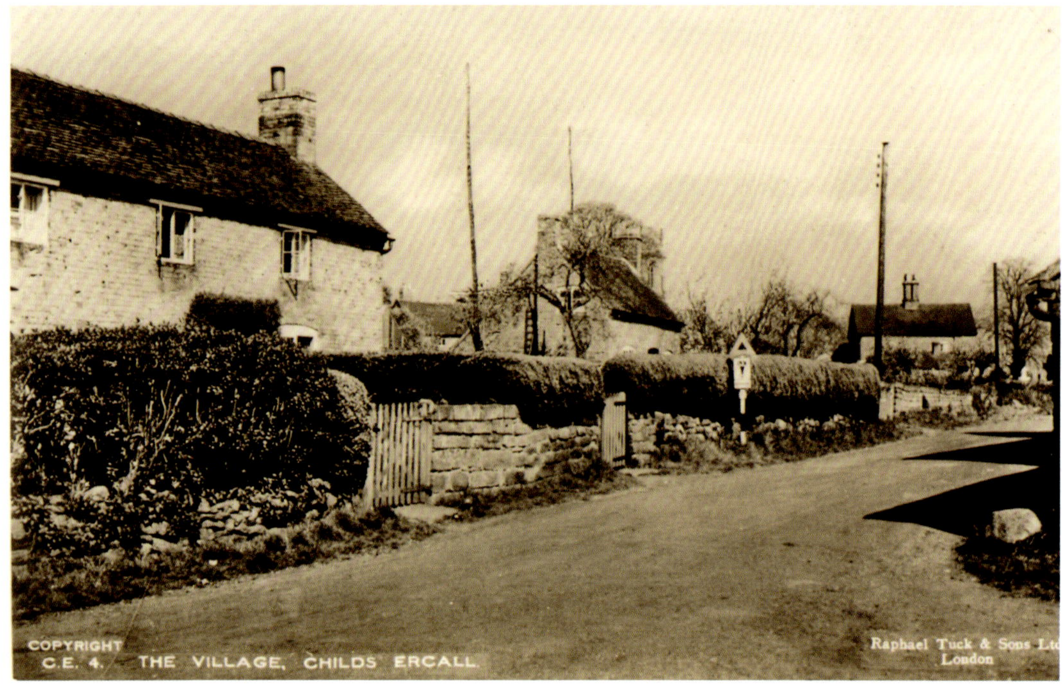



## Childs Ercall and Rowton

Not all settlements in the Telford borough have been absorbed into the conurbation. Many villages have managed to preserve their rural ways of life. Childs Ercall (above) and Rowton (below, with a monument to its famous son, the 'Protestant Divine' Richard Baxter (1615-1691), curiously chaplain to both King Charles I as well as Oliver Cromwell during turbulent years in the seventeenth century) are but two.

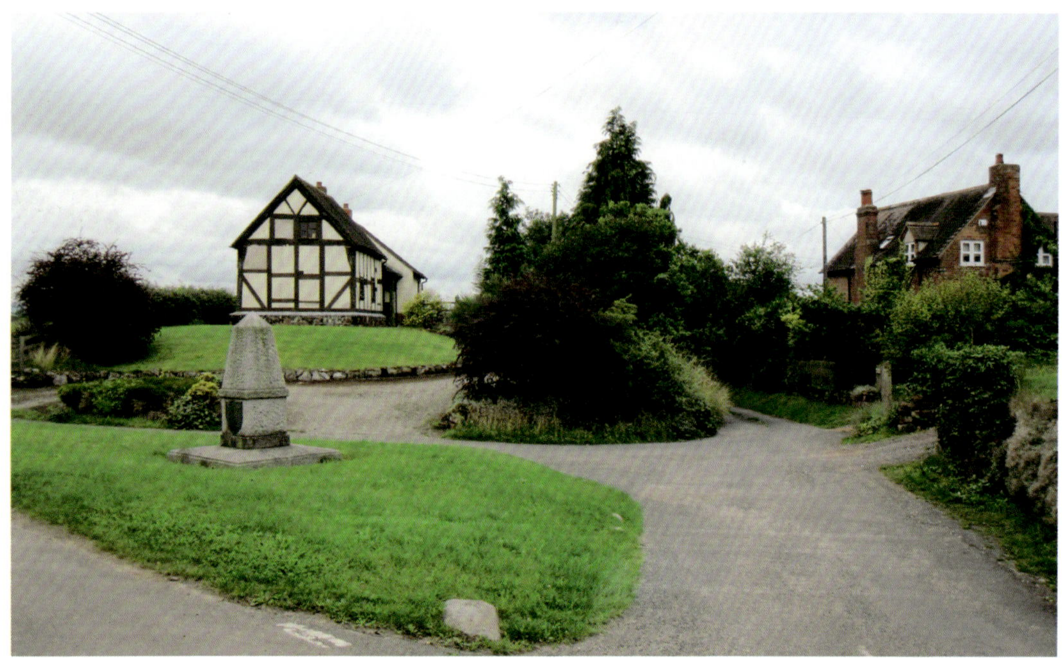

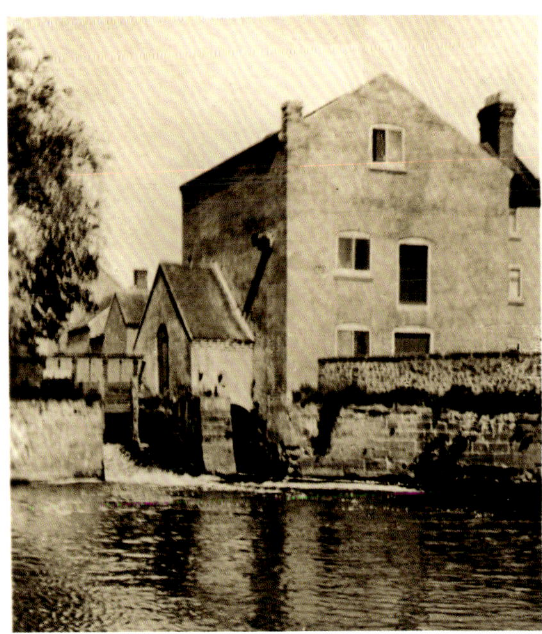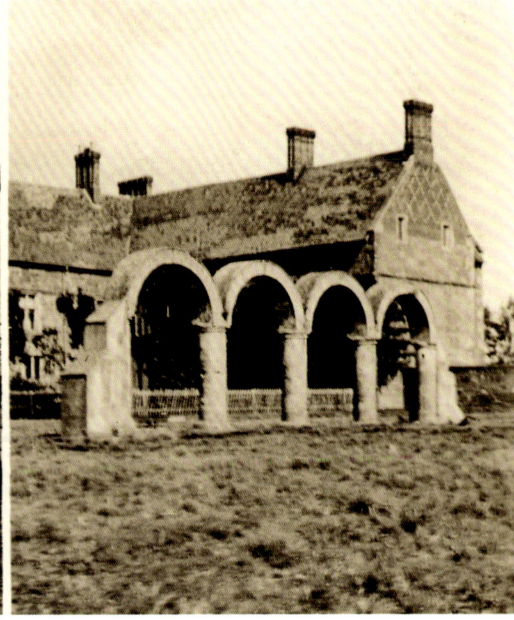

## High Ercall and Bolas

High Ercall dates back to beyond Norman times and has a large parish comprising numerous villages. Situated on the River Roden, it once had two mills. The village and High Ercall Hall suffered from English Civil War skirmishes. Nearby in Bolas, the village postman stands by while children and their teachers enjoy an open air lesson, *c.* 1905.

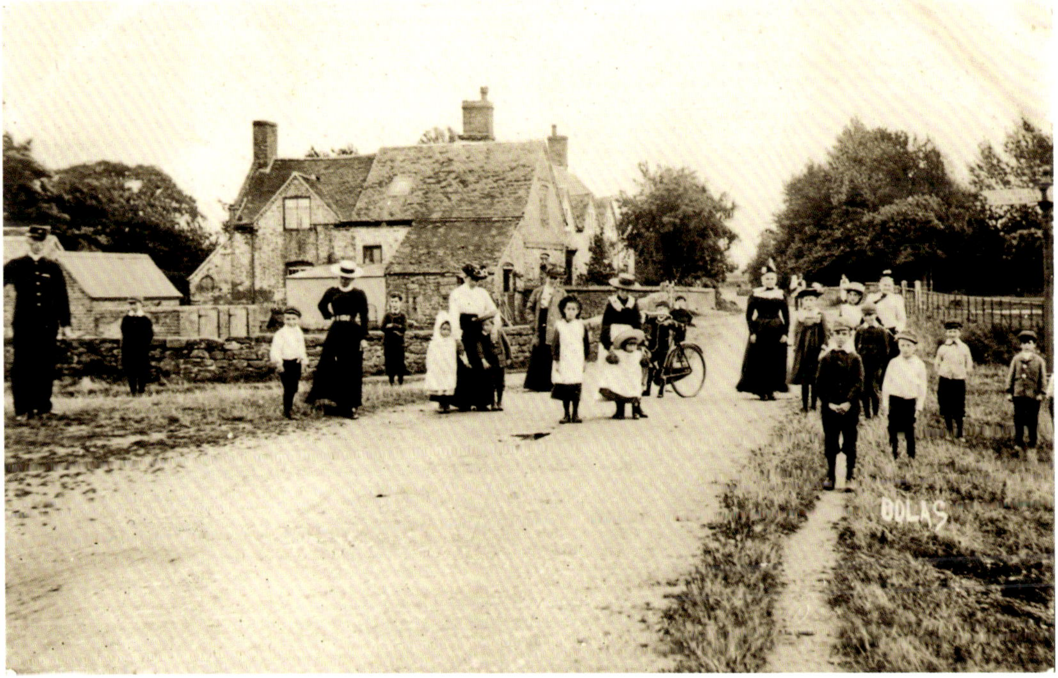

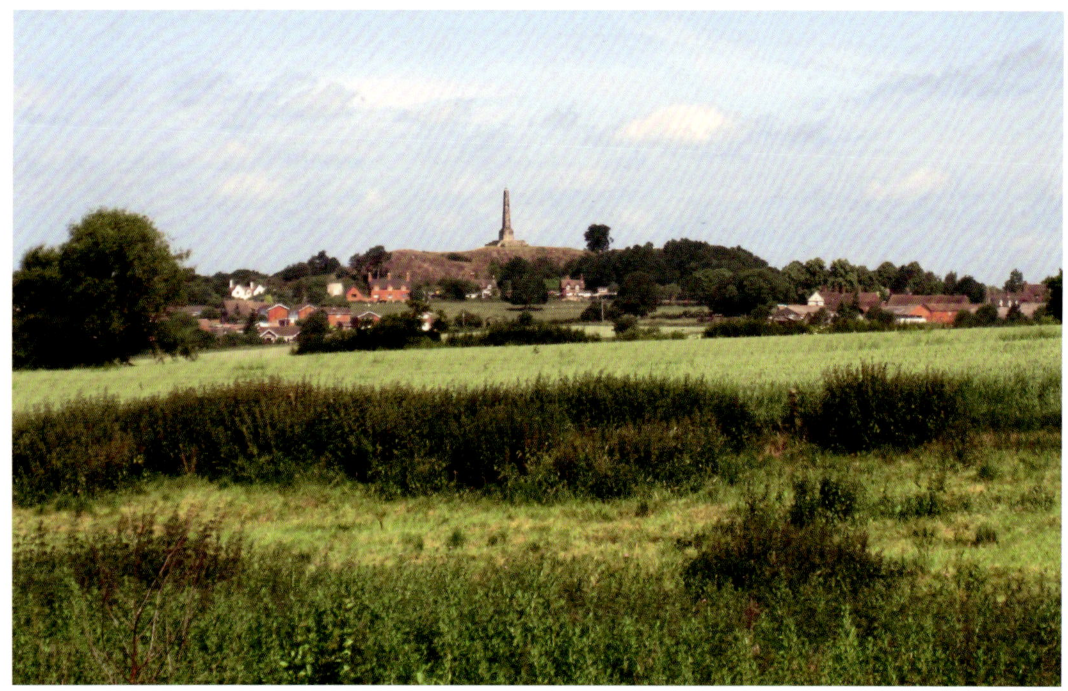

### Lilleshall and Tibberton

Both these villages lie towards the eastern edge of the Weald Moors and date from Saxon times. Lilleshall clings to a central hill surmounted by an obelisk paid for by tenants in memory of the first Duke of Sutherland. The village itself has no public houses because one of the Dukes disliked them. Ironically, the Sutherland Arms is the name given to pubs at nearby Tibberton (below) and Muxton.

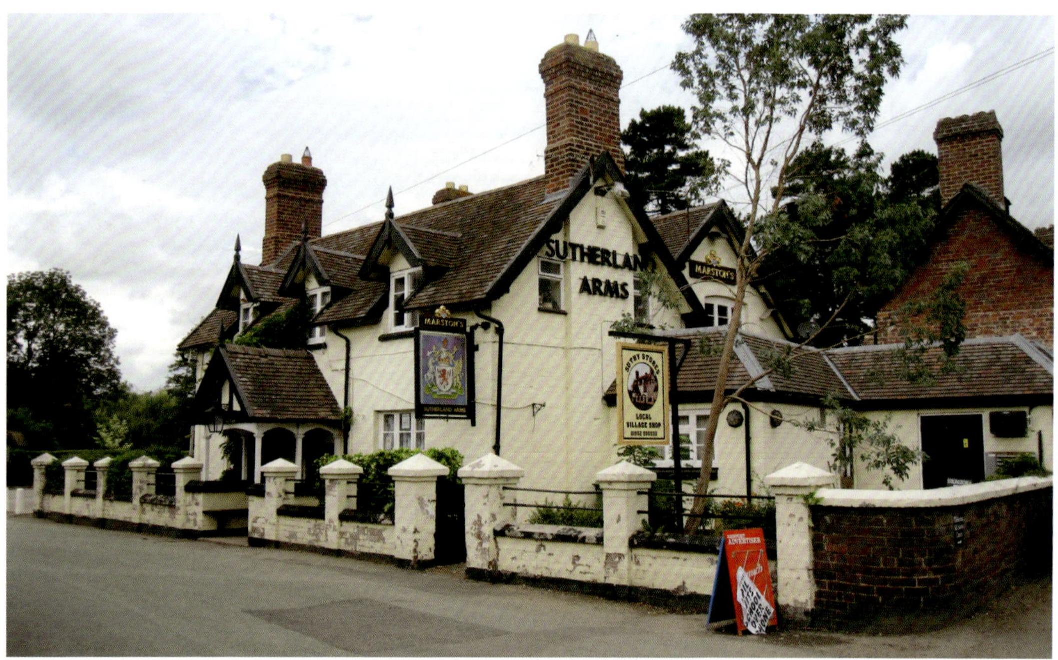

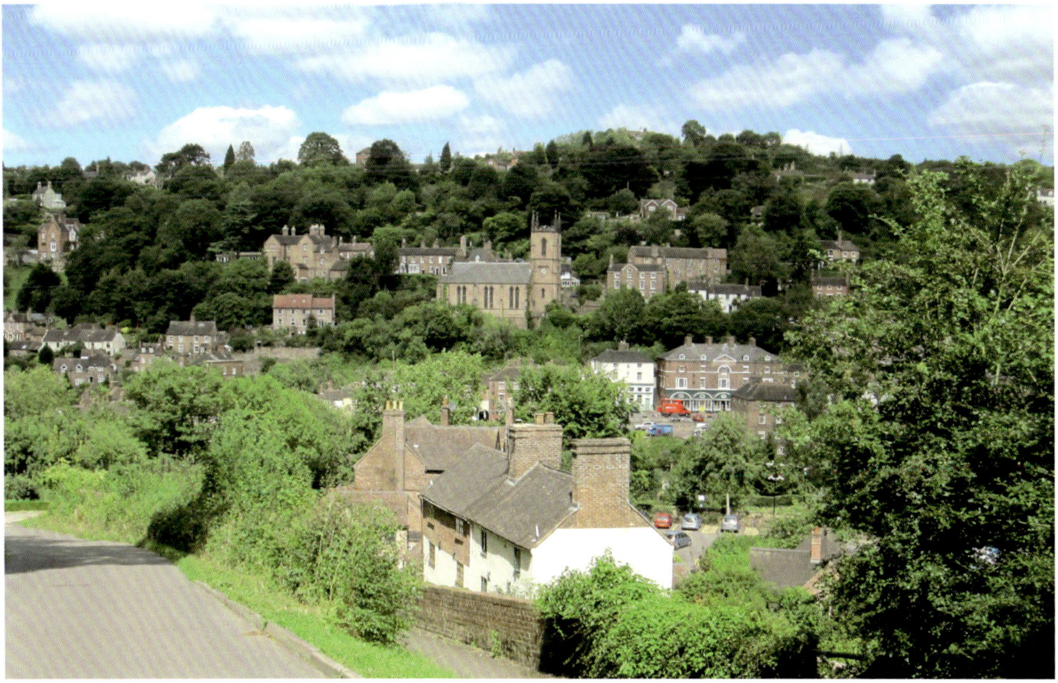

## Ironbridge

Named after the bridge made of cast iron in 1779 and simplistically credited with being the 'birthplace of the Industrial Revolution', Ironbridge has been heavily promoted to encourage visitors to this picturesque town which had become entirely neglected by the 1950s. From a historical point of view, there are many more places within the area far more interesting... but few so scenic.

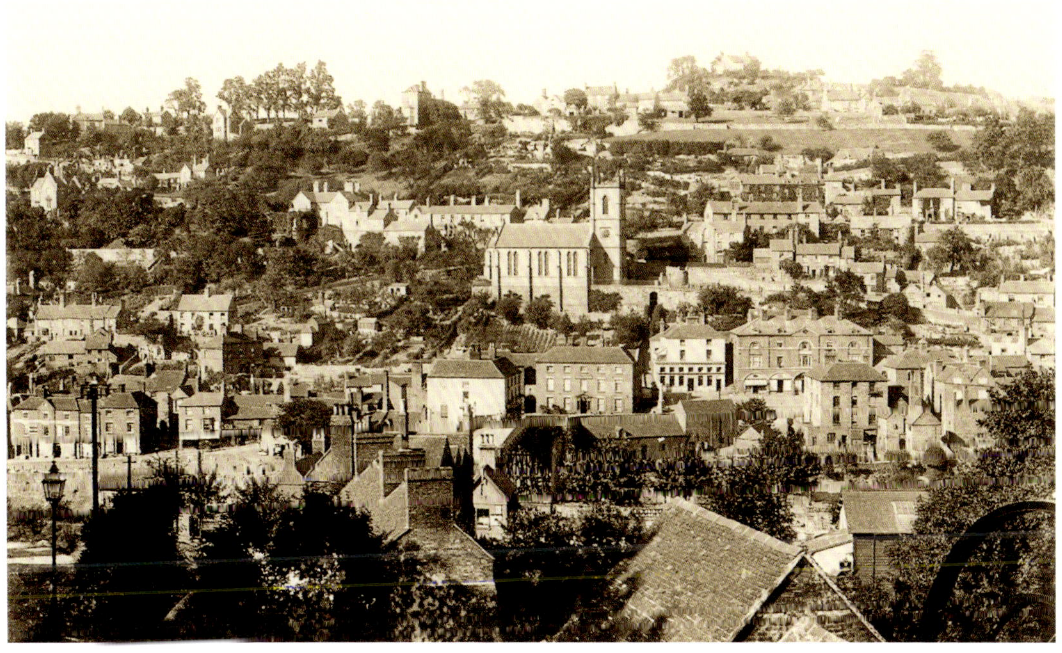

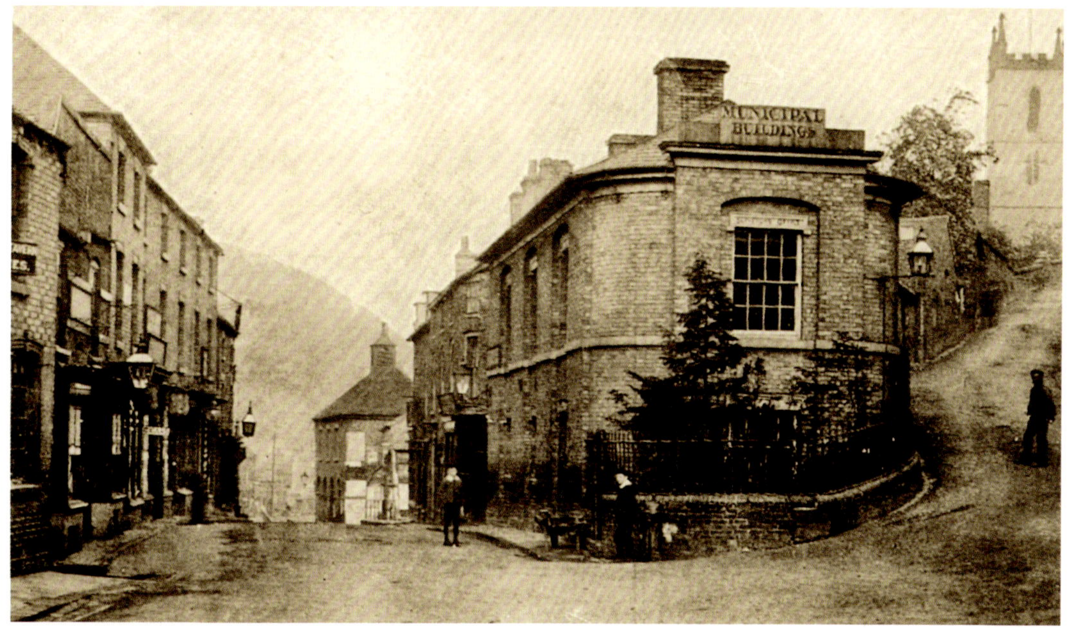

## High Street and Church Hill, Ironbridge

Between High Street on the left and Church Road (leading to St. Luke's) on the right, the Municipal Buildings began life as the town's dispensary in 1828. They later became council offices for Wenlock before demolition for road improvements. High Street catered well for drinkers: on the extreme left, the Railway Tavern lay a few doors away from The Vaults (which still exists), which itself was a few yards from the (Old) Queen's Head, which was near The Three Tuns Hotel (now a café).

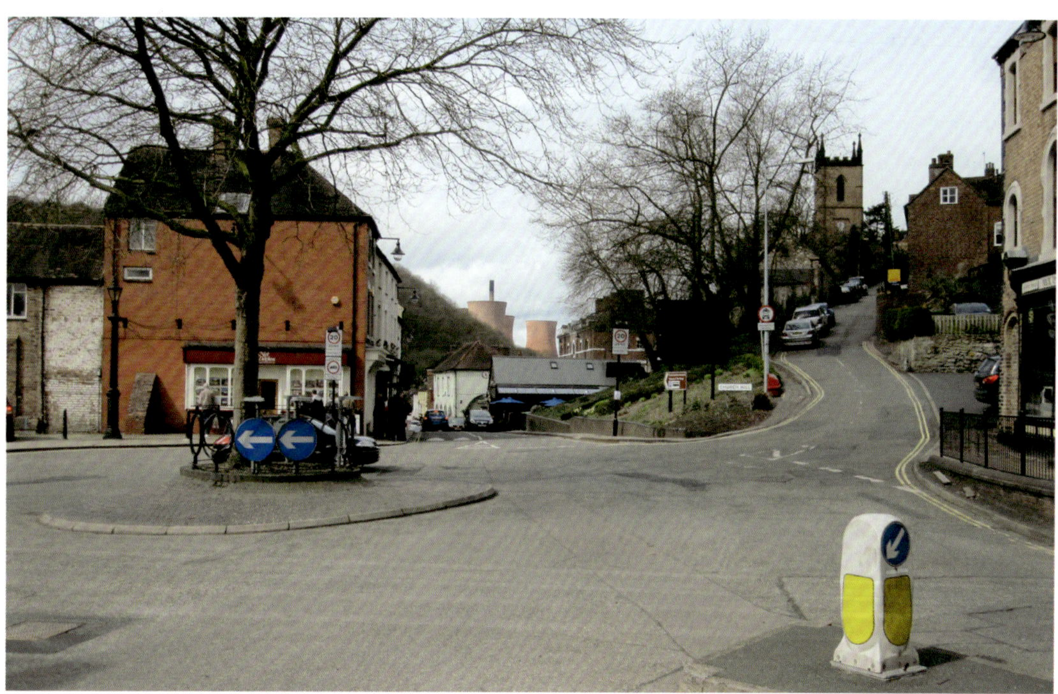

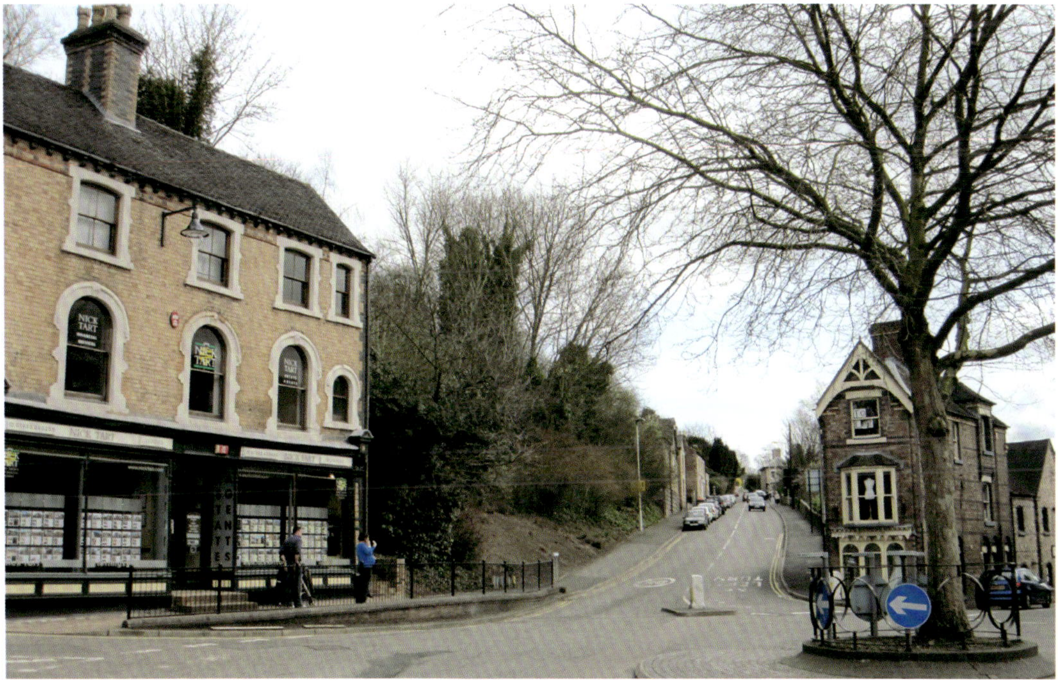

## Madeley Road, Ironbridge

The view opposite that on the previous page looks northeastwards towards Madeley and was, before Ironbridge came into being, part of Madeley Wood. The estate agent's building on the left was, until relatively recent years, next door to the (New) Queen's Head Inn (as opposed to the 'Old' one in High Street) which became a Wrekin Brewery hostelry during the 1930s. The building on the right awaiting a new tenant next to the entrance to Waterloo Road was Woolley's clothing stores for around fifty years.

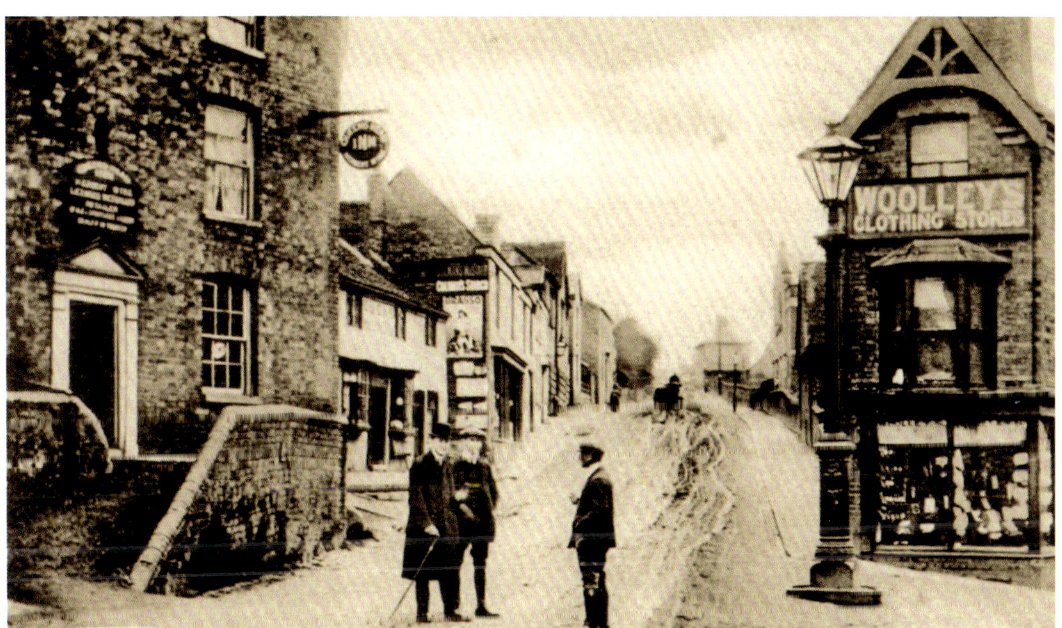

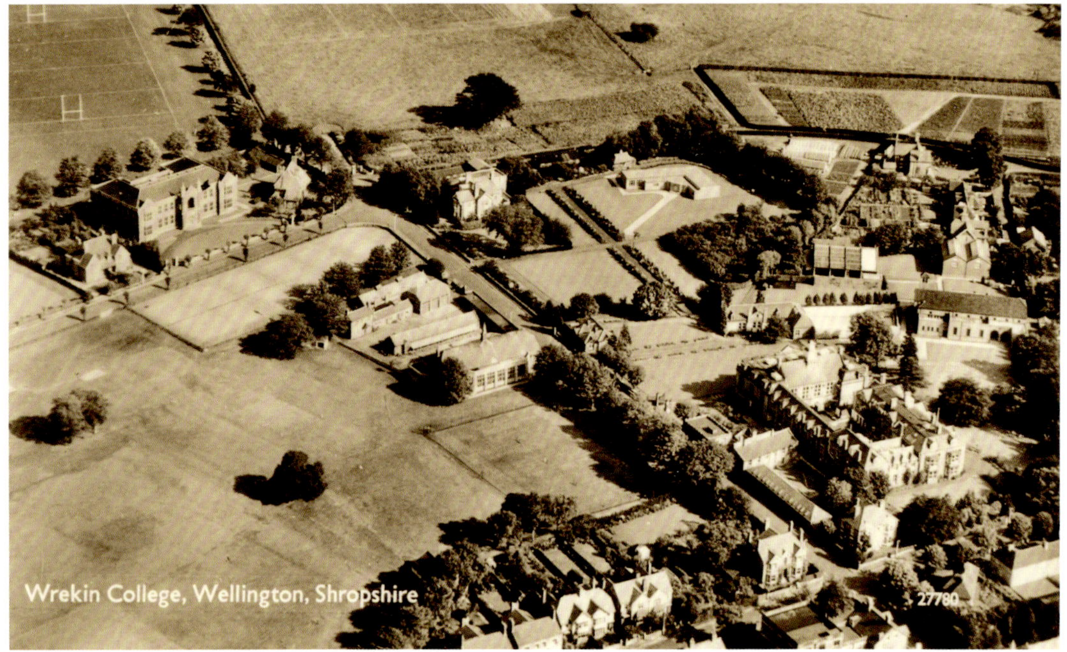



### Schools Old and New

Telford has had many schools scattered around the district, including private schools like Wrekin College (above, founded in 1880 by John Bayley). Originally named Wellington College, it changed its name in January 1920 to avoid confusion with Wellington College in Somerset. The trend for local authority schools in recent years has been towards building large complexes (such as the Hadley Learning Community, below, being constructed in 2006) under Private Finance Initiatives.

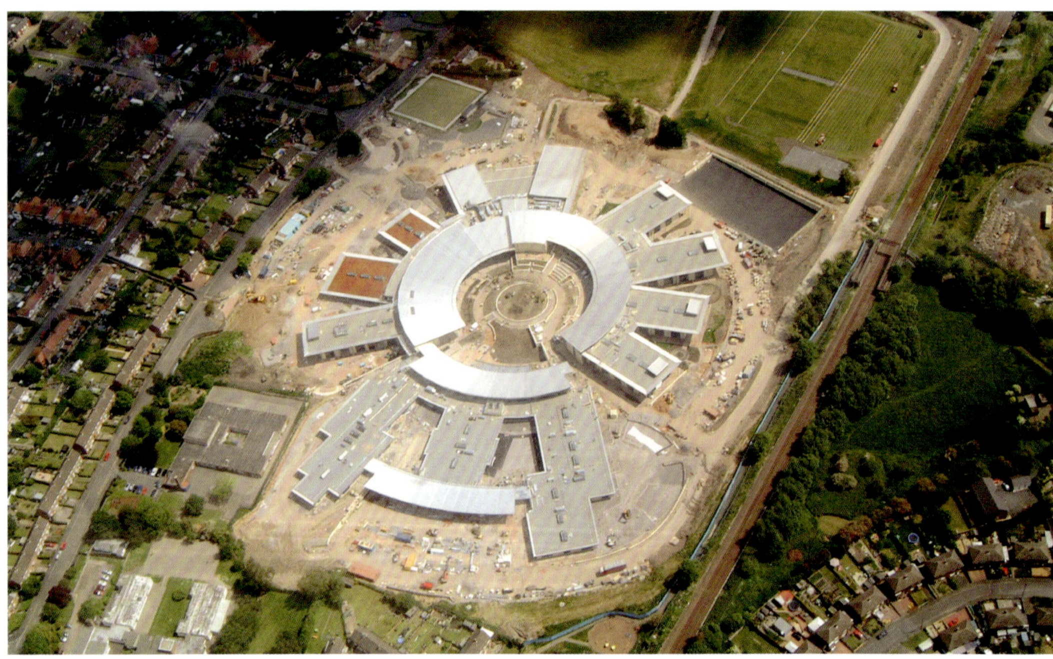

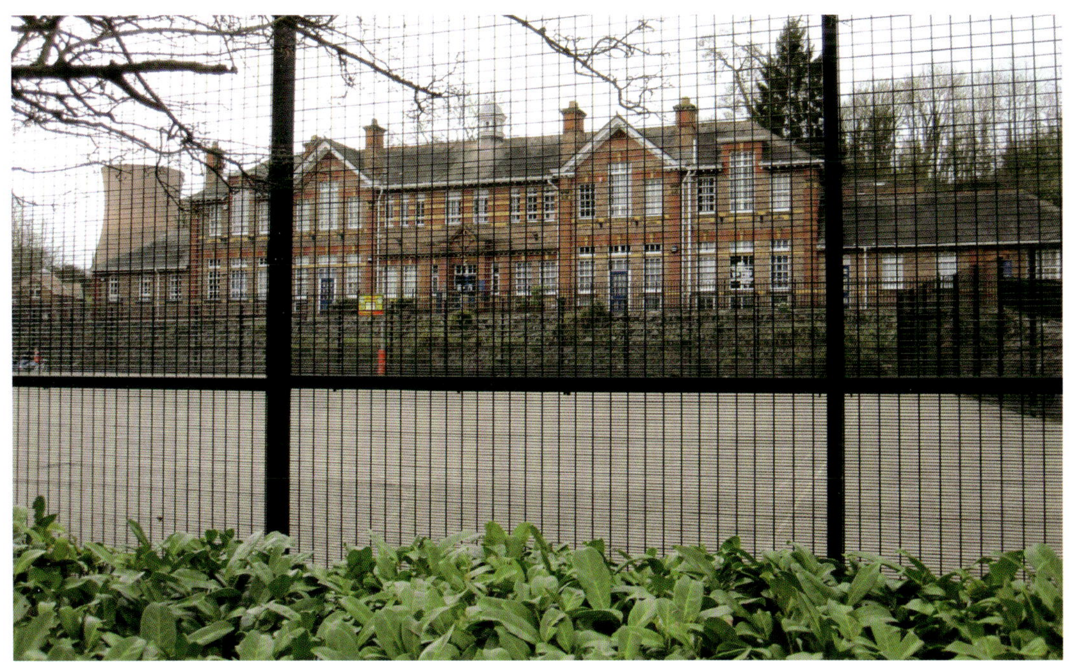

## Coalbrookdale

Coalbrookdale High School opened in 1911, with girls separated from boys as was common practice at that time. In 1965 it merged with Madeley Secondary Modern to become the Abraham Darby Comprehensive school, although first and second year pupils continued to be taught here until 1968. The premises are now home to Coalbrookdale and Ironbridge (C of E) Primary School. Note the 1960s Ironbridge Electricity Generating Station cooling tower, and prison-like fencing in the modern scene.

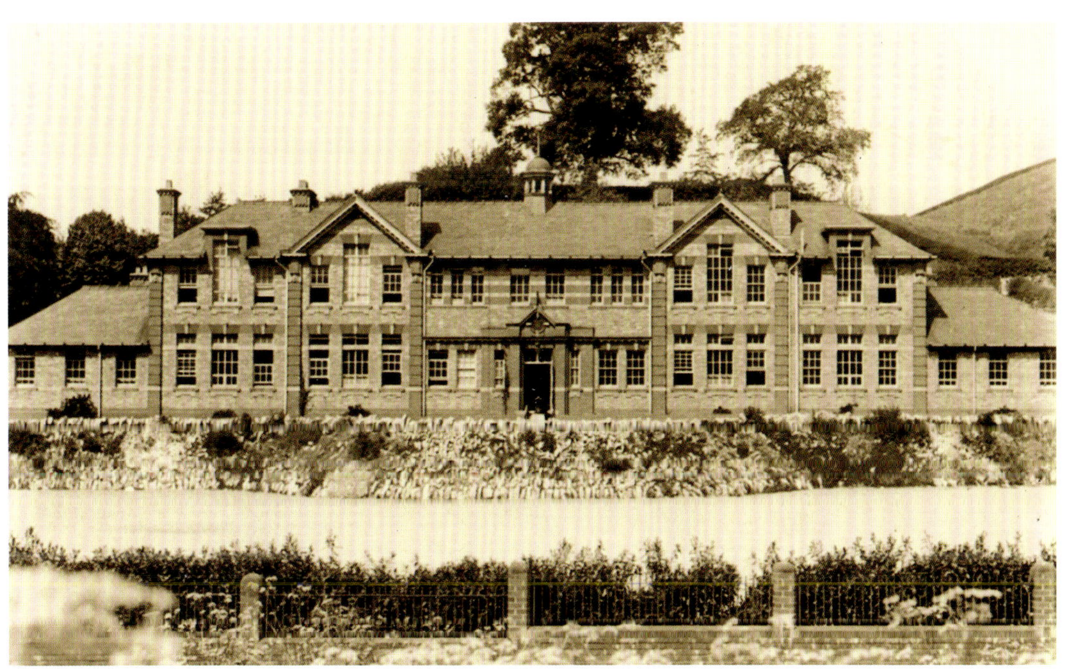

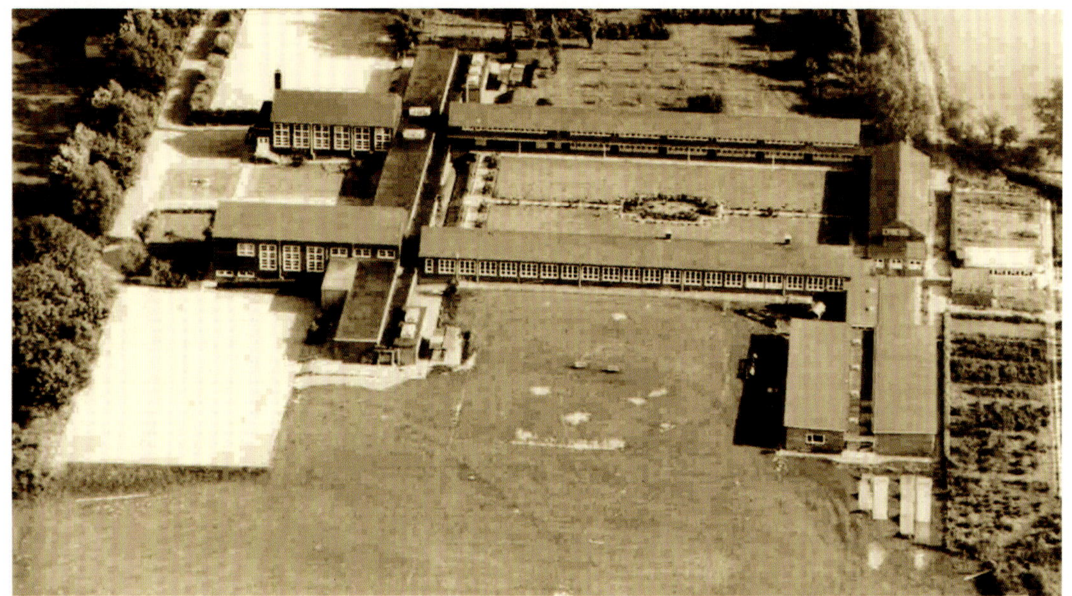

## Wellington Modern and Grammar Schools

Both the Orleton Lane Mixed Secondary Modern (above) and Golf Links Lane Boys' Grammar schools opened in 1940, having previously been based respectively at Constitution Hill and King Street, the latter remaining a Girls' High school. The grammar school closed in 1975 when the New College took over the Girls' High school premises to become a mixed sixth form college. The premises in Golf Links Lane later became Ercall Wood junior school which has since assumed Technology College status. Modern school girls left Orleton Lane for a new girls school at Dothill, which became the Charlton school in 1974. Orleton Lane pupils moved to the Hadley Learning Community and the old premises were demolished.

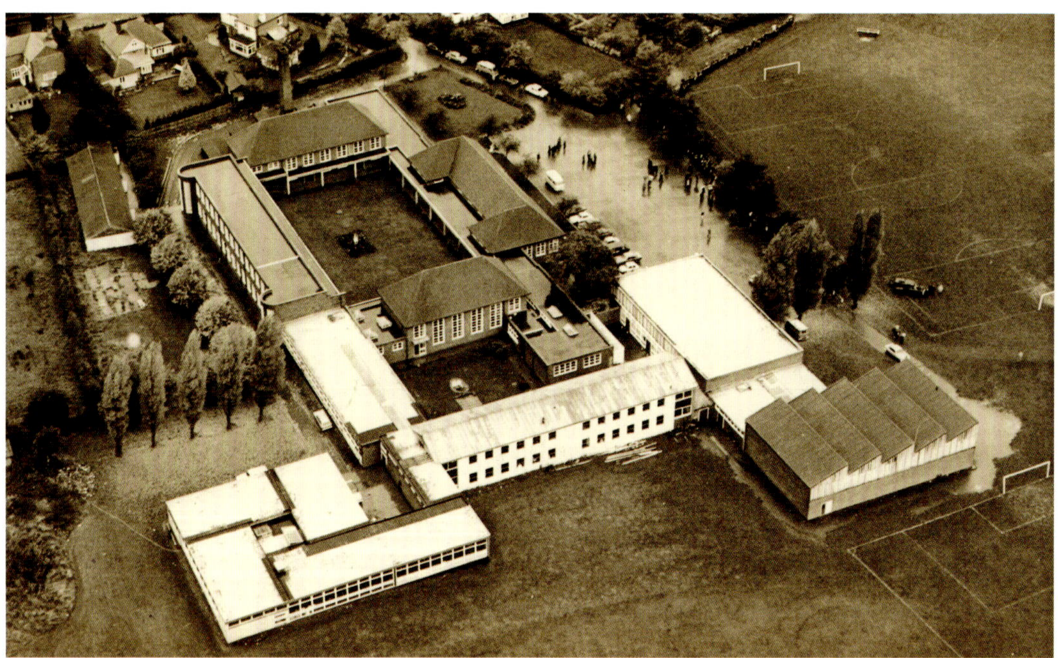

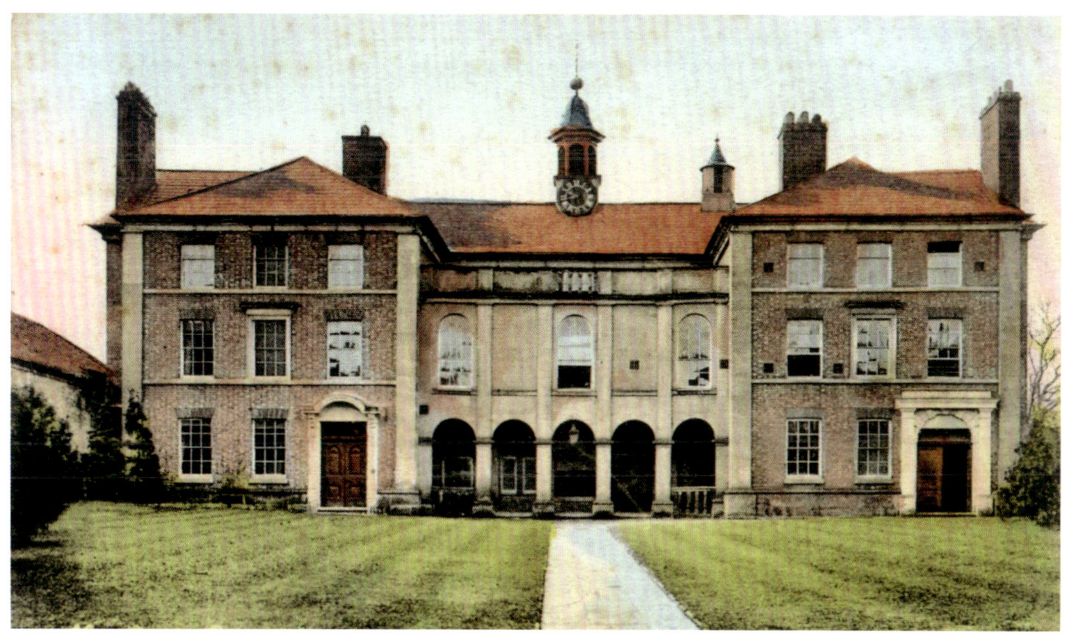

### Adams Grammar School, Newport

Founded by Newport-born wealthy haberdasher William Adams in 1657 after receiving permission from Oliver Cromwell, this selective state school continues to provide a high standard of education for day- and boarding boys; juniors board about a mile away at Longford Hall. Together with Newport Girls' High and Thomas Telford schools, Adams continues to rank among the best performing educational establishments in the borough. Seventeenth century spy and writer Matthew Smith, satirist Tom Brown ('I do not love thee, Doctor Fell') and radio disc jockey Simon Bates are among the school's alumni. Note the almshouses on either side of the school entrance.

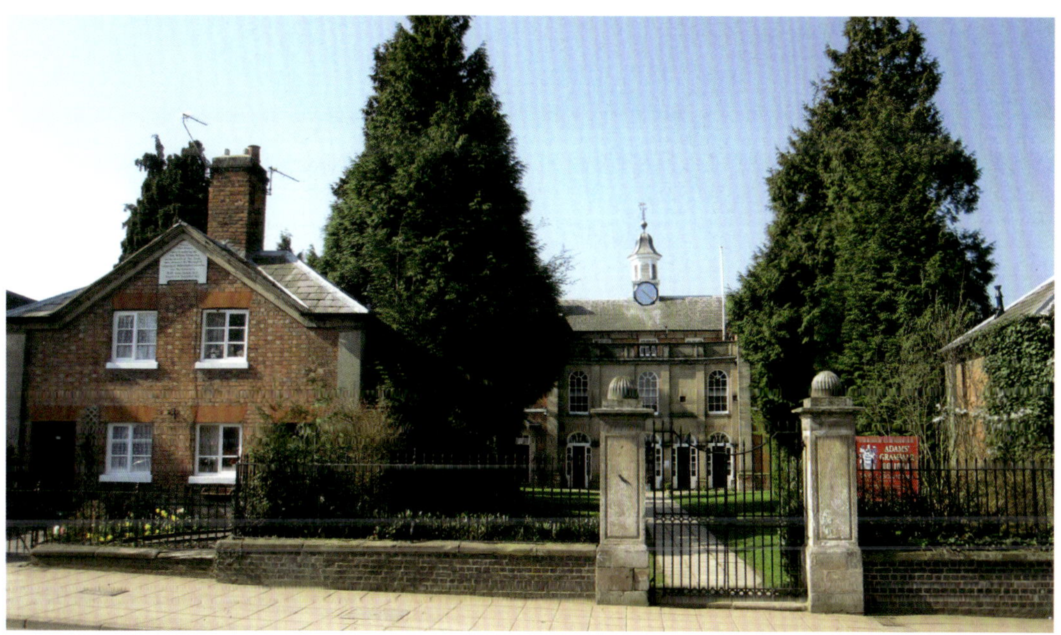

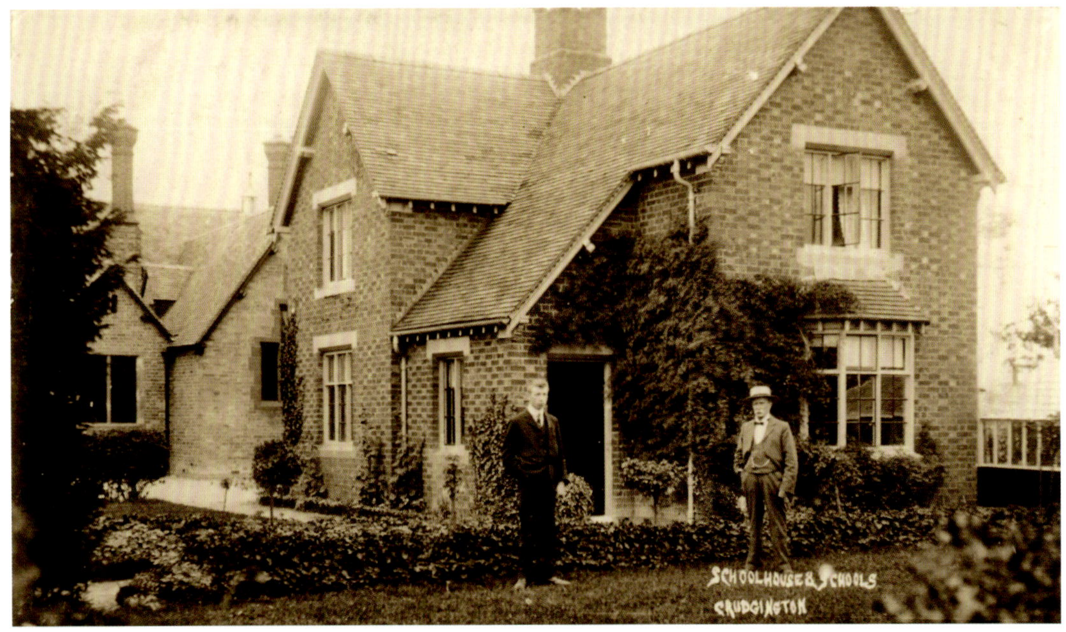


## Mixed Fortunes: Crudgington and Priorslee

Built in 1877 for ninety pupils, Crudgington Public Elementary school (with head teacher Edgar Percy Davies believed to be standing right in the above *c.* 1910 photograph by esteemed Wellington photographer W. Cooper Edmunds) still exists as Crudgington Primary. However, Priorslee National School, erected by the Lilleshall Company in 1872 and subsequently enlarged to accommodate 444 children, was demolished in 1958 because of falling numbers, probably due to a serious decline in the local economy at that time.

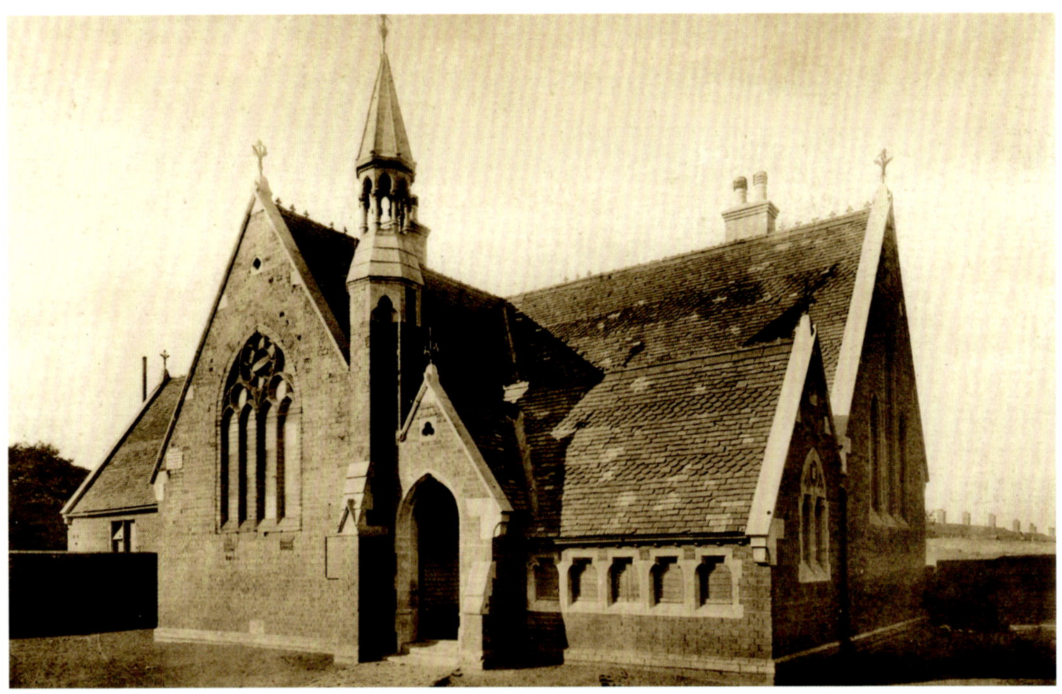

## Wrockwardine Wood Glassus School

Children from the Edwardian era have their photograph taken on the side of the Wombridge Canal which linked up with the Donnington Wood Canal and the Trench Inclined Plane prior to the latter's closure in 1921. Behind them is the tall Donnington Wood Flour Mill, also known as Bullock's Mill, which operated from 1818 until the 1970s and whose buildings have been converted into accommodation. To the right of both scenes stood the Donnington (sometimes called Wrockwardine) Wood Glassworks with its bottle kilns; it was in business from about 1792 until the early 1840s. Besides manufacturing green bottles for the French wine trade and numerous fancy items (including doorstops) the works also made sheet glass for windows. However, the Window Tax (repealed in 1845) and the Napoleonic Wars crippled trade. The Glasshouse (or 'Glassus') school, built in 1830 for employees and other children living nearby, was demolished in 1967. The canal has been filled in to create a curved footpath.

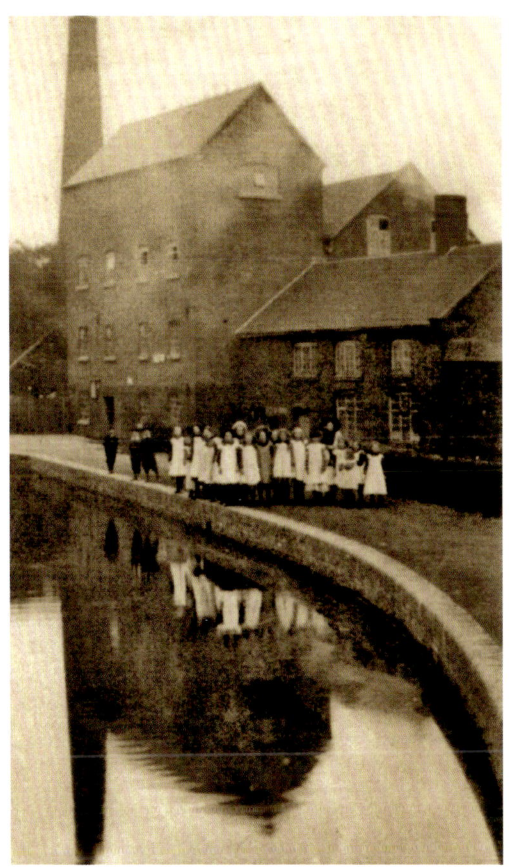

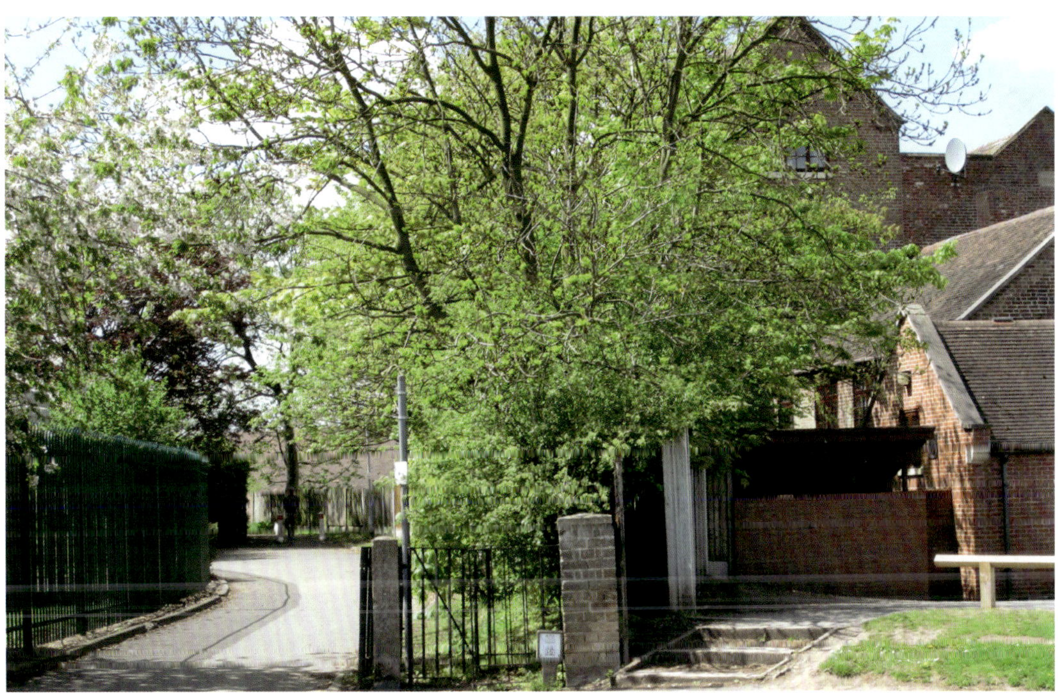

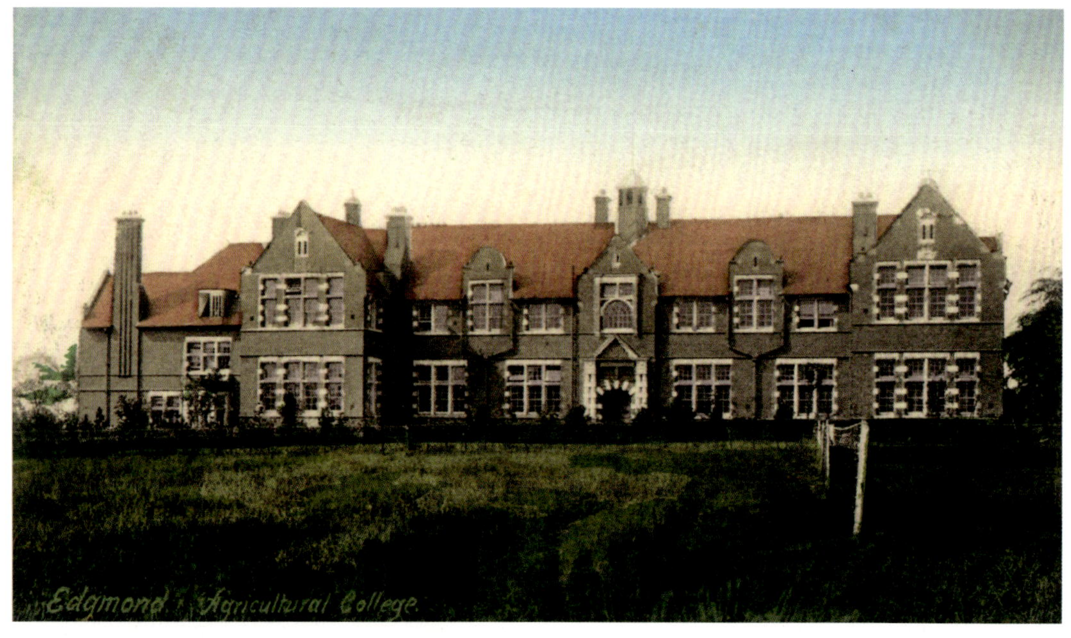


## Harper Adams Agricultural College, Edgmond

When Shropshire gentleman farmer Thomas Harper Adams died in 1892, he left his estate 'for the purpose of teaching practical and theoretical agriculture'. The college at Edgmond opened in 1906 with six male students (women were admitted from 1915); there are now 4,000, including post-graduates. World wars and recessions have affected progress at times but the college has more than made its mark. In addition to teaching all aspects of modern farming (livestock, poultry, arable, etc.), rural enterprise, management and marketing, research work of national importance is also undertaken.

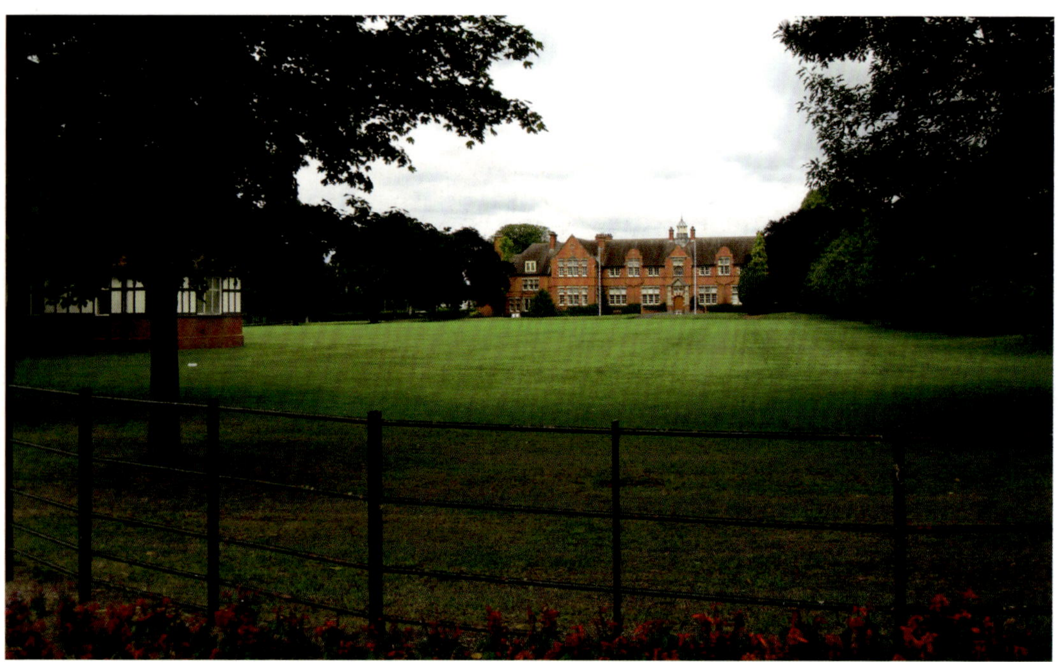

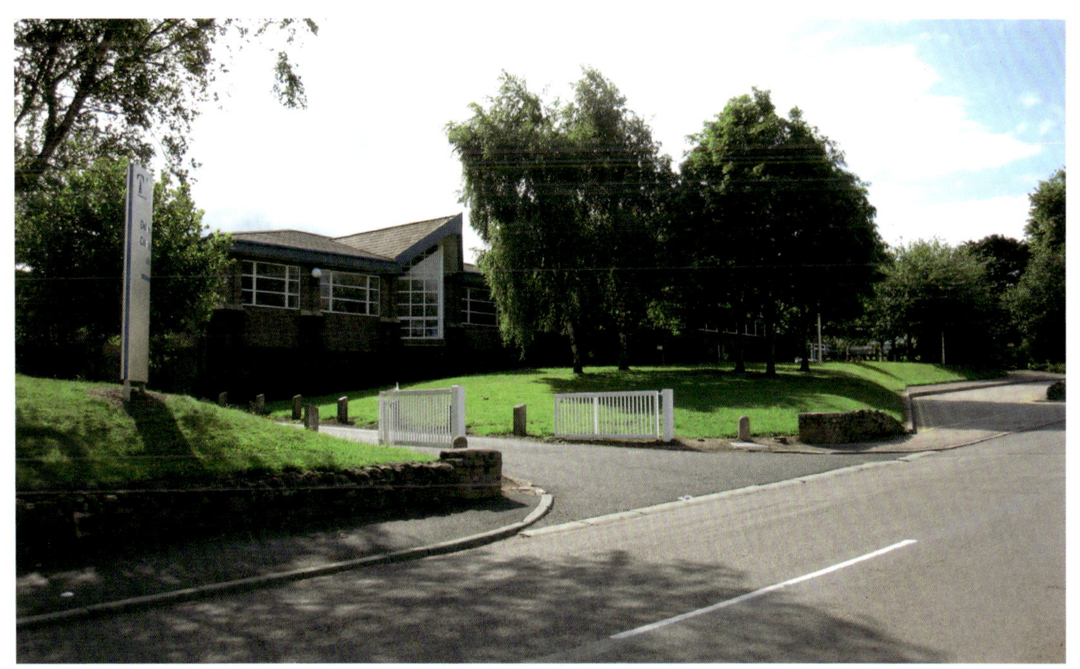

## Walker's Legacy: Oakengates and Wellington

Charles Walker, director of C. & W. Walker Ltd., Donnington, provided a number of educational establishments before the Walker Technical College opened in 1927 at Hartshill, Oakengates, as the county centre for mining engineering. The range of subjects taught expanded, requiring newer, larger premises to be erected in Haybridge Road, Wellington, in 1962. The Hartshill building continued to have various educational uses but is now empty and dilapidated. The Haybridge Road site has been expanded over the years and now constitutes the Telford College of Arts and Technology.

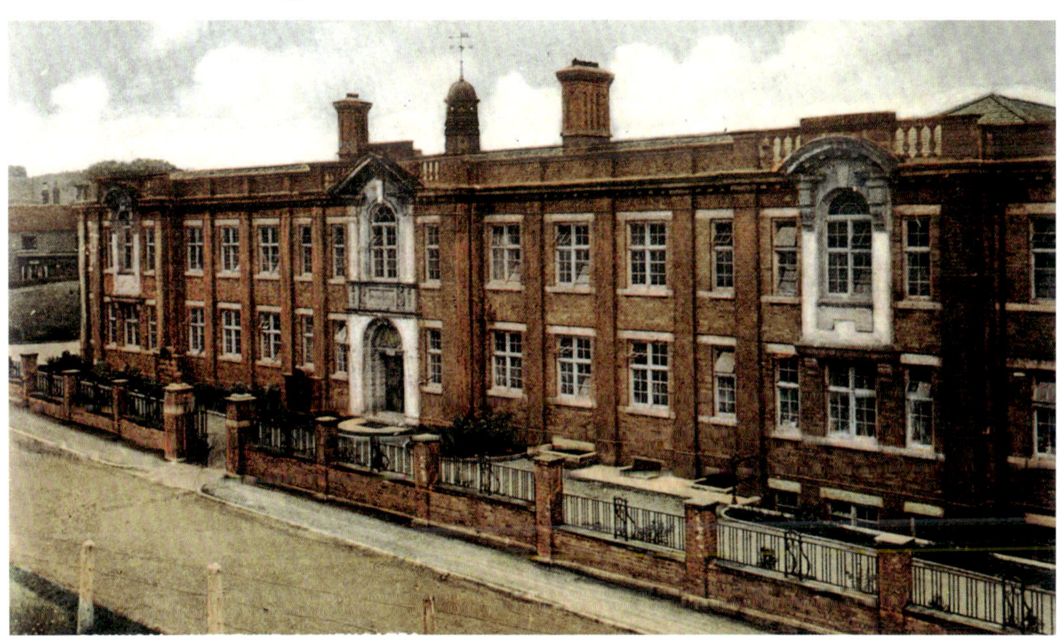

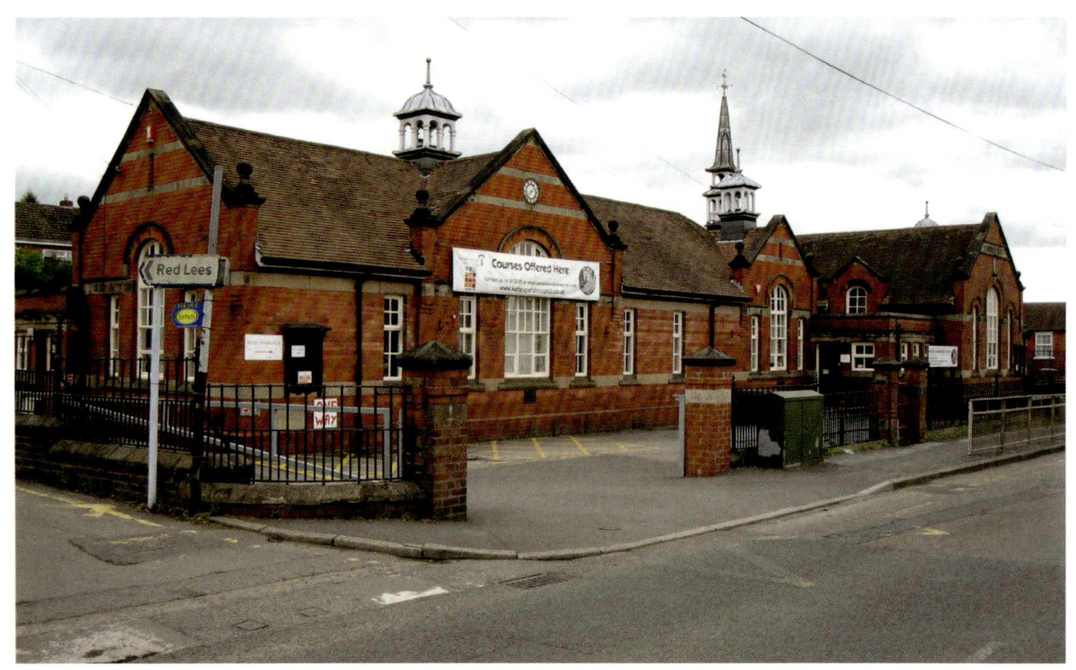

## Old Schools, New Uses: Ketley and Wellington

Several schools originally built in Victorian times survive... but no longer as schools. Ketley Juniors has now become home to Ketley Parish Council. The old buildings are now used for a variety of purposes, including a community hall. Prince's Street, Wellington (below), was built by Wesleyan Methodists in 1858 and brought into council control in the 1890s. It closed in 1971. The former school is now known as The Belfrey Theatre and Arts Centre, home of the Wellington Theatre Company.

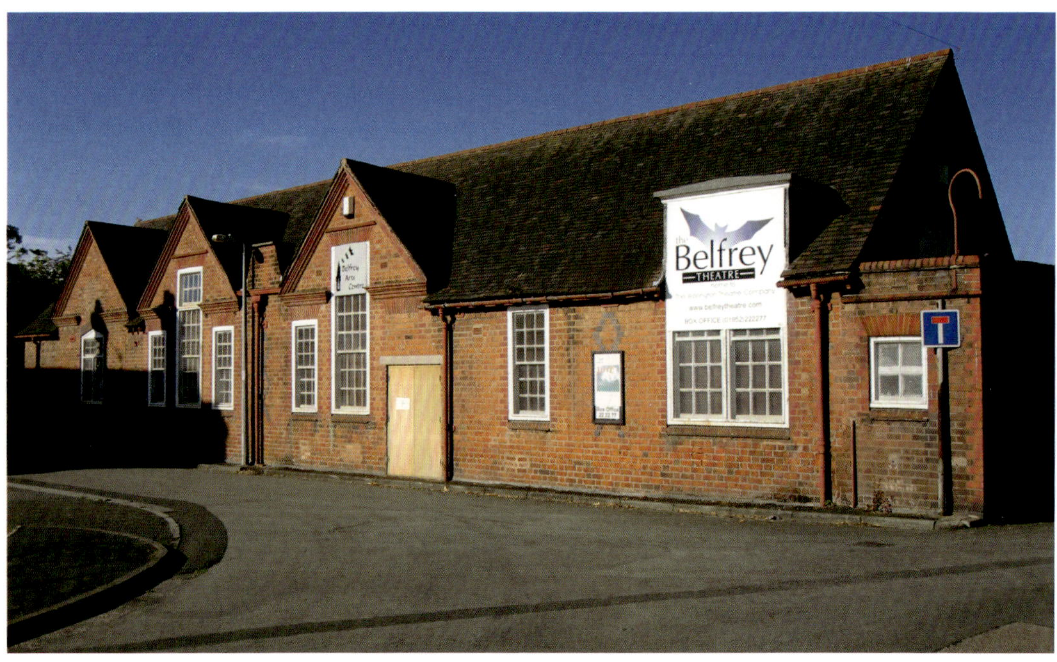

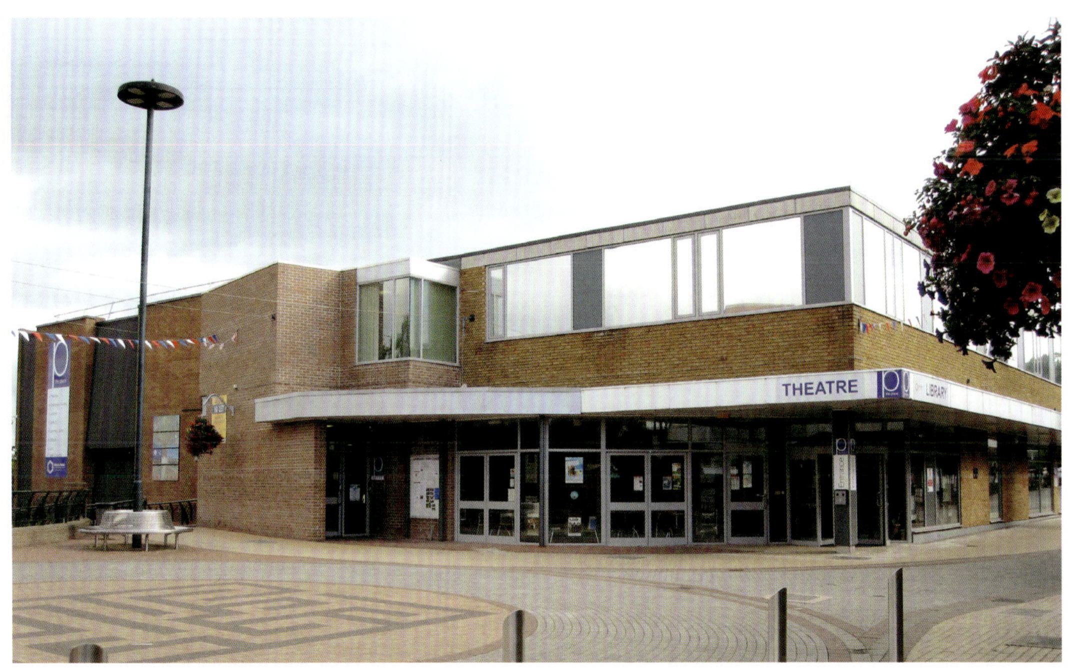

## The Place, Oakengates and Little Theatre, Donnington

Oakengates Theatre @ The Place (above), which reopened after extensive refurbishment and was renamed in 2005, having originally been built in 1968 as Oakengates Town Hall, is a major venue for performing arts from stand-up comedians to plays to popular singers, dance and classical music. Conversely, the Little Theatre's amateurs at Donnington have been captivating audiences with their operettas and plays for over sixty years in a converted army hut. Telford Sea Cadets meet in the hut on the left.

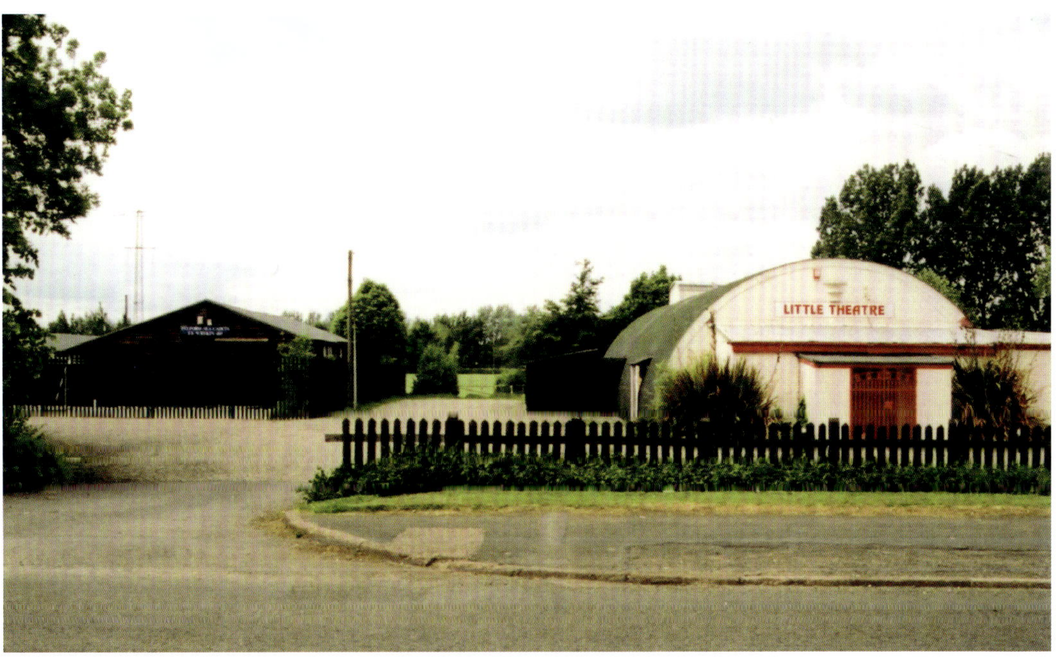

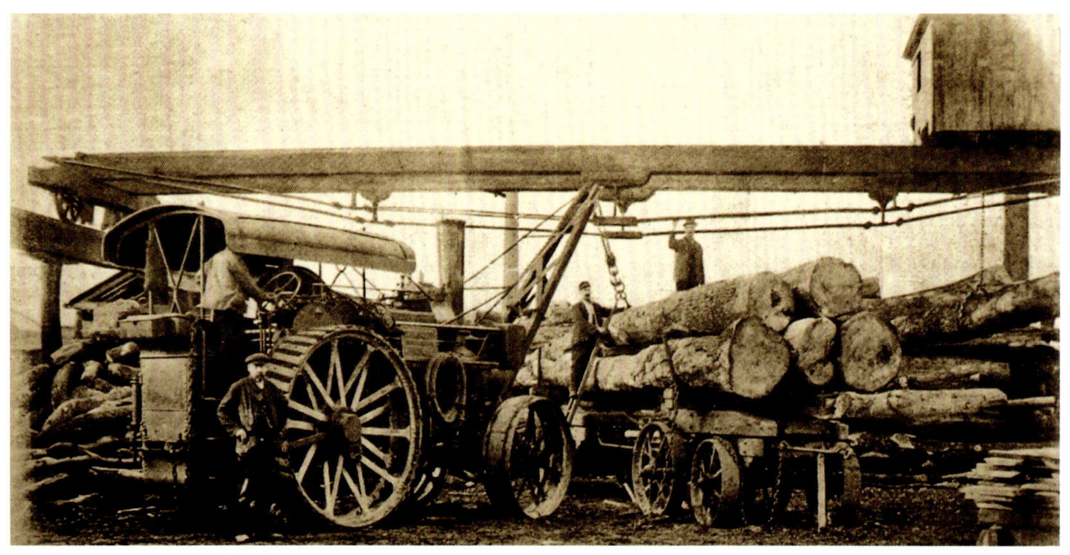

## Earliest Industries: Timber!

The Wrekin (below, as seen from the south-east in 2006) and its extensive Medieval Royal Forest provided a living for many centuries. Charcoal burning provided fuel to fire iron furnaces until coke and coal took precedence, but careful husbandry of the woodland enabled Richard Groom's Wellington timber works to thrive. The 1905 eight-wheeled steam wagon above enabled vast logs to be hauled from hill to the yard.

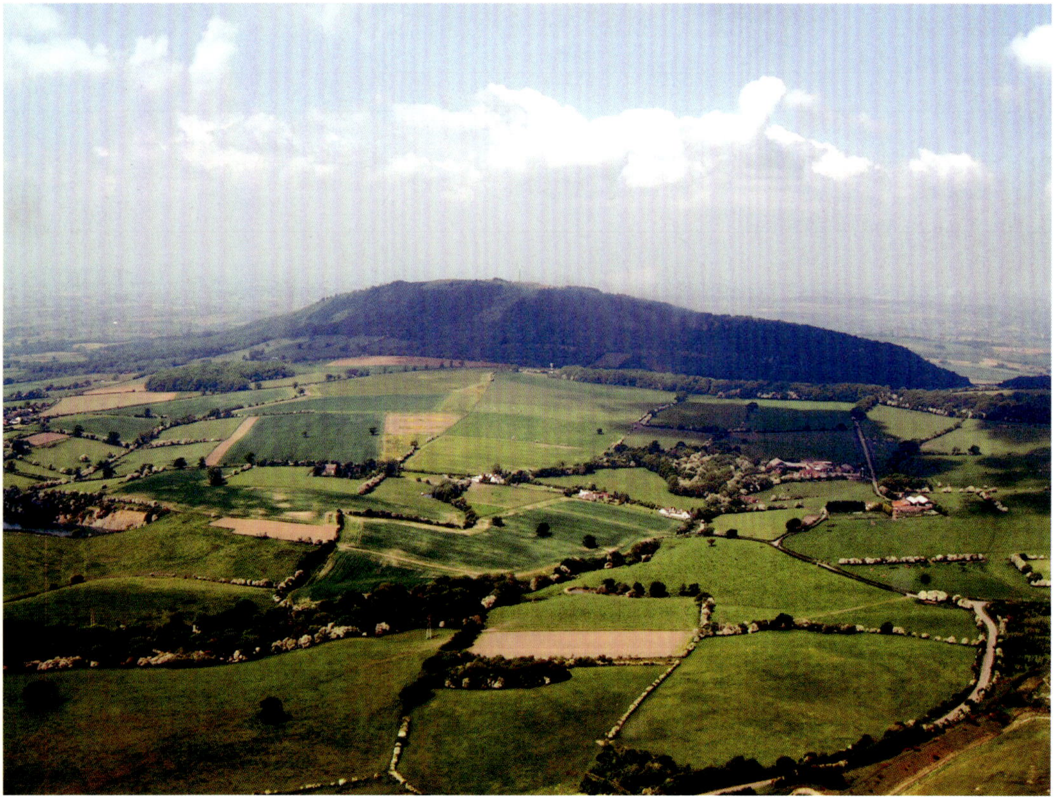

## Arable and Pastoral Farming

Historically the principal town in the Telford conurbation, Wellington has served the needs of the varying communities comprising its hinterland. Farming was the mainstay of trade, even after intense industrial developments on the adjacent coalfield got under way from the eighteenth century onwards. Samuel Corbett's engineering works in Park Street, Wellington, became famous throughout the world for its labour-saving mechanical contraptions, for which it won many awards during the nineteenth and early twentieth centuries.

Wellington's Smithfield livestock market, originally begun by John Barber in the 1850s to combat corruption among cattle dealers, moved to the site now occupied by Morrison's supermarket in 1868 and became the largest Smithfield outside London. The scene below is of the last day of trading on 30th January, 1989. Trade in the town undoubtedly suffered as a consequence.

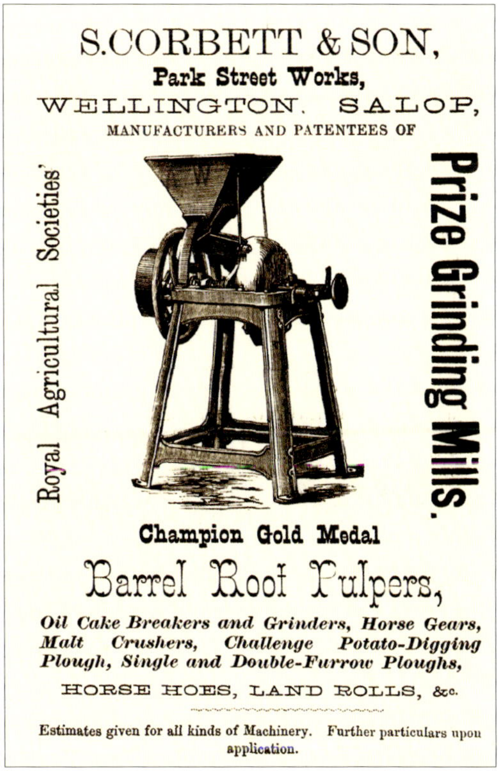

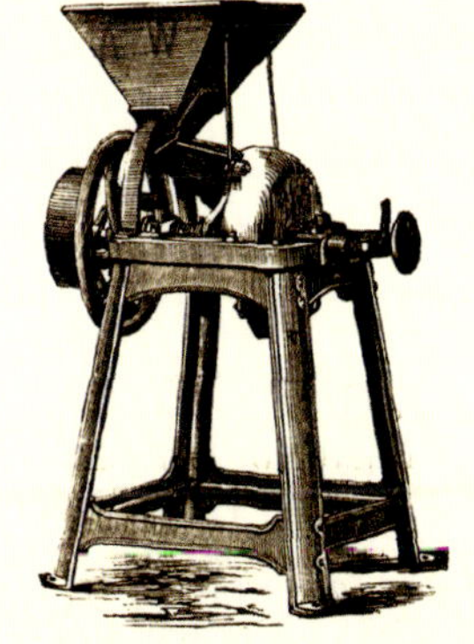

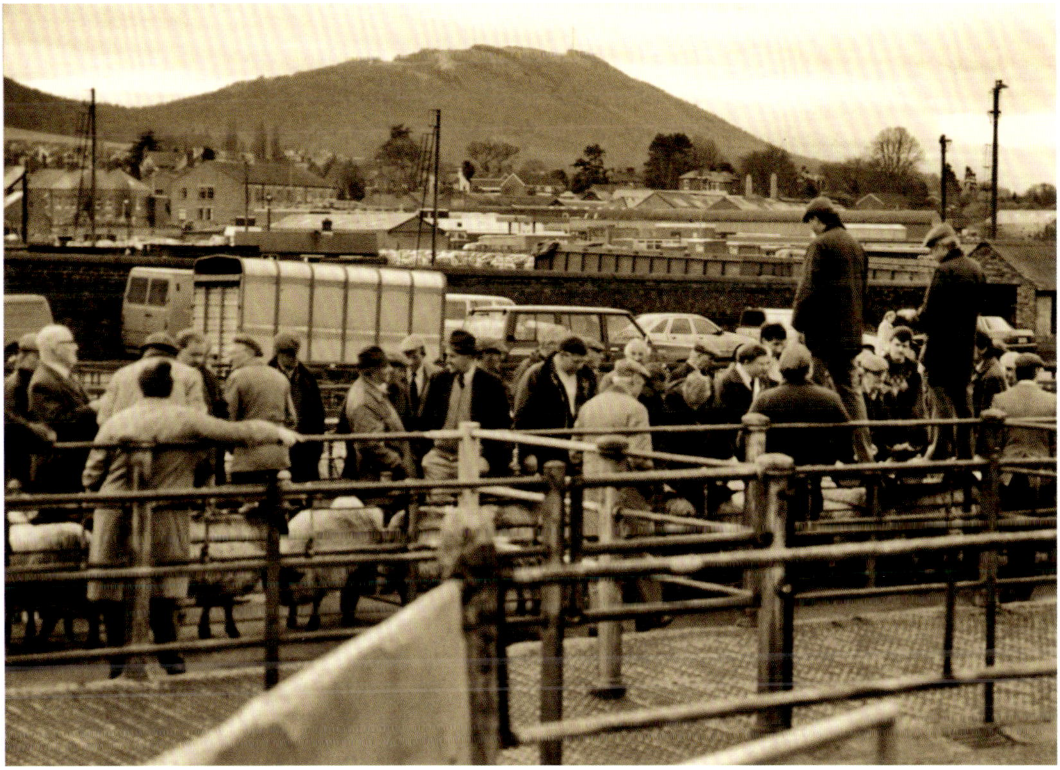

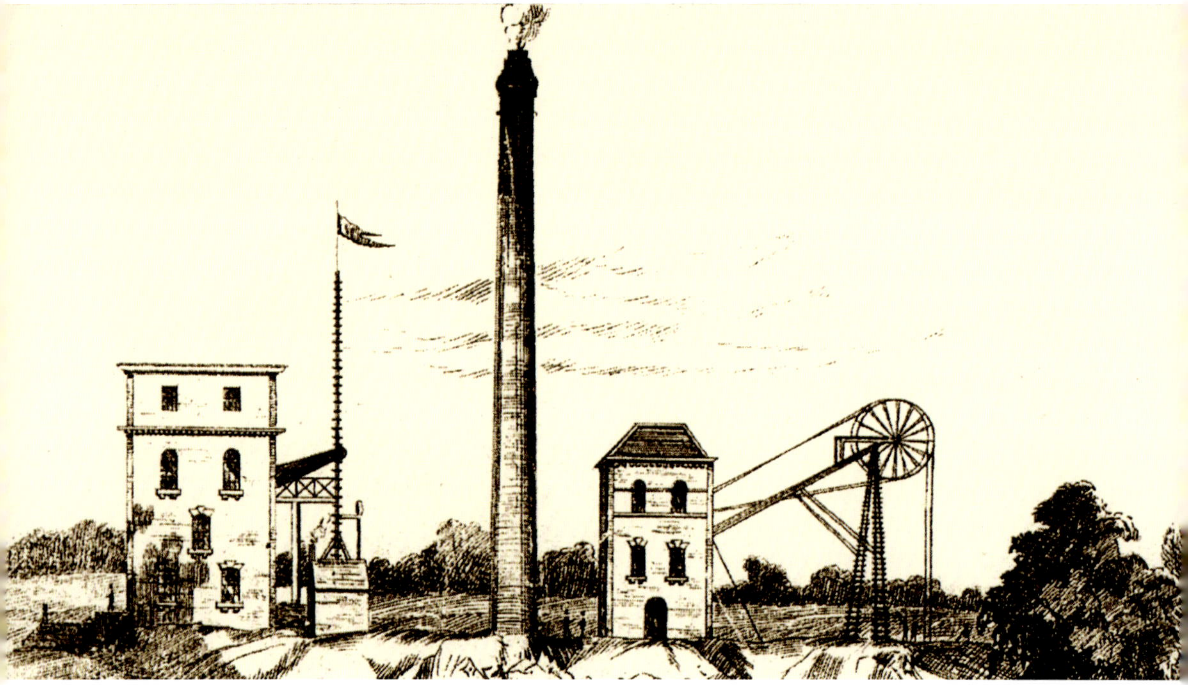

## Coal and Iron Mining: Granville Colliery

With its name preserved in a country park between Muxton and Donnington Wood, Granville Colliery began sinking shafts between 1854 and 1860. These scenes show the views in 1864 and *c*. 1979, the year in which this last surviving colliery in Telford closed. Originally operated by the Lilleshall Company, it was nationalised in 1947.

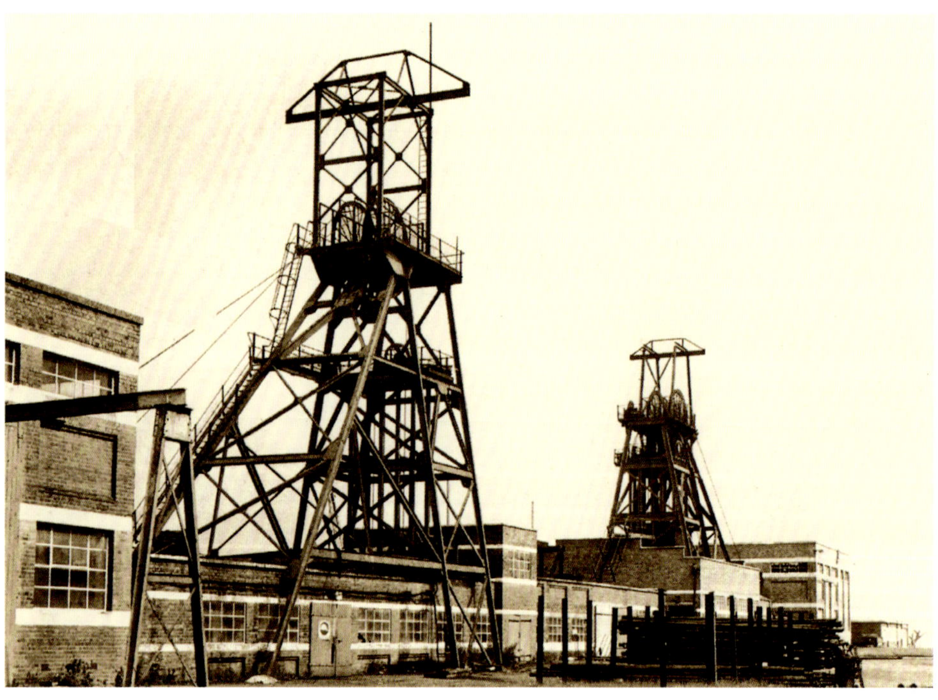

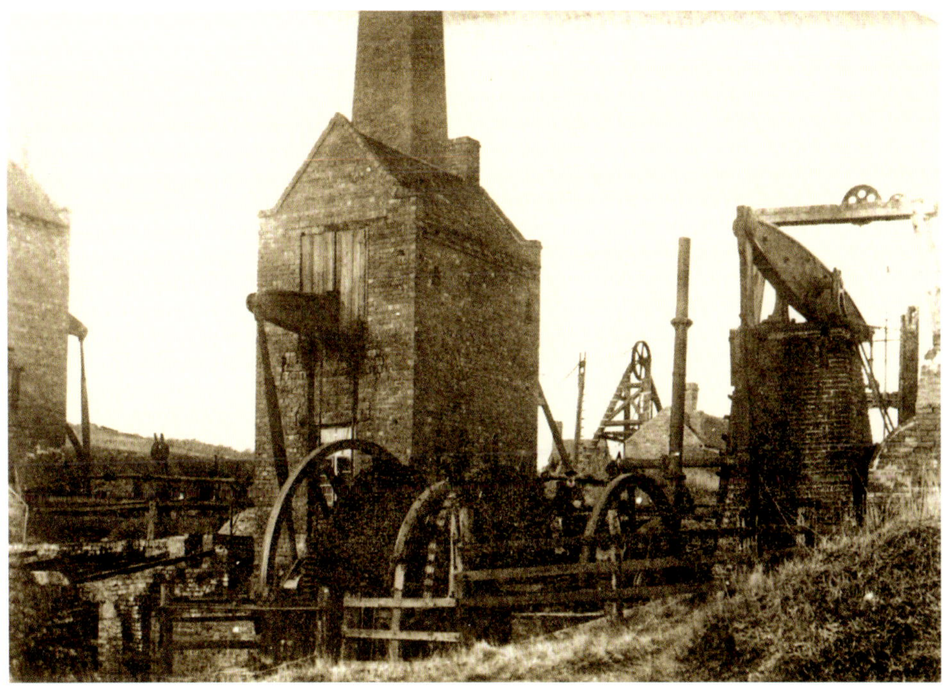

## Other Collieries: Madeley and Old Park

It may have seemed like it at the time, but official statements during the 1960s that Telford would be built largely on land blighted by mining activities was simply untrue. However, the east Shropshire coalfield gave rise to innumerable coalpits and collieries from Roman times until 1979. Incredible as it seems, most of these pits were uncharted and often run in the nineteenth century under the chartermaster system (indeed, the author's great great grandfather ran a mine at Newdale in the 1830s until his house blew up in an explosion). These views show mining at Madeley Court Colliery (*c.* 1900) and at Old Park (mid 1940s).

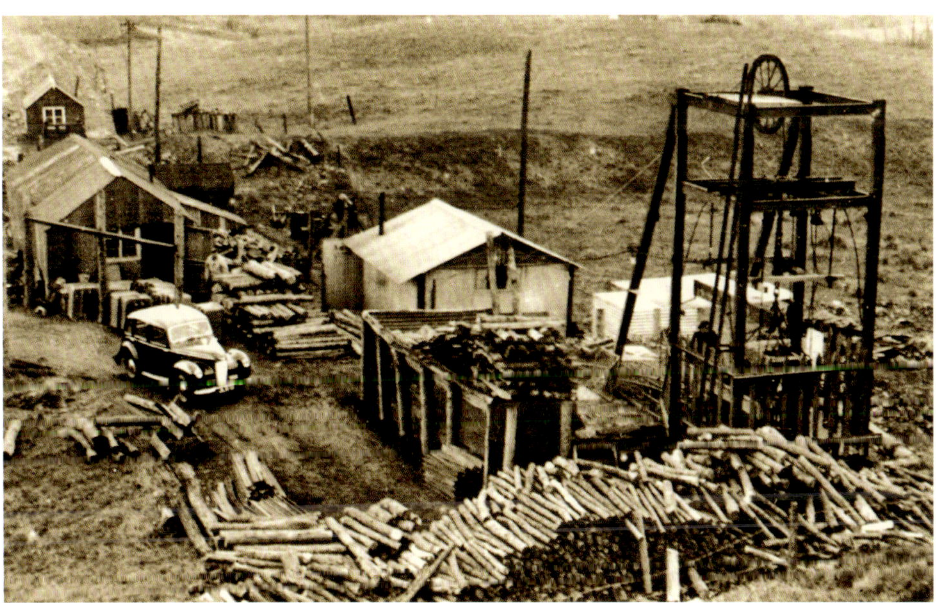

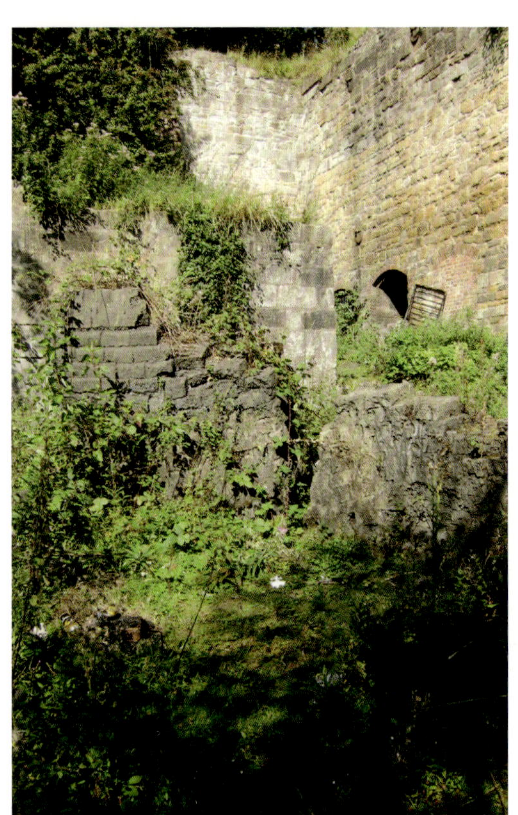

## Blast Furnaces: Donnington Wood

In some parts of the area, collieries weren't so much noted for the coal they extracted but rather for their iron ore. Mines around Donnington were essential for the amount of iron they provided for furnaces from Donnington itself to other parts of the district, including Coalbrookdale whose fame became assured when the Coalbrookdale Company cast the world's first iron bridge – and successfully erected it – in 1779.

The Lodge furnaces at Donnington Wood were erected in the early days of the Lilleshall Company and were expanded several times as the demand for iron grew. Iron, coal and limestone were brought by Lilleshall Company canals and railway. However, a severe economic downturn led to this magnificent structure having its furnaces blown out (closed down) in 1888. Substantial quantities of Grinshill sandstone were carted away for building projects elsewhere (including an extension to St. Matthew's church, Donnington Wood.) Only ground level ruined structures remain.

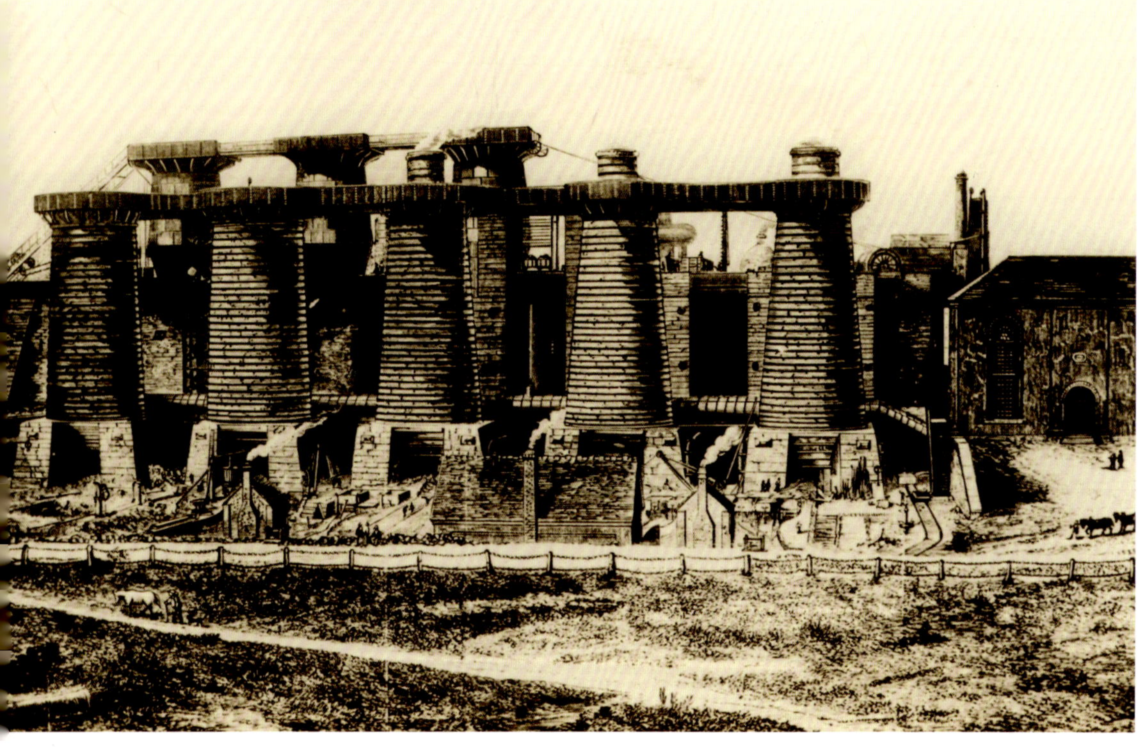

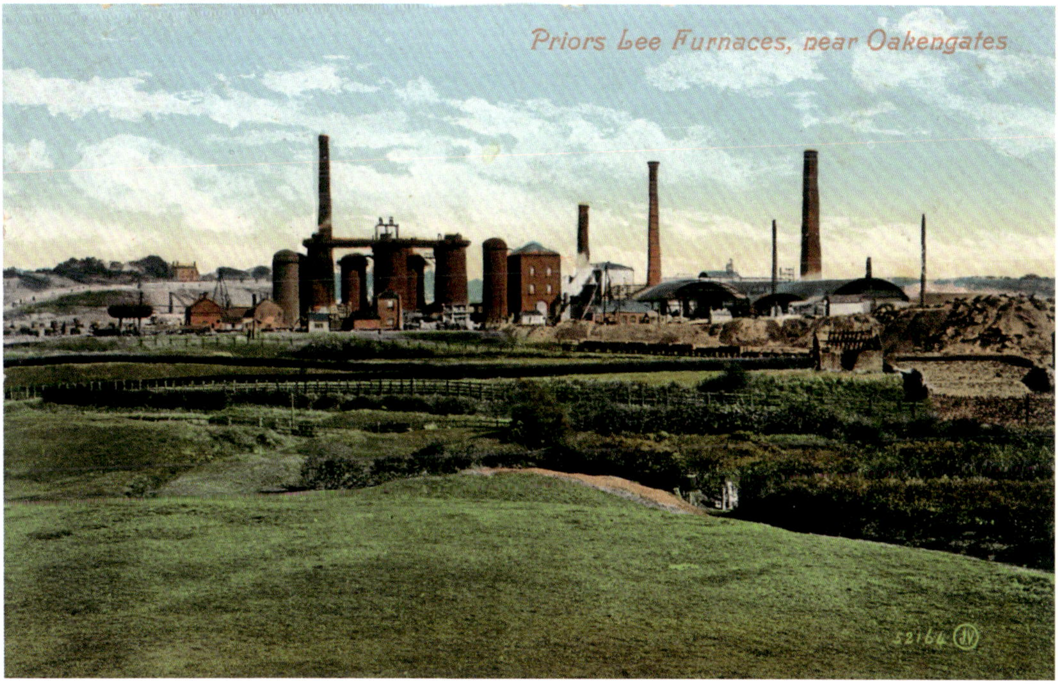

### Blast Furnaces: Priorslee

Erected in 1851 by the Lilleshall Company and later expanded and converted to produce Bessemer steel, the last incarnation of these furnaces finally closed in 1970, possibly because the author had a student holiday job here as a fitter's mate during the summer of 1969. Central Park offices now occupy the site.

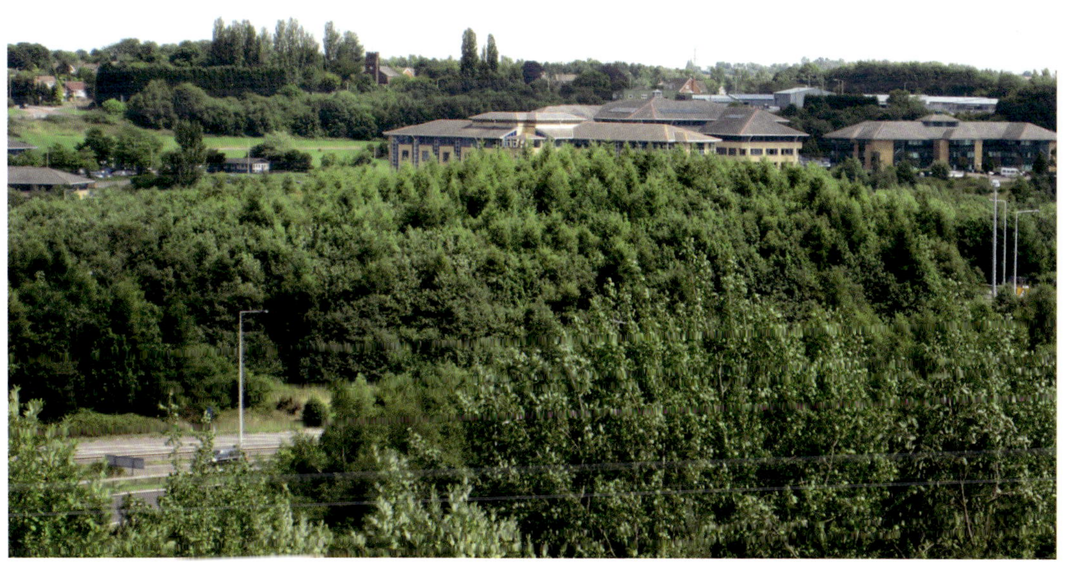

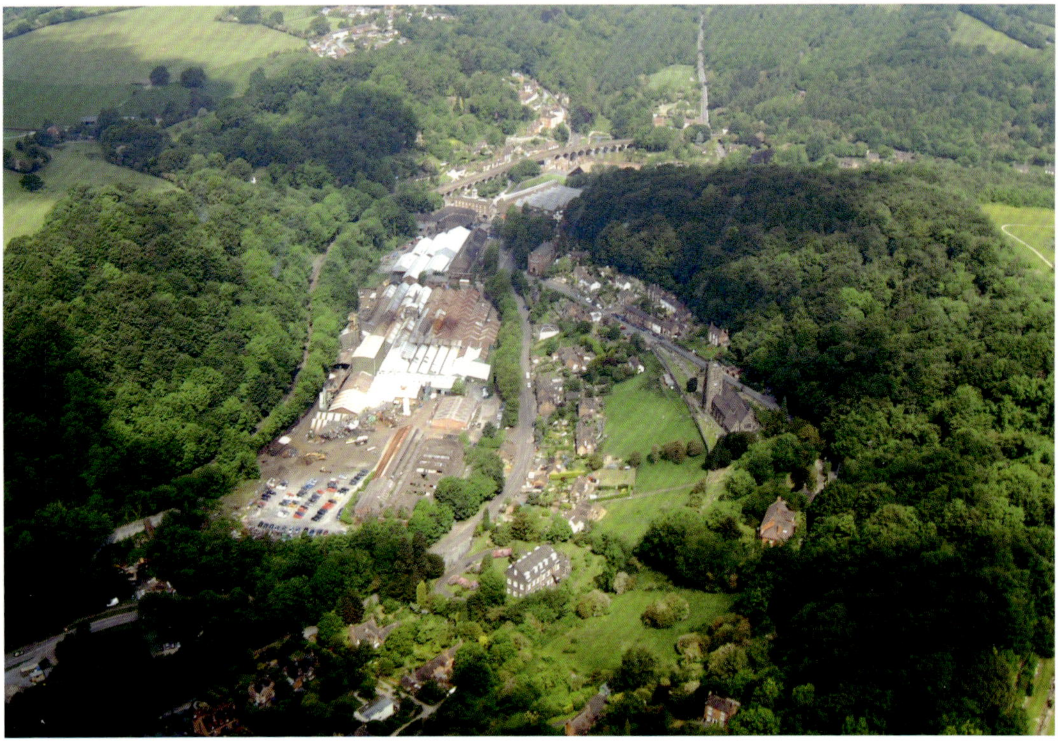

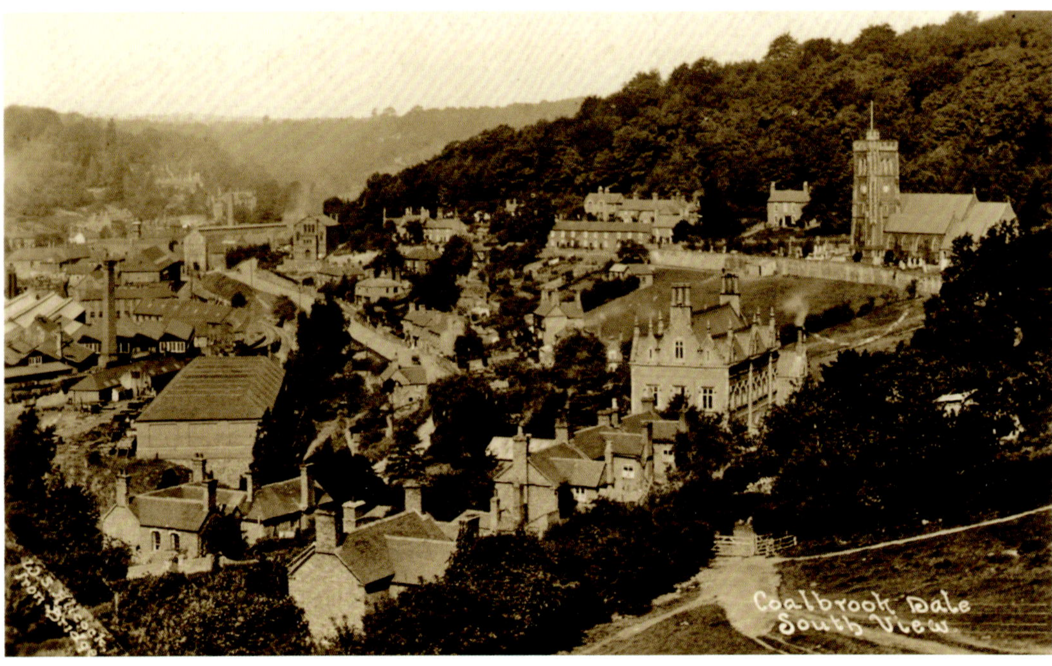

## Coalbrookdale

Coalbrookdale was just one centre of cast iron production in the Telford area but has been allowed to survive and promoted as the Coalbrookdale Museum of Iron where the castings for the iron bridge were made. 100 years separate these scenes.

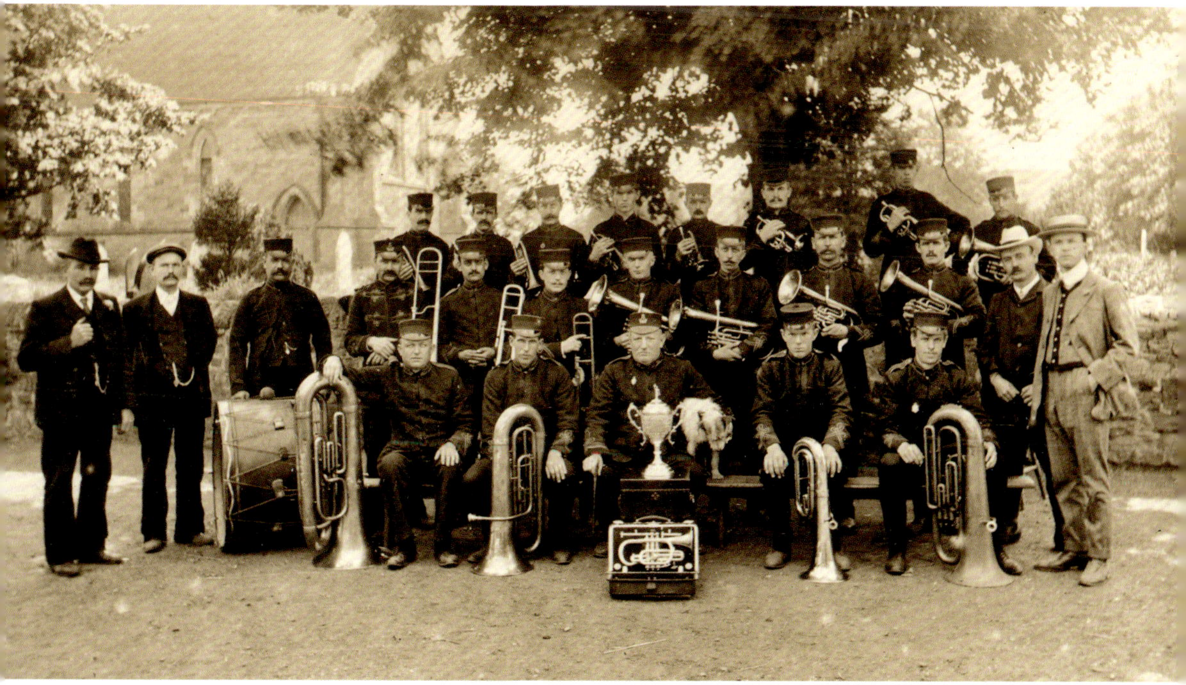

## Brass Bands

In common with countless mining communities elsewhere in England, Donnington Wood (above, *c.* 1908) and Jackfield (below, 1906-7) at the opposite end of Telford were just two local brass bands which won many competitions, some of which took place in The Quarry, Shrewsbury. Rivalry could be intense.

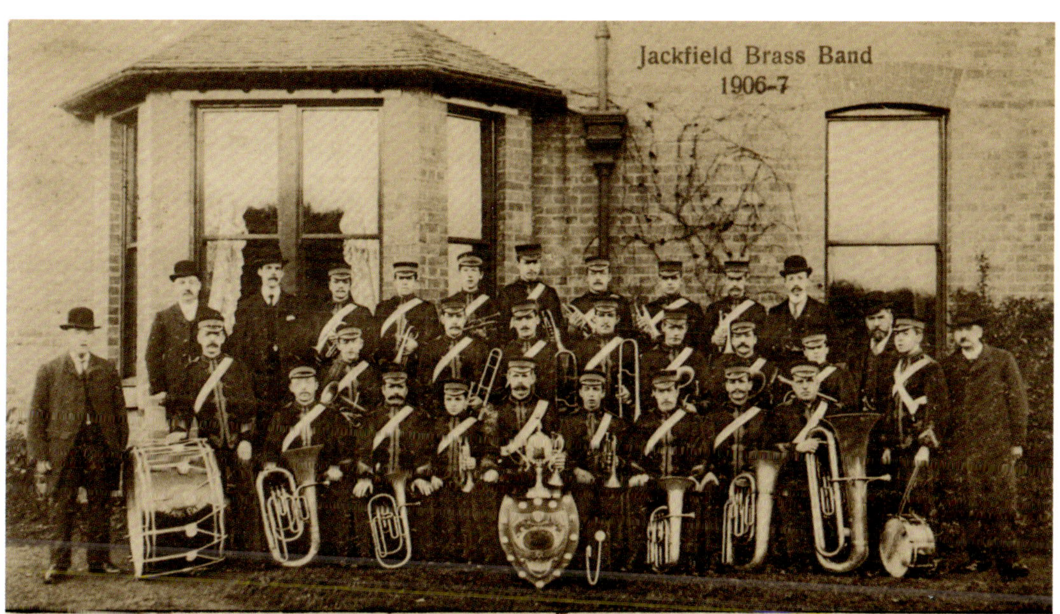

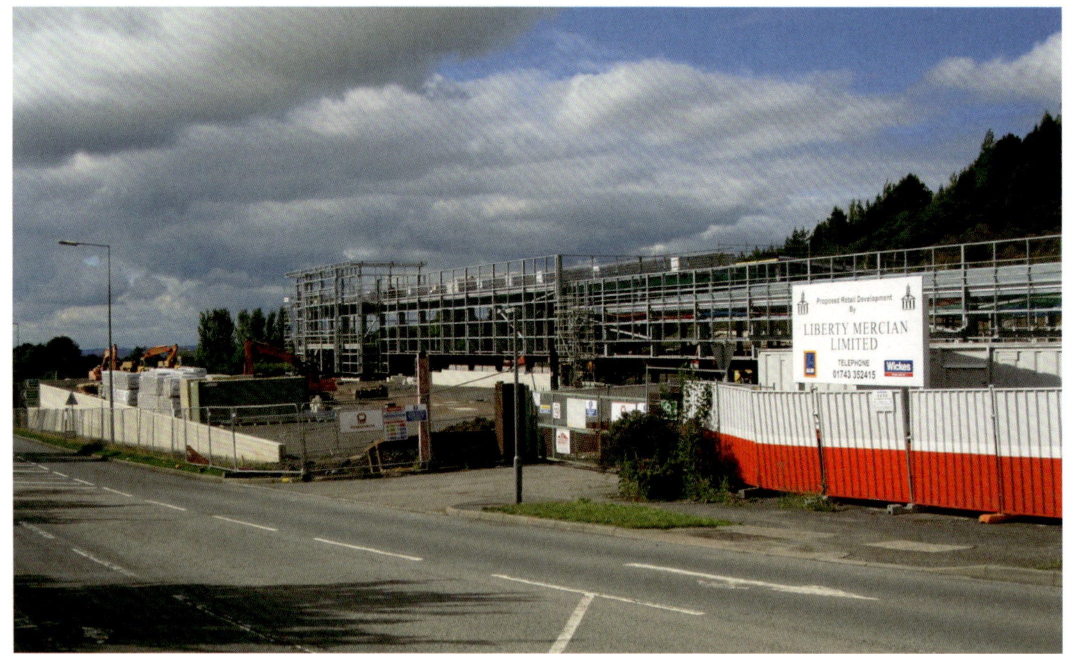

## Snedshill Brickworks

This former Lilleshall Company site suffered extensive fire damage when acting as a small industrial centre around January 2006. The company's 'clay department' at Snedshill Brickworks didn't just make excellent building bricks; it made salt-glazed pipes, refractory bricks, tiles and sanitary ware. The brickworks struggled to survive from the 1950s onwards as stainless steel and plastic products gained popularity and restrictions were placed on deep-mined clay extraction, upon which the company had relied for decades. Ceramic production ended here in 1977. The site is now being prepared for occupation by Wickes hardware and ALDI supermarket stores.

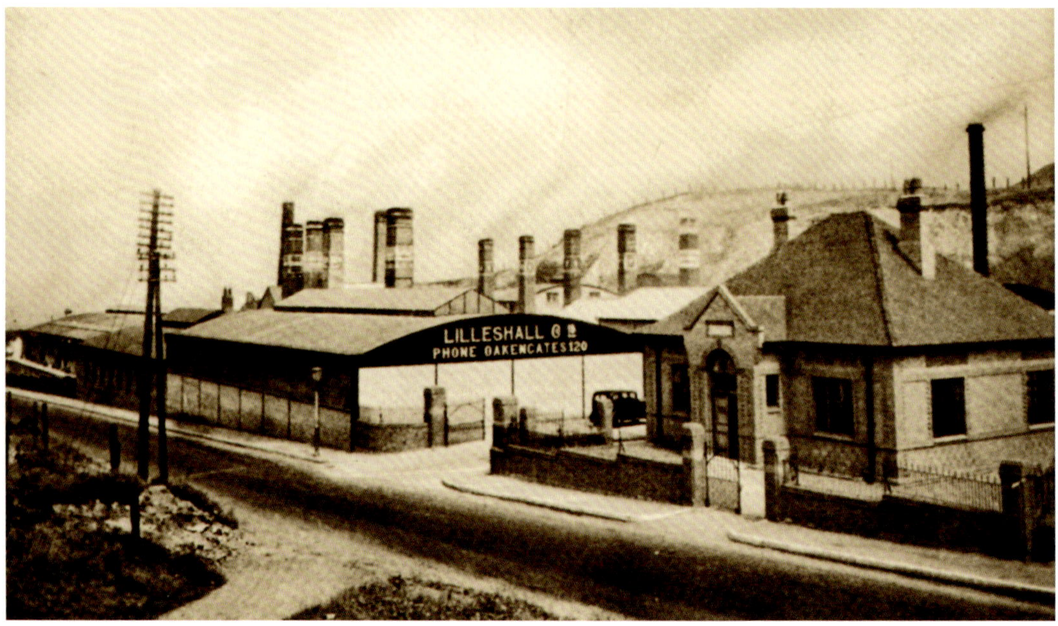

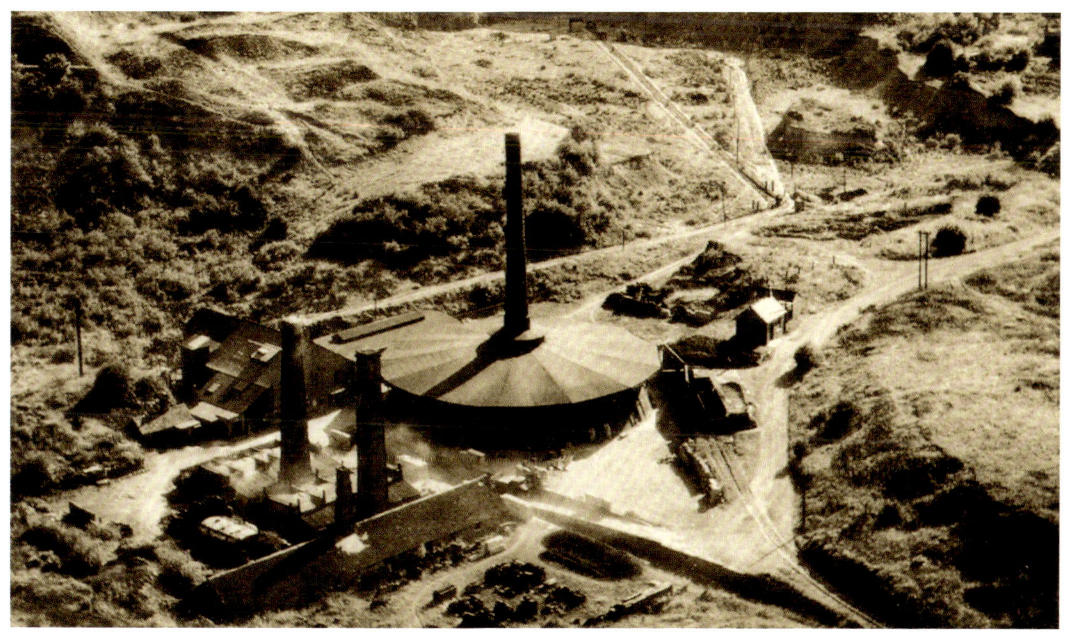

### The Rookery Brickworks and Coalport China

The Lilleshall Company also had a major brickworks at The Rookery, on the border between Donnington Wood and St. Georges. That area had been associated with brick production before The Rookery was erected in 1850 and took advantage of local marl and sand pits for making high quality bricks for export even as far away as Russia. Coalport China is renowned worldwide for the quality of its decorated tableware. Founded by John Rose, the factory on the banks of the River Severn opened around 1800 and used the river to receive raw materials and transport finished goods to Bristol and beyond. The original factory buildings are now one of the Ironbridge Gorge Museums and still make collectable ceramics.

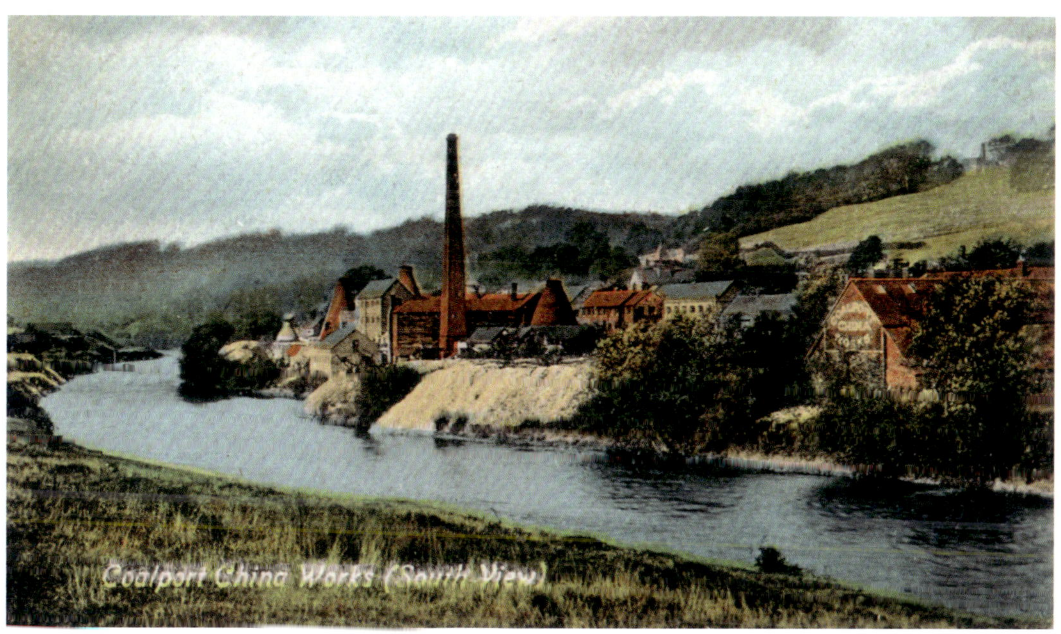

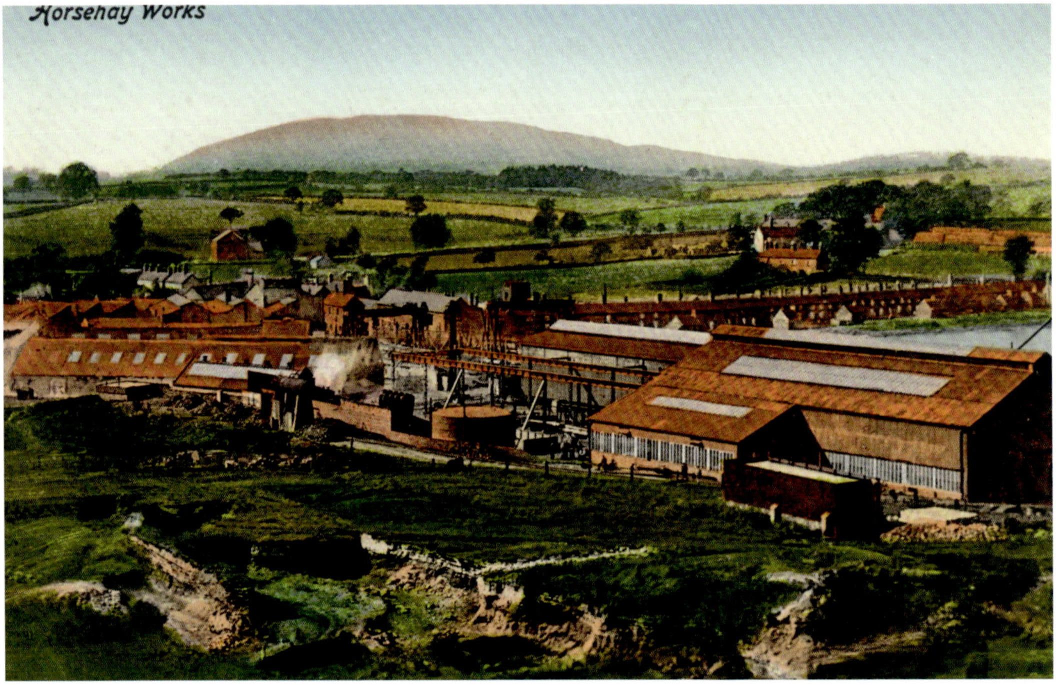

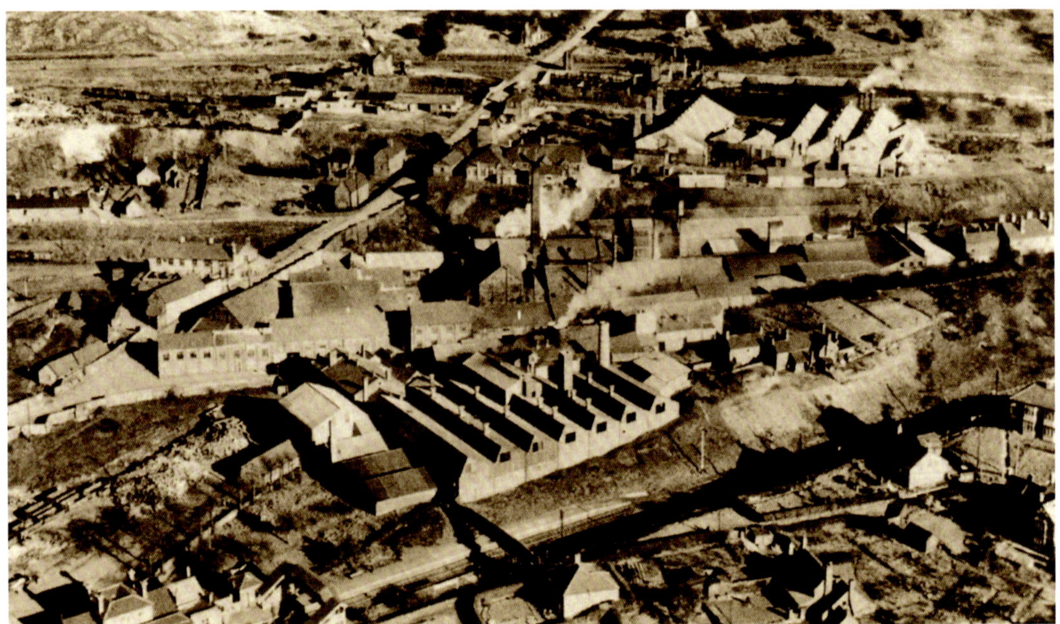

## Bridges, Cranes and Castings: Horsehay and Oakengates

Horsehay Works (above, known by several names between when it began in 1755 under Abraham Darby I and its closure in 1986 when owned by Adamson Alliance) was famous during its life for the making bridges and cranes (and the inconvenience caused to motorists when transporting excessively long loads by road). John Maddocks at Oakengates (below, centre), at the opposite end of the scale, specialised in nail manufacture and malleable iron castings, like parts for bicycles and pipe fittings. The company operated from 1878 until the late 1980s.

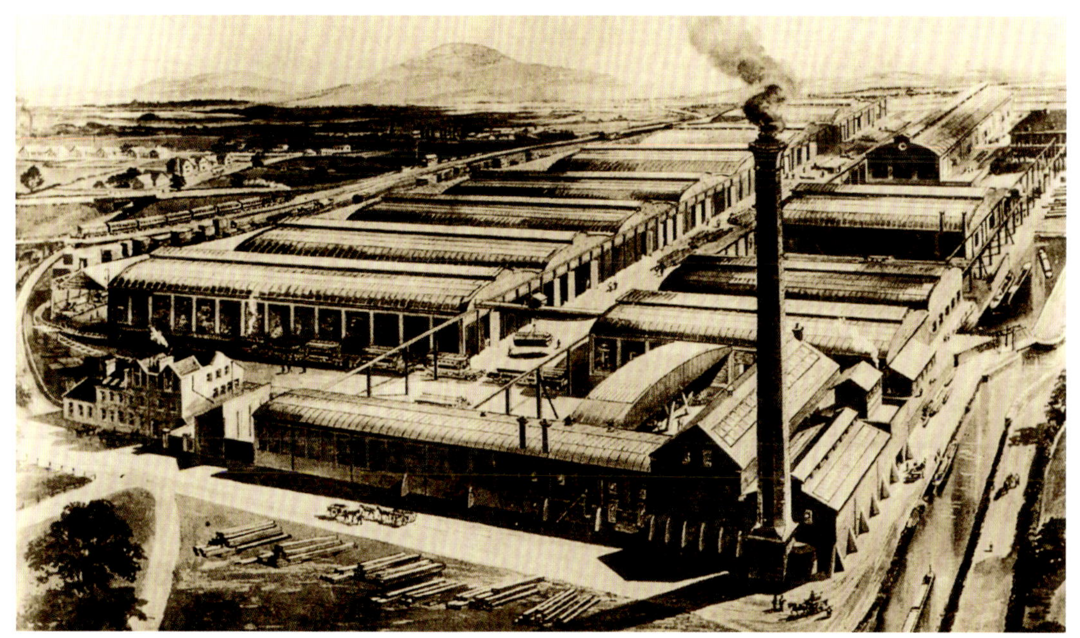

## Trams, Wheels, Spitfires and Army Vehicles: Sankeys, Hadley

Ultimately the factory with the largest ever number of employees in the district, in 1910 Sankey's acquired the Castle Car Works (above) where trams had previously been made. During the Second World War, the author's father was a draughtsman who designed fuselages and other parts for Spitfire production here. Over the years, washing machines, beer casks and an abundance of car parts (especially wheels) have been manufactured in these extensive works (below), as well as various types of army vehicles.

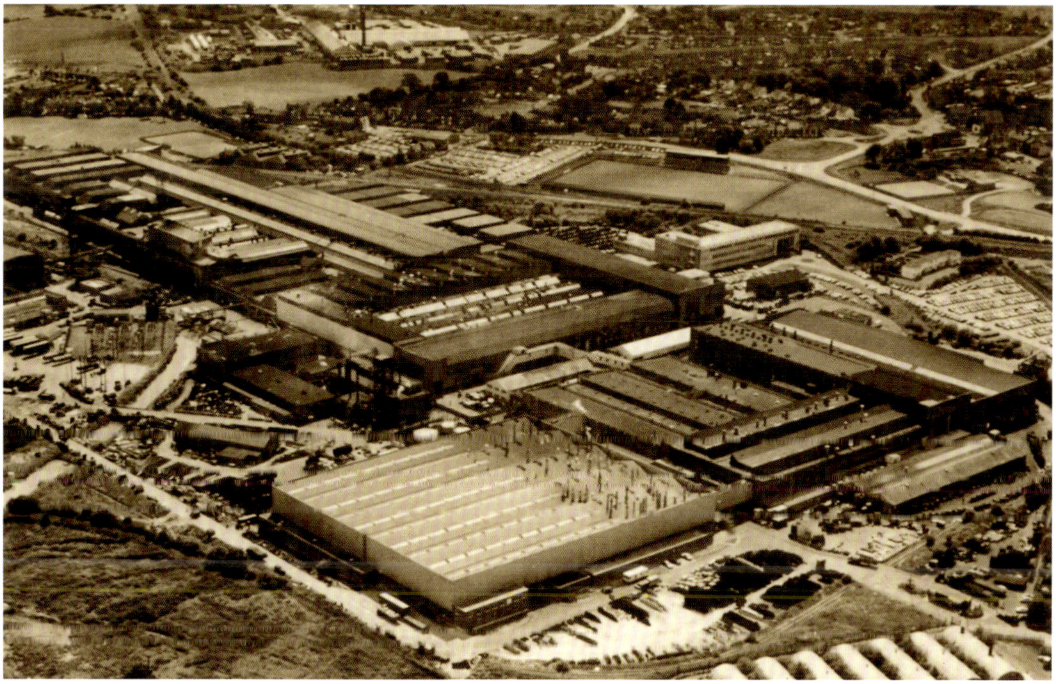

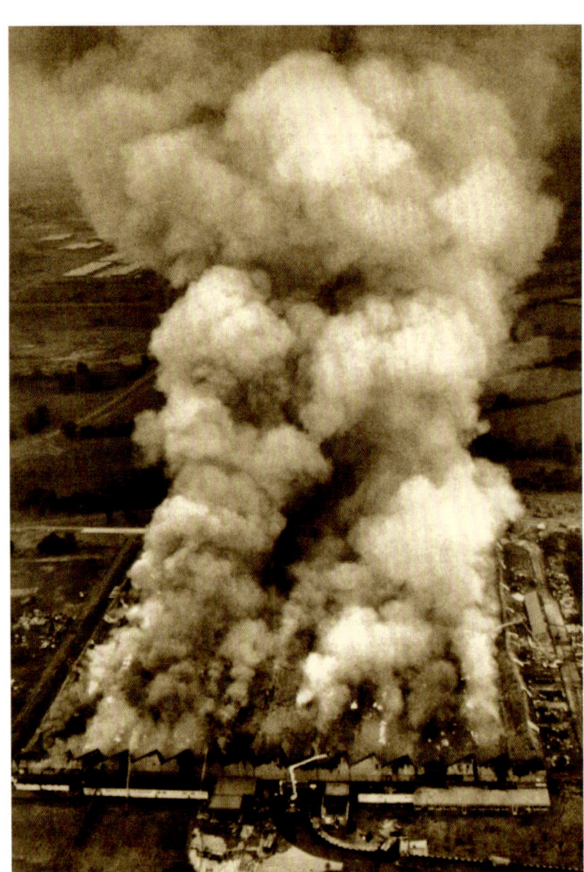

## Ordnance and Batteries

The Civilian Ordnance Deport (whose name has been changed several times over the years) was opened at Donnington on the edge of the Weald Moors as part of the nation's preparations in readiness for the outbreak of the Second World War. Second only to Sankey's for the size of its civilian workforce (it also has an army presence), The Dump (as it was known colloquially) suffered two enormous conflagrations, the worst in 1983 (aside) which destroyed millions of pounds worse of equipment but only cost a fraction of the total value lost to restore (a lot of things were out of date or not worth replacing).

The Ever Ready factory at Hinkshay near Dawley made dry cell batteries for domestic and industrial use from 1956. It had been intended to provide work to replace jobs lost by a decline in traditional heavy industry, and didn't rely on local raw materials. Like so many other Telford factories, it no longer exists.

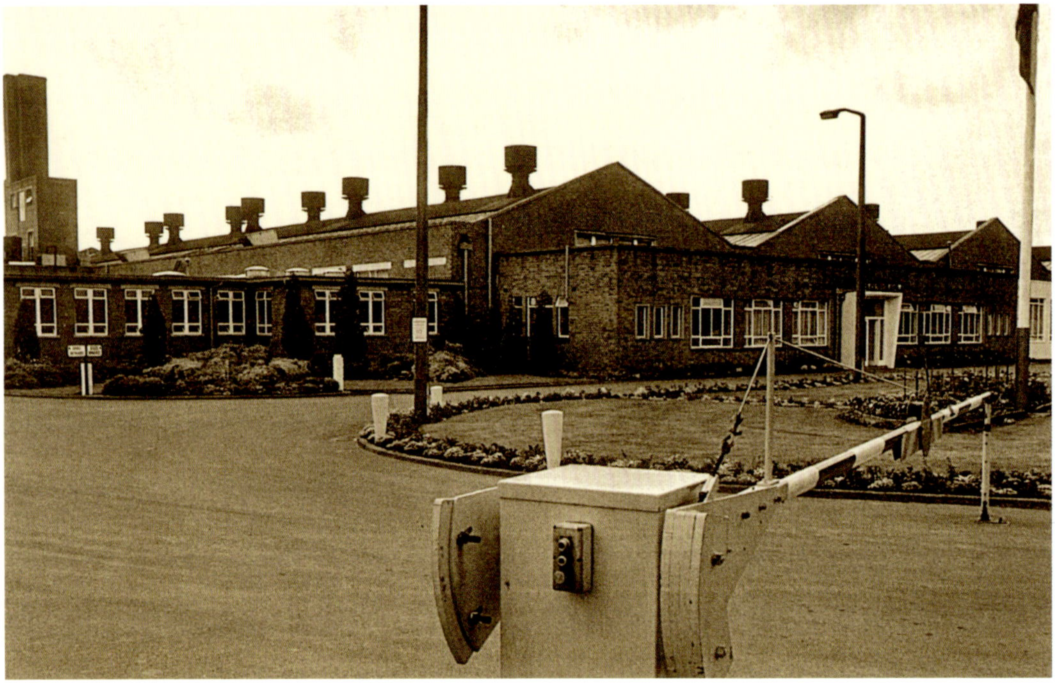

### Modern Industrial Sites

Whereas old, usually heavy, industries sprang up not far from raw materials or the rail and canal networks, modern manufacturing tends to be confined to specific 'enterprise zones' based mainly at Stafford Park (below, with Priorslee Balancing Lake at top right) and Halesfield.

This poster was supposed to entice 'industrialists' wearing bowler hats to set up businesses in Telford, taking advantage of attractive incentives. Reality was not quite so rosy. The caption 'For people on the move' was perceptively interpreted by one witty urban district councillor as meaning that no one in their right minds would want to settle in one of Telford's modern, future slum, housing, let alone lease a commercial workshop beyond the period of twelve months reduced (sometimes free) rent.

As with all things human, time heals. The population is growing to take advantage of increased housing, and there will always be 'industrialists' willing to run their own businesses.

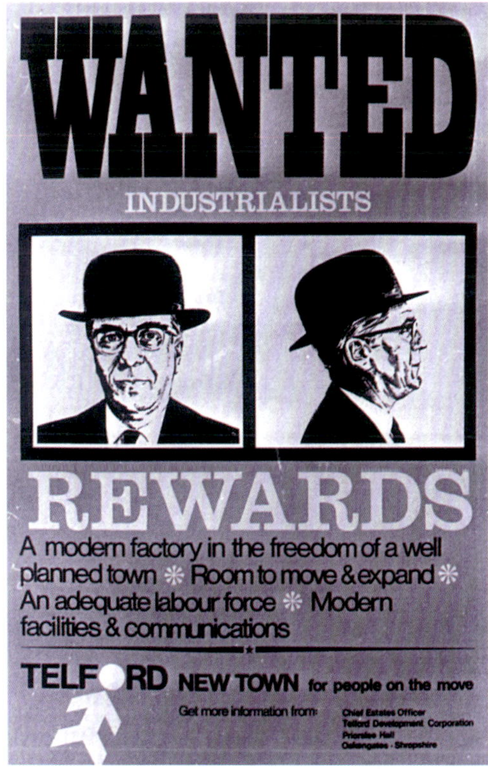

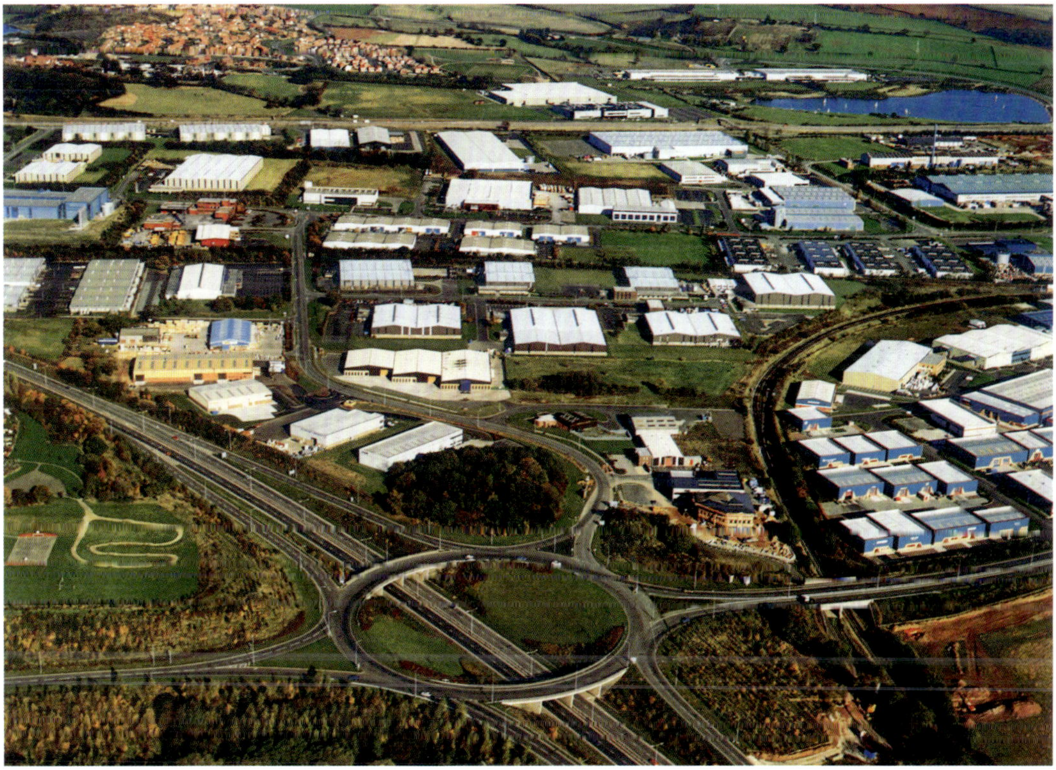

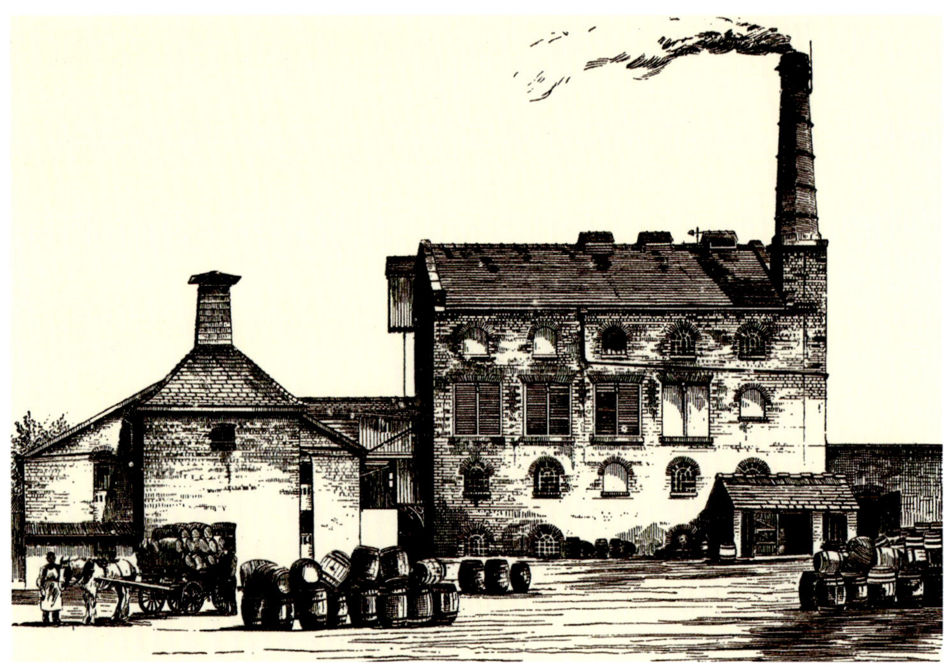

## Brewing: From Wellington to Ironbridge...

The Shropshire Brewery at Wellington seems to have been the first purpose-built (in 1851) brewery in the area and became part of a drinks empire created by O. D. Murphy after the former mineral water manufacturer moved from his Long & Co. pop works at Ironbridge in the early 1900s. Oddly, he wasn't allowed to brew beer at the Shropshire Brewery... so he used it as a bottling plant for firms like Guinness.

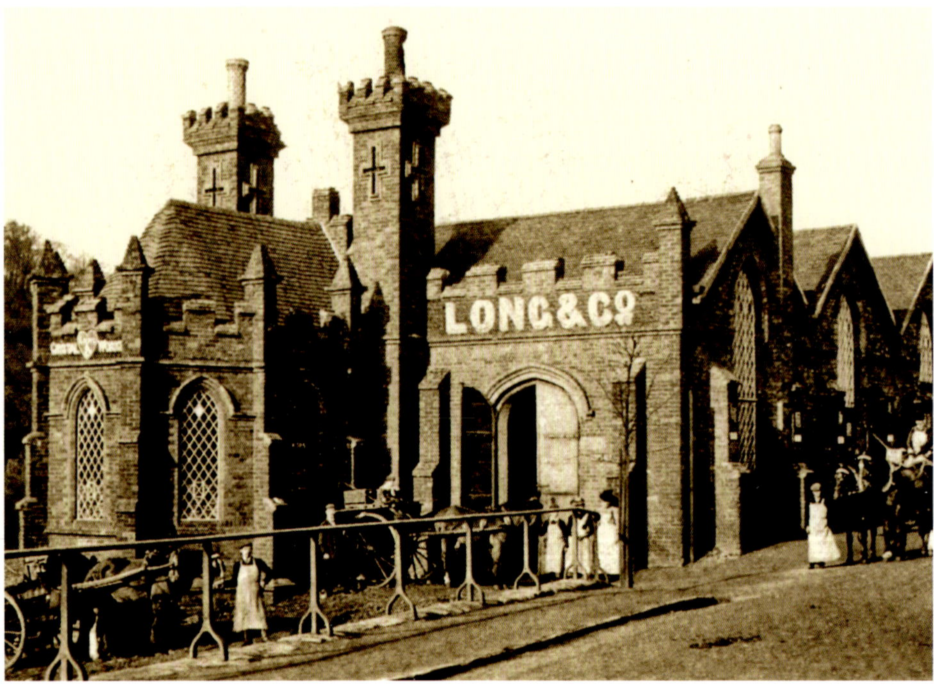

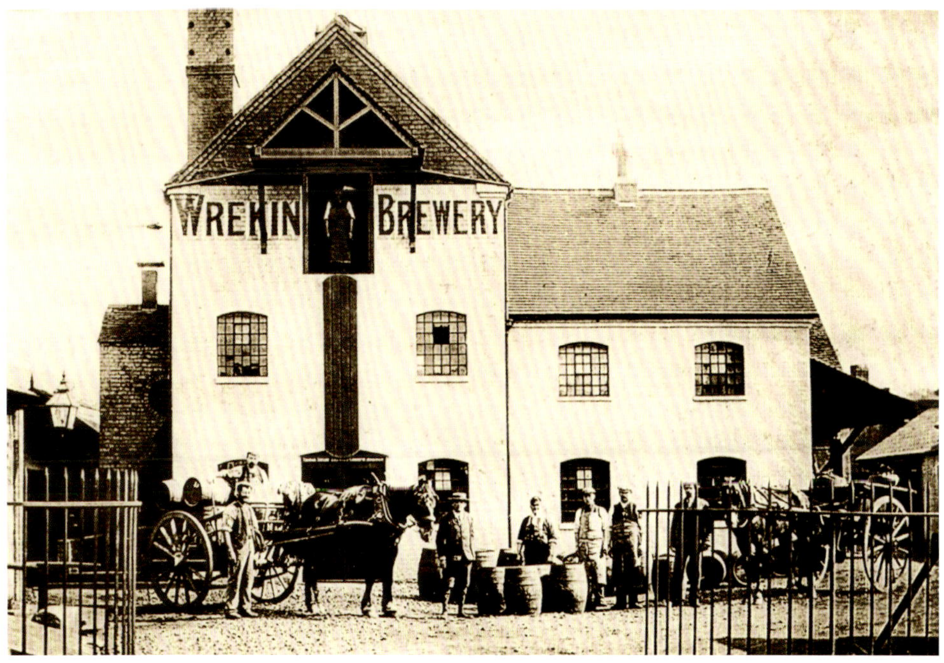

## ...and Wellington to Rowton

Having cornered the soft drinks market, O.D. Murphy turned to brewing and acquired the Wrekin Brewery (established in 1871) in the 1920s. It became the largest privately owned brewery in the country but was closed in 1969 after Greenall Whitley took it over in 1966. Nowadays, 'micro' breweries producing 'real' ales exist at Ironbridge, Madeley (All Nations) and Rowton (below, with brewer Jim Preston).

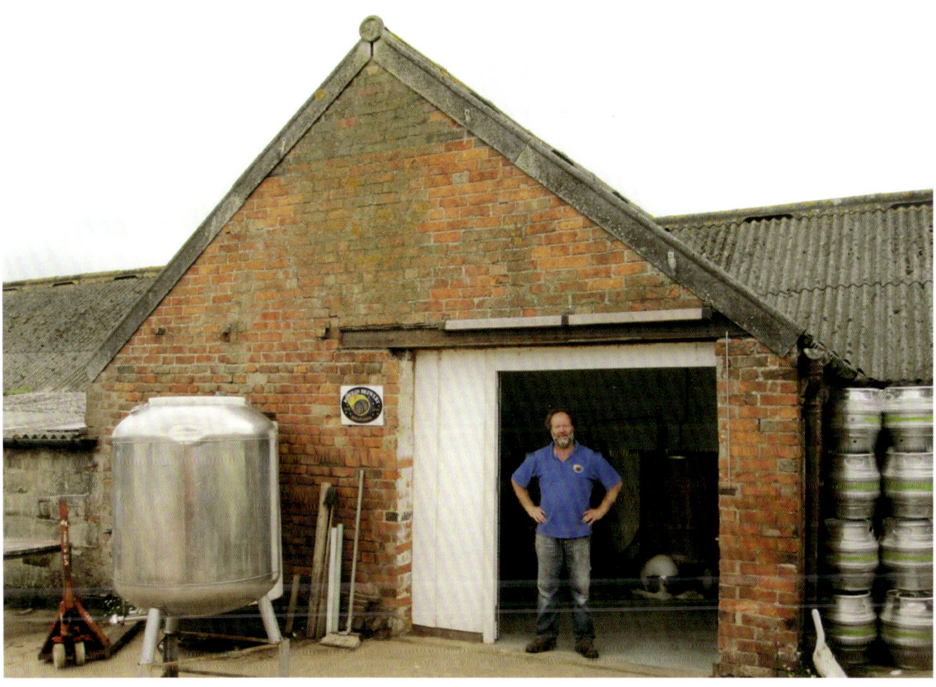

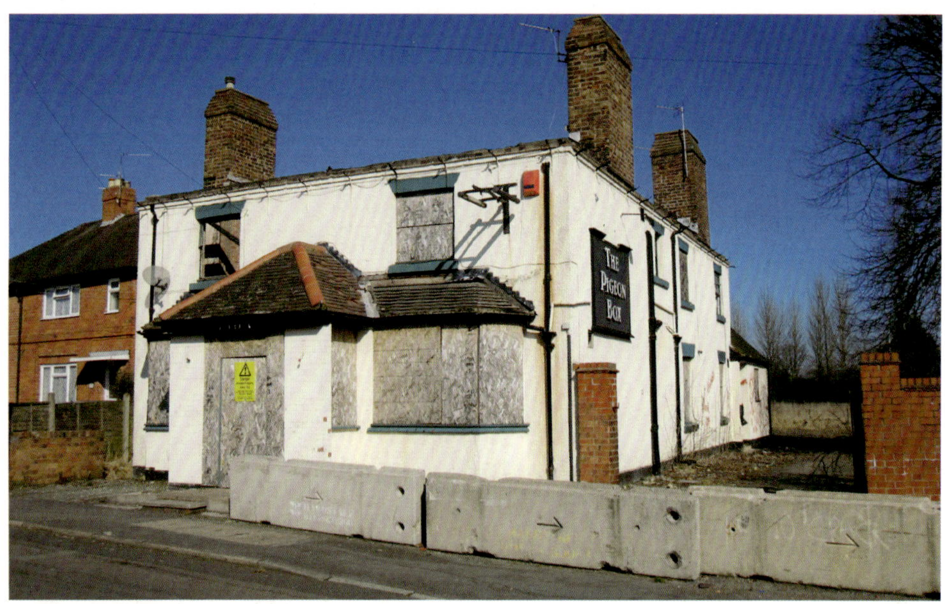

## Pubs: Fire Damage

The number of pubs was once a good indicator of the sense of community in a town. It has been asserted that Telford Development Corporation was responsible for the loss of about 100 pubs as it sought to create a middle class standard of living in the area. In recent years, social, economic and political changes have led to the demise of many more hostelries. A surprising number have suffered fire damage despite stringent fire and other safety regulations, and apparently even insurance cover isn't enough to enable repairs to be made and a pub reopened for business. The Pigeon Box at Priorslee (above) is awaiting demolition to enable over 100 new homes to be built behind its derelict remains, while the respected Charlton Arms at Wellington (below) has resisted attempts by its present property-developing owner to turn it into apartments.

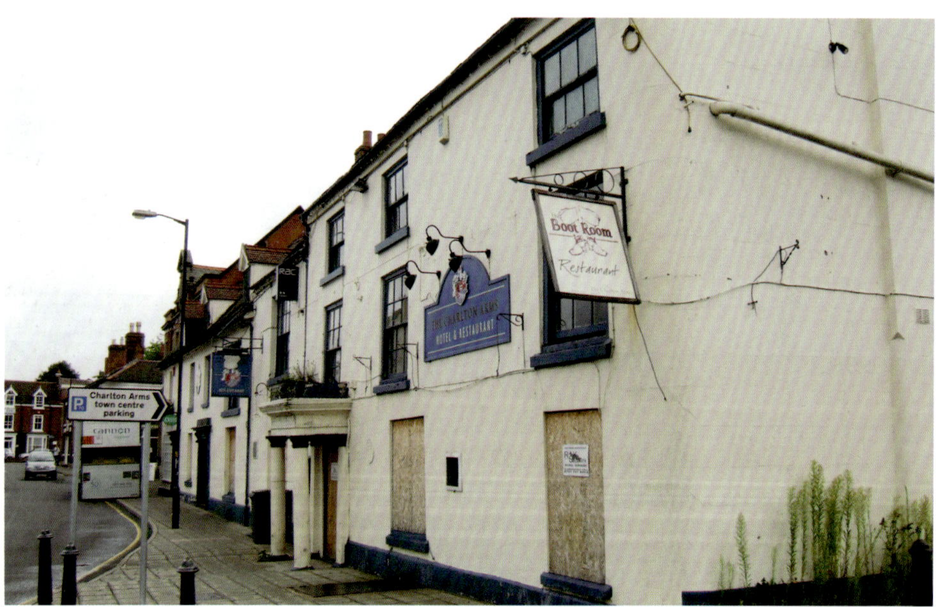

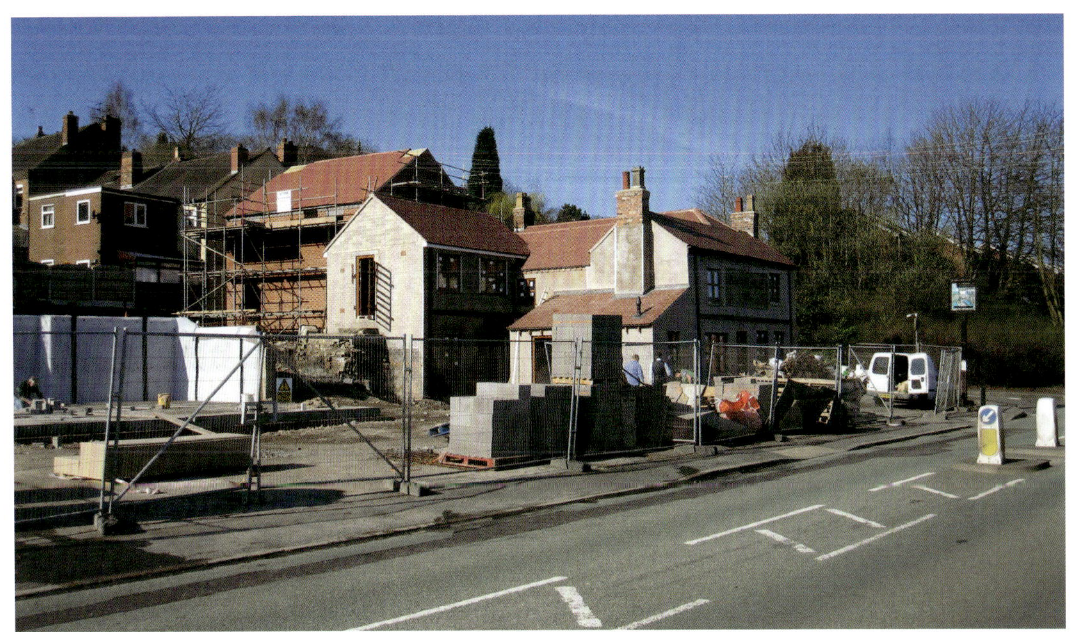

## Pub Conversions

Not all pubs come to a sticky end. The site of the Pear Tree Bridge at Ketley is currently undergoing conversion into various accommodations. The original public house on the right and even its signpost have been preserved, while new buildings occupy the former car park and garden. The Queens Hotel in Wellington, in existence for well over a century and in recent years known as 'The Queens' and 'Porters', has been given a complete and sympathetic facelift by its present owner and reopened as the Taj Mahal Indian restaurant  It has already gained an excellent reputation.

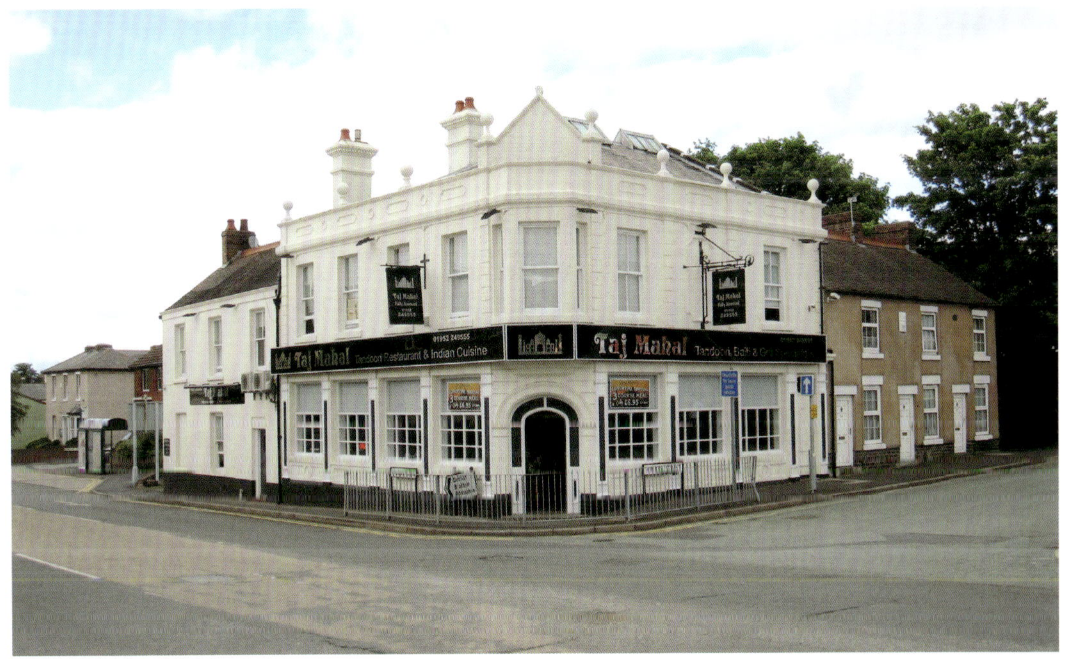

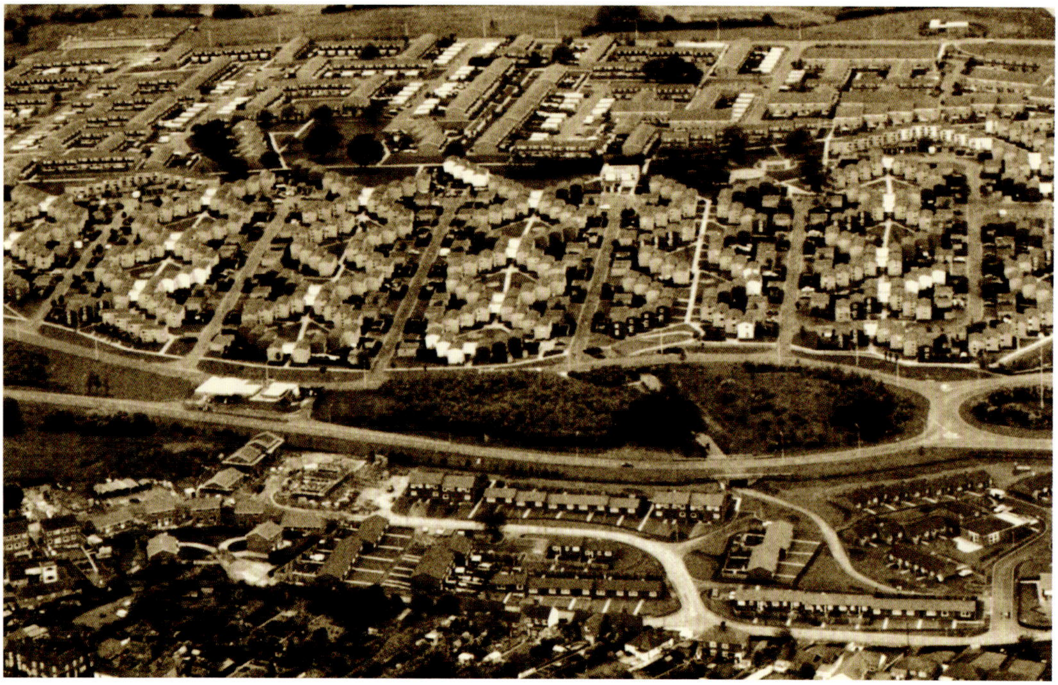

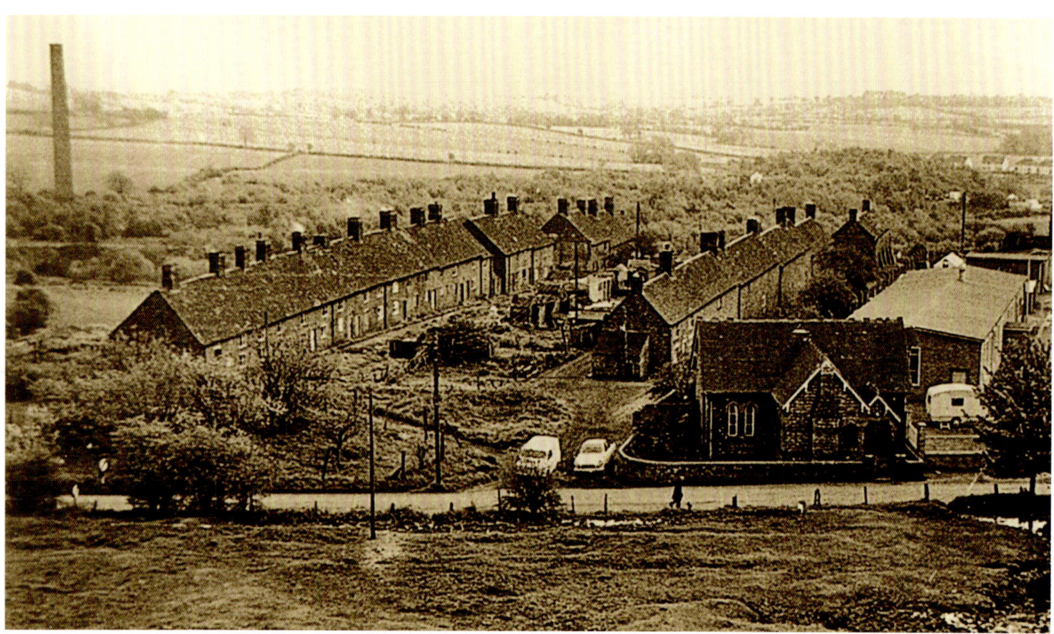

### New Slums for Old? Hinkshay and Woodside

One of the most abrasive observations made by the public and pre-Telford councillors was that Dawley (and its successor Telford) Development Corporation were demolishing old communities like that at Hinkshay (below, now part of the 'town centre' park) and replacing ostensibly sub-standard dwellings with 'slums of the future' like those on the new estate at Woodside (above), where architects separated car parks from homes and designed complex pathways to create inhospitable warrens.

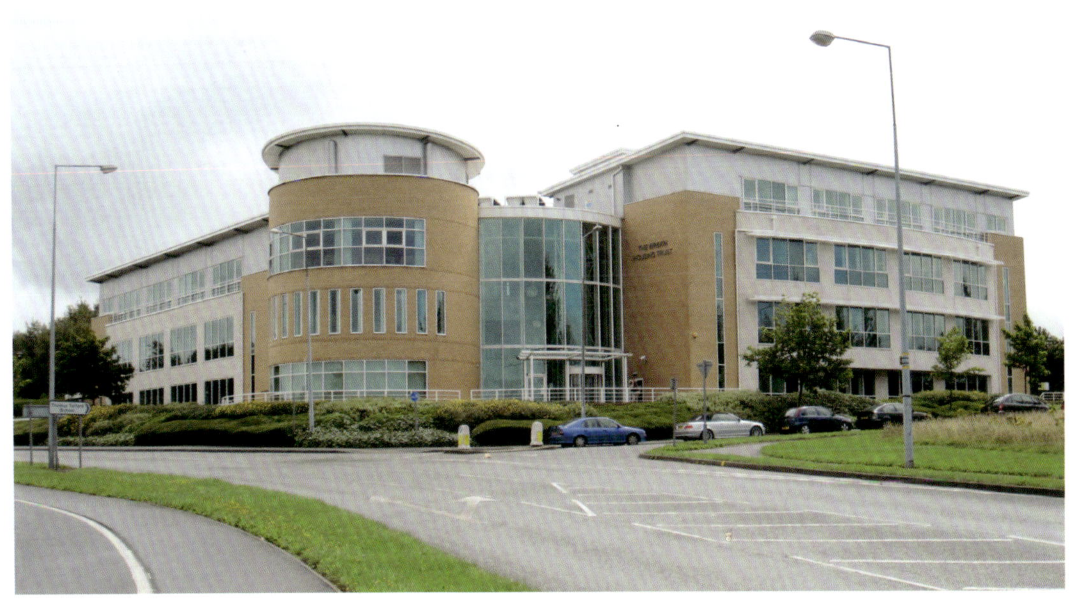

## Local Government

Non-profit making Wrekin Housing Trust moved into its present home (above) in 2001, having been established in 1999 when over 13,000 properties were transferred from Telford & Wrekin Council, whose own home at Malinslee House (below) was created in 1976 for its predecessor, Wrekin District Council. The Malinslee House site is currently being considered for a new ASDA supermarket, which will entail the council relocating elsewhere in the Telford conurbation.

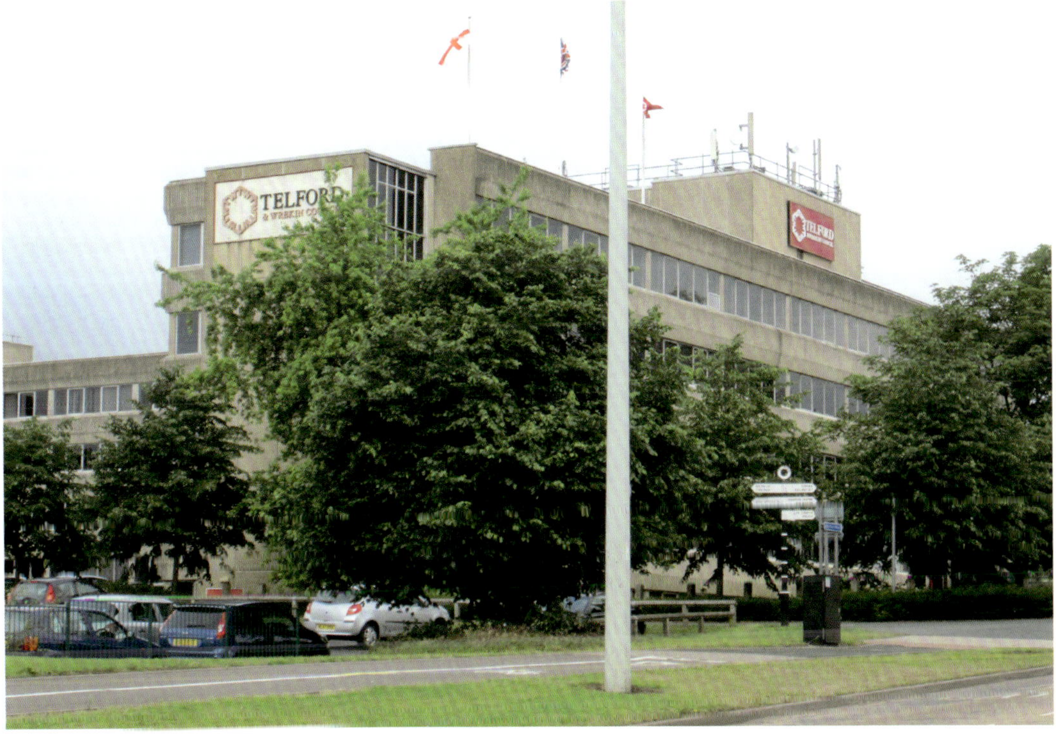

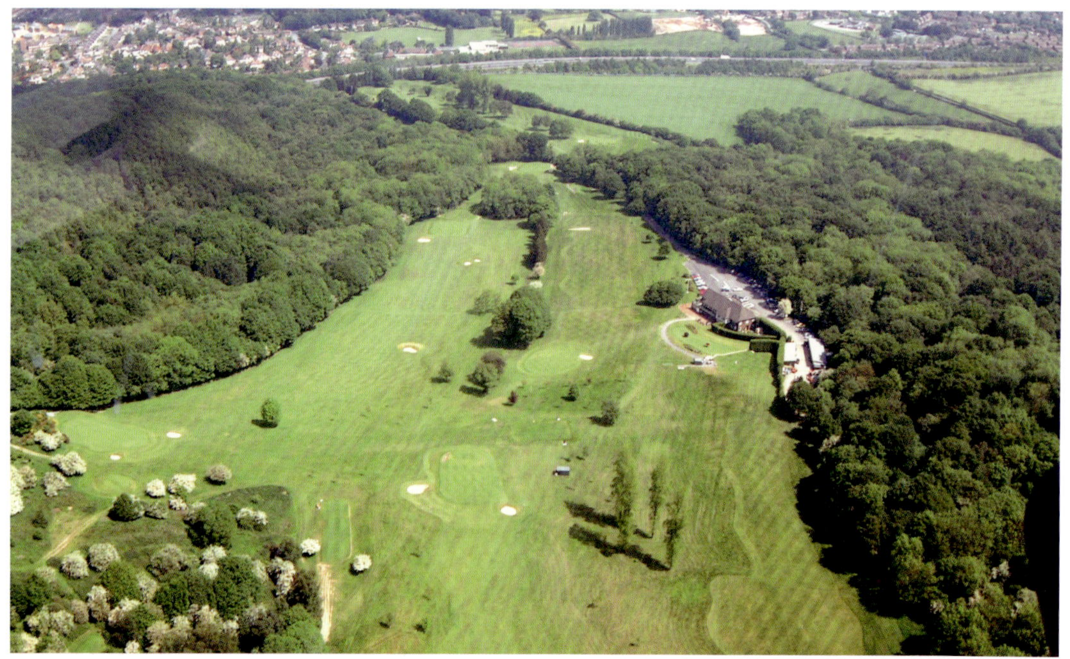

## Sport for All: Golf

Wrekin Golf Club (above) moved to the slopes of Ercall Hill in 1908 and originally catered for the sporting needs of those who were well-heeled and had time to spare. The clubhouse moved to its present location away from the M54 after the motorway was created in the 1970s. The course is considered to be one of the most scenic in England. Over the last forty years, several new courses have opened (some municipal, others private), like the one south of the Sutton Hill housing estate (below).

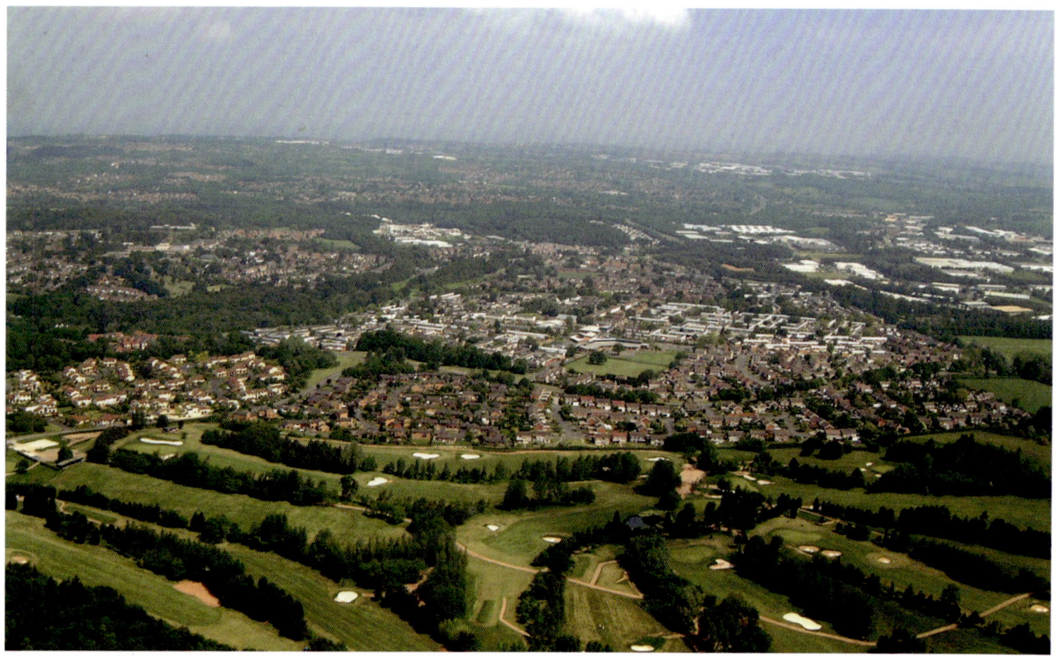

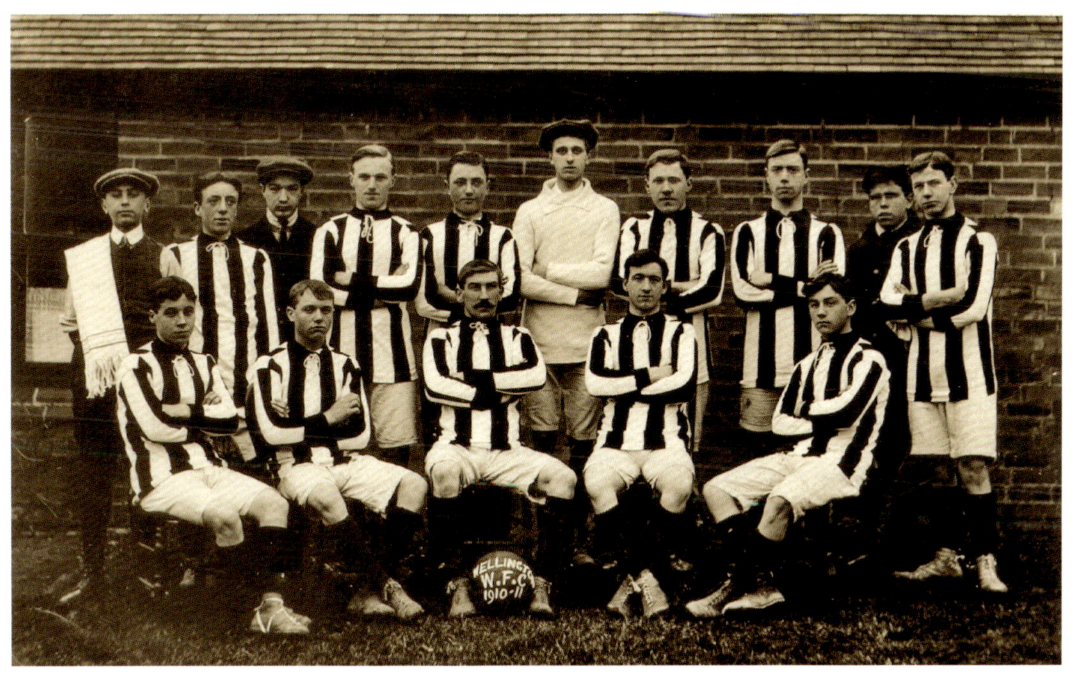

### From WTFC to AFC Telford United

Wellington Town Football Club, for a while known as The Lilywhites, evolved from a team formed at All Saints parish church, Wellington, probably in the 1870s. When this photograph of the 1910/11 team was taken, they had already won the Welsh League and went on to win many more trophies. In 1968 their name was changed to Telford United but in more recent years the club suffered financial problems. Now called AFC Telford United (below), the club still plays at the Bucks Head ground in Wellington.

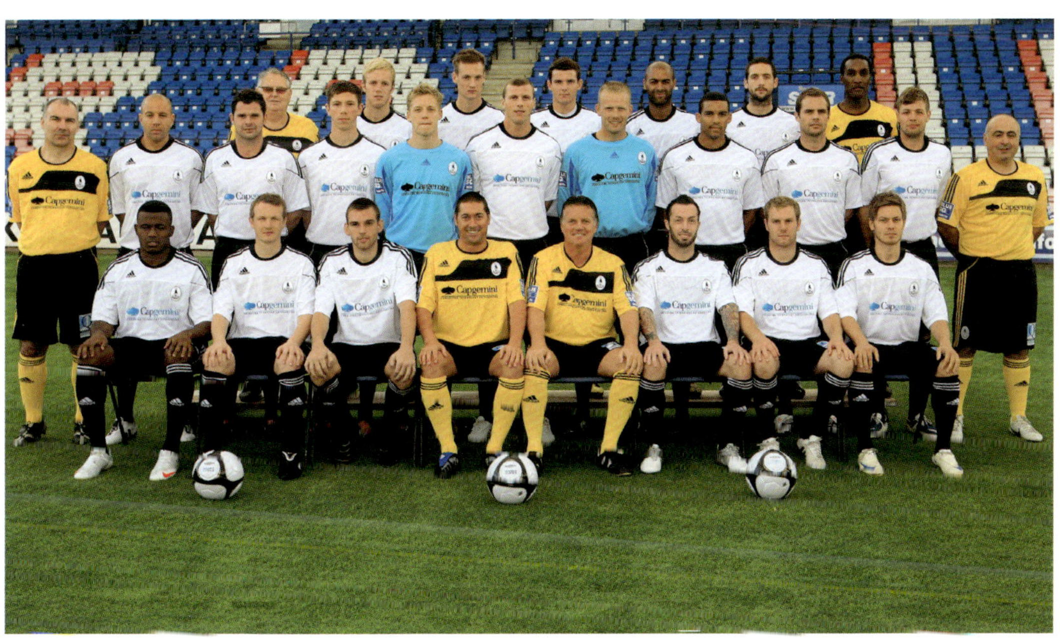

# Acknowledgements

In addition to the support given by the author's wife Dorothy and his extensive collection, grateful thanks are extended to the following for their help in the gathering of old illustrations and information for this book: Barbers, James Bayliss, G. Evans, B. Felton, Ironbridge Gorge Museum Trust, Leisure Connection, Madeley Library, P. Morris-Jones, Old Ben Homes, M. Roberts, Shropshire Archives, Shropshire Museums, *Shropshire Star*, SLR Consulting, *Telford Journal*, *Telford Observer*, R. Tranter, *Wellington Journal* & *Shrewsbury News*, Wellington Library, *Wellington News*, Wrekin Housing Trust.

Attempts have been made to trace copyright where appropriate and apologies are extended to anyone who may have inadvertently been omitted from these acknowledgements.

# About the Author

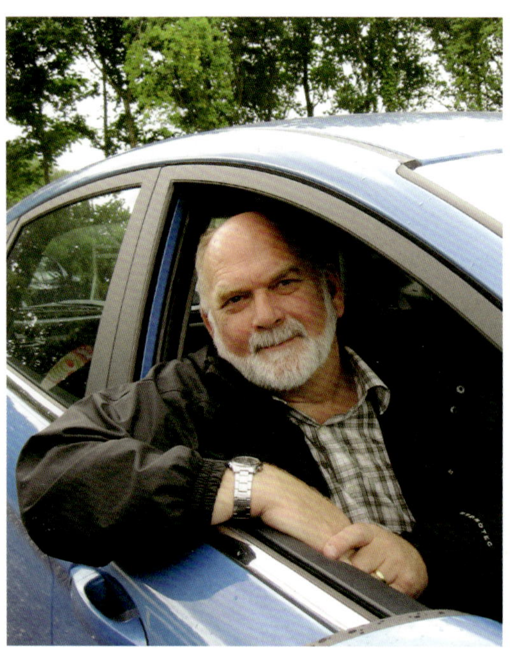 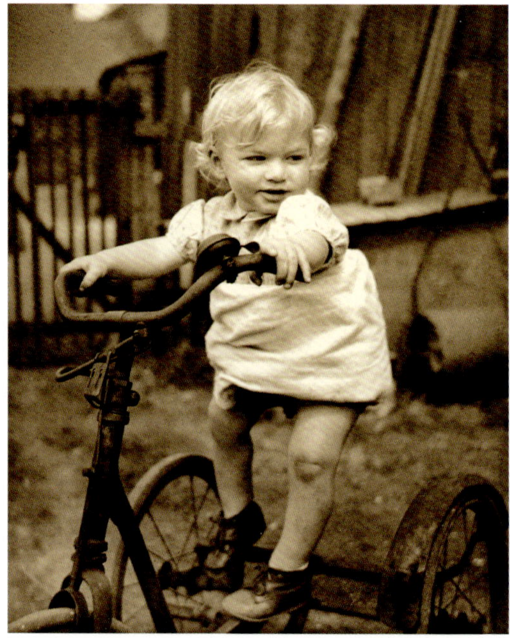

Allan Frost through time… in 2010 and 1950. The author grew up at his family's home in King Street, Wellington, and has lived in the area all his life (so far). His ancestors have also lived in the present Telford district since the 1730s. It is because of this long connection that he is so interested in local history, particularly that of Wellington, the conurbation's principal township.

Allan Frost has written many books on the area in addition to novels and other works. A popular speaker, he is current chairman of Wellington History Group.